Cooking with Sunshine

Cooking with Sunshine

Recipes from the Sunkist Kitchens

NEW YORK *Atheneum* 1986

Library of Congress Cataloging-in-Publication Data

Cooking with sunshine.

Includes index.
1. Cookery (Citrus fruits)   I. Sunkist Growers, inc.
TX813.C5C66   1986   641.6'435   86-47684
ISBN 0-689-11809-0

Photographers: Elmer Moss (Jacket photographs and Fresh Lemon Meringue Pie)
George Selland (All other color photography)
Illustrations: Robert Drake, Artist
Sumie Mishima and Kimberly A. Walker, Visual Resources, Inc.
Recipe Coordinator and Food Stylist: B.J. Doerfling
Recipe Testing: Cindy Ray Mansfield, Sunkist Home Economist, Shirlee Kelly, and Marlyne Selk
Research/copy writer: Holli Pfau
Special Assistance/Sunkist Staff: Barbara Robison, R.D., Cindy Maynard, M.S., R.D., Ruth Mann, and Lisa Tait

Sunkist, Sunkist, and SNACKER are trademarks of Sunkist Growers, Inc., Sherman Oaks, California.

Copyright © 1986 by Sunkist Growers, Inc.
All rights reserved
Published simultaneously in Canada by Collier Macmillan Canada, Inc.
Composition by Westchester Book Composition, Inc.
Manufactured by Fairfield Graphics, Fairfield, Pennsylvania
Designed by Cathryn S. Aison
FIRST EDITION

THIS COLLECTION OF FOODS AND FLAVORS, PREPARATIONS AND PRESENTATIONS IS DEDICATED TO THE NEARLY 6,000 GROWER MEMBERS OF SUNKIST GROWERS, INC., THE MEN AND WOMEN IN CALIFORNIA AND ARIZONA WHO NURTURE THE GOODNESS FROM THE EARTH.

Contents

Introduction	ix
Citrus: The Source	3
The Sunkist Family of Products	11
Appetizers and Soups	15
Fish and Seafood	39
Poultry	61
Beef, Lamb, and Pork	77
Vegetables, Pasta, and Rice	99
Salads and Salad Dressings	123
Eggs and Breakfast or Brunch Ideas	147
Sandwiches	161
Preserves, Relishes, and Marmalades	171
Quick and Yeast Breads	181
Desserts and Ice Creams	197
Cookies and Confections	215
Cakes and Frostings	229
Pies and Pastries	247
Beverages	263
Fresh Citrus Garnishes	285
Citrus Preparation Techniques	303
Western Citrus Information	311
Equivalent Measures	321
Index	323

Introduction

Welcome to the pick of *our* crop: the best recipes from the Sunkist kitchens. Many of these favorite dishes, developed by our home economists, are based on generations of good recipes shared with us by our own growers, citrus enthusiasts, and friends. This collection combines the best of old-fashioned goodness with the new flavors and techniques of contemporary cuisine. Since citrus is very useful in flavoring lower-calorie and lower-sodium meals, some recipes have been especially developed to fit in with today's preference for lighter eating.

We have carefully tested all the recipes, using Sunkist fresh citrus and processed citrus products. We recommend the ingredients and methods that give the best results, based on our generations of experience. Sunkist was one of the first major food companies to have test kitchens, staffed by professional home economists. Since the 1920s, Sunkist has shared nutritional data about citrus as well as ideas for its use. This information first appeared on the tissue wraps that protected our fruit in its wooden shipping crates, and later in booklets and pamphlets written for consumers and health professionals. We have always believed that attractive, good-tasting food can also be good for you.

You'll find many different kinds of recipes in *Cooking with Sunshine*. You'll appreciate the delicious quick-and-easy dishes on busy weeknights, and enjoy preparing other elegant, more involved presentations for special, festive occasions. While many dishes were born in California and Arizona citrus country, others—like Greek lemon soup, Mexican salsa, Italian marinated mushrooms, and Ger-

Introduction

man-style hot potato salad—are the heritage of other cultures. Today they're all a flavorful part of our new way of eating.

There are some special things you can count on when you use oranges, lemons, grapefruit, or tangerines in your menus.

fragrance—Nothing smells as good as fresh citrus in the kitchen, especially if it's in lemon bread or orange muffins baking in the oven.

color—Brightly colored citrus fruits in a basket on the table or in a chilled fruit punch or a shimmering marmalade invite your family and friends to taste and enjoy.

freshness—This quality more than any other makes citrus almost indispensable. From a squeeze of fresh lemon over salads and vegetables to a sprinkling of freshly grated orange or lemon peel with chicken and fish, fresh citrus makes everything taste fresher.

versatility—You may be pleasantly surprised to find oranges in omelets, grapefruit in salads, or lemon in meatloaf. Once you've tried our recipes, you'll appreciate the true versatility of citrus.

Citrus fruits have a unique ability to complement and enhance other foods and flavors. Many times you won't even detect a prominent citrus flavor, just something delightful and fresh about a dish. That's the subtle difference citrus can make.

Come share our country heritage and the goodness of Sunkist's wholesome products. Our high standards of quality—for our fruit, our products, and our recipes—let you cook with confidence.

Welcome to the Sunkist kitchens. We hope you'll enjoy cooking with us.

B.J. Doerfling
Supervisor
Consumer Test Kitchen

Barbara C. Robison
Manager
Consumer Services

Cooking with Sunshine

Citrus: The Source

On this morning, there's no other place in the world that citrus grower Tony Wisniewski would rather be. The fingers of first light are barely touching the trees, heavy with fruit. The air is still and fragrant with the richness of the earth—dark soil, green grasses, fresh citrus, and life.

In an hour or so a crew of pickers will arrive to harvest this year's orange crop. But for the next few minutes Tony can savor the beauty of the fruit on the acres of groves just outside his door.

It's been a good year. It's been the kind of year that growers dream of, and pray for. The trees are healthy, and the fruit is bursting with sweetness and juice.

As he wanders down a row of trees, Tony picks an orange, inspecting it critically. The fruit is brilliant, round and firm. A smooth cut with his fruit knife reveals the meat of the orange, rich in color and flowing with juice. Sampling the fruit, Tony smiles. He knows that when his oranges are eaten at breakfast or in a salad, with an entrée or for dessert, they will bring more smiles.

Later today Tony Wisniewski will probably visit the packinghouse, just a few miles down the road from his home and his groves. He'll want to see his fruit as it gets packed for market. He knows the packers will treat his fruit with the same care that he has for the past year. They will be reminded by a lettered sign that hangs just inside the door of the packinghouse: "Mind the Fruit."

Most citrus growers, like Tony, count on their crops for their family's livelihood. So they have to become experts in agricultural practices and the economics of the business. But underlying this knowledge and dedication is a real love of the outdoors and life on a citrus ranch.

When you talk with a grower family, you learn a lot about citrus. Because, for them, it's like knowing the family genealogy. And although it's a business, it's also a way of life with roots over 2,000 years deep.

Citrus was once a rare and prized commodity—mysterious, satisfying, coveted, and symbolic of wealth, status, and power. Imagine yourself living in an ancient civilization, and encountering a luscious golden orange for the first time. Imagine holding an almost perfect globe, the color of a tropical setting sun. Firm but not hard. Almost smooth, but with a decided texture. A rich, refreshing fragrance suggests the wonders inside. But how could you ever guess what is hidden beneath the protective peel? Segments of pure nectar—sweet, juicy, thirst-quenching, and satisfying, all at once.

As you experiment with the fruit, you find that it adds flavor to your food, fragrance to your room, color to your table, soothes your parched throat, and satisfies your hunger. So it's little wonder that when you and your countrymen of the ancient world travel to new horizons, you take your wonderful discovery with you.

THE ANCIENT ORANGE

All citrus varieties probably evolved in the regions of India and the Orient. While there is less recorded history of the lemon, grapefruit, and tangerine, the orange has left a lengthy legacy.

The ancestors of today's orange were flourishing in China centuries ago. The earliest reference to oranges is found in the second book of the "Five Classics," believed to have been edited by Confucius in 500 B.C. The word "orange" itself evolved from Sanskrit, where it was first recorded in a 2,000-year-old medical book. In many ancient civilizations, oranges were considered the fruit of the gods, but it was centuries before they became a staple in the everyday diet.

As generations of dreamers and explorers pushed civilization westward, the orange migrated, too. Orange seeds and trees traveled on the tides of exploration and colonization. From the Orient through southern seas, across African deserts, to the fertile Mediterranean, and aboard sailing vessels to the New World, oranges moved with man.

This westward migration put oranges on the porches of sunny Italian villas, in the great halls of Moorish castles, and in the royal courts of Europe. The fruit was first used decoratively, and the aroma was considered a disinfectant and deodorant. Later the orange became prized for its flavor.

Every culture amassed its own beliefs about citrus. Some thought citrus eaten before a meal made one resistant to all poisons. Others saw the fruits as cures for fever, colic, and dehydration. Citrus compounds were used as laxatives and to reduce enlarged spleens. The seeds were believed to be the antidote to scorpion bites and were a source of lamp oil as well.

There are also substantial references to the romantic properties of oranges and blossoms. For centuries, love and the fragrance of citrus have been entwined. Perhaps this romantic vision inspired the construction of orangeries in the gardens of royal palaces. Charles VIII of France built the first orangerie and touched off competition across Europe. The elaborate architecture afforded protection for the warmth-loving citrus trees and provided the ruling families with beautiful green foliage in their gardens and luscious fruit for their tables.

Other citrus varieties followed the migration of the orange. Lemons are believed to have originated in India, arriving in Palestine and Persia in the twelfth century. The tangerine arrived in Europe from China in 1805, and migrated to the United States from the Mediterranean in the mid-nineteenth century. The grapefruit's ancestor, the pomelo, moved westward from China and the Malay Peninsula, arriving in the Americas in the seventeenth century. The grapefruit was first recorded in Jamaica and named for the way it grew, in grape-like clusters.

A NEW FRUIT IN THE NEW WORLD

The first citrus probably arrived in the Western Hemisphere when Christopher Columbus introduced it to the Caribbean. These plantings soon spread throughout the islands, and were an important reason why sailing ships stopped there during long voyages. The discovery that citrus not only prevented but relieved the symptoms of scurvy, made Caribbean groves essential medical stations for sailors.

Ponce de Leon may have brought citrus to the North American mainland when he discovered Florida in 1513. During this period of exploration, sailors on Spanish ships were required to carry 100 orange seeds, and later seedlings, for planting on arrival. The trees flourished, and in the 1800s the Florida citrus industry took root.

WESTERN HORIZONS

Oranges also arrived in California with the Spanish explorers. Franciscan missionaries migrated northward along the Pacific coast, bringing the culture and foods of Spain. In July 1769, they established the first California mission in San Diego and planted orange seeds in the mission gardens.

The seedlings flourished in the Western sun and grew to bear crops. In 1804, the first full grove of trees was planted on 6 acres at the San Gabriel mission, 200 miles north of San Diego, near Los Angeles. In 1841, former Kentucky trapper William Wolfskill began an experiment, starting the first commercial grove with seedlings from the San Gabriel mission. The business was successful, and Wolfskill's original 2 acres of trees rapidly grew to 17,000 trees on 76 acres.

At about the same time, the gold and silver deposits of California's Mother Lode were drawing thousands in search of their fortune. With rugged living conditions and an inadequate diet, California's prospectors began to suffer the same malady as the early sailors: scurvy. Enterprising growers and importers in California and Mexico soon made San Francisco a major citrus port, supplying lemons and oranges for delivery upriver to the gold mining towns.

In 1873, a new variety of orange arrived from Brazil to change the U.S. citrus market dramatically. Presbyterian church missionaries in Bahia, Brazil, advised the United States Commissioner of Agriculture of a unique kind of orange tree bearing seedless fruit. Twelve trees arrived in Washington, D.C., for evaluation.

Three of the budded trees were sent to the Tibbets family,

one of a group of New Englanders establishing a colony in what is now Riverside, California. One tree died, but after careful tending, the other two trees bore the first navel oranges in California in 1875.

News of the beautiful color and flavor of the seedless fruit traveled throughout California, and the Tibbets began selling budwood to other growers. The California navel orange burst upon the market and by 1905 the Riverside area alone was shipping 5 million cartons of fruit a year, while plantings reached valleys and hillsides throughout the state.

The entire Western navel orange industry traces its origin to the two Tibbets trees in Riverside. Today one remarkable tree still remains, in Tibbets Park; it is carefully tended and protected as a living patriarch.

THE SUNKIST HERITAGE

The citrus industry spread through the fertile lands of California and into Arizona. The soil and climate were ideal and the trees thrived. But as the volume of marketable fruit increased, so did the problems for growers.

Erratic fluctuations in supplies, prices, and available markets forced growers to develop a more reliable way to market their fruit. On April 4, 1893, a group of 60 growers met in Los Angeles to organize a system of cooperative marketing from which all could benefit. A plan was approved on August 29, 1893, and the Southern California Fruit Exchange was born.

As activities expanded throughout the state, the name evolved to the California Fruit Growers Exchange, and the brand name "Sunkist" was adopted. This trademark became a symbol for premium-quality citrus products from California and Arizona, and, in 1952, the Exchange's Board of Directors changed the corporate name to Sunkist Growers, Inc.

The history of citrus in California and Arizona is linked with the innovations and marketing successes of the cooperative. As the group solved problems and seized opportunities, their creativity and tenacity improved the industry for all growers.

• In 1908, the Exchange tested the power of advertising in developing new markets. In a joint effort with the Southern Pacific

Railroad, shipments of oranges to Iowa were heralded by the nation's first newspaper advertisement for a produce item, proclaiming "Orange Week in Iowa." The experiment was a success, increasing sales by 50 percent.

• In 1916, the Exchange developed an entirely new use for oranges, by designing and manufacturing the first glass citrus reamer, and by showing people how to "Drink an Orange."

• In 1926, the Sunkist brand was first stamped directly on oranges. This trademark replaced the earlier tissue wraps that had sported the Sunkist name.

• Sunkist supported early research into the healthful properties of citrus, especially vitamin C, and provided information to consumers and the medical community in brochures and advertisements.

• Sunkist's sister company, Fruit Growers Supply Company, also aided the growers' efforts by providing reasonably priced agricultural supplies. They built lumber mills to produce wooden shook for the early cartons, and they obtained scarce oil to fuel orchard heaters during winter freezes.

SUNKIST TODAY

Sunkist Growers, Inc., is the oldest and largest citrus cooperative in the world. Members market 68 million cartons of fresh citrus each year in the United States and Canada and 27 countries overseas. In an average year, one million tons of citrus are processed in Sunkist plants and marketed worldwide for use in thousands of products.

The success of all these efforts starts with the grower. Before the oranges ever reach your table, the grower invested at least five years and a lifetime of knowledge. A good orange—or lemon or grapefruit or tangerine—starts with a good tree with sound roots. Some varieties of root stock are resistant to disease and pests, while other varieties of citrus produce the best fruit. So most commercial trees are the result of a budding process. A small slip of budwood from a good fruit-producing variety is grafted onto a hardy rootstock and becomes the bearing part of the tree.

It then takes five to seven years for the tree to reach maturity and bear a commercial crop. Each day during this time the grower must maintain an appropriate irrigation, feeding, pruning, and pest control program.

Occasional chilly weather—even in the warm valleys of the West—requires sophisticated frost protection. Wind machines keep warmer air circulating close to the ground. Sprinkler systems also help to maintain above-freezing temperatures in the groves.

Picking the fruit isn't easy, either. Thorny lemon and dense orange trees challenge the pickers, who wear gloves to protect the fruit and snip each piece with special clippers. Often temperatures above 100 degrees drive pickers from desert groves. And the morning dew in California's central valley can delay the start of picking, to avoid moisture that could cause decay in transit.

Once the fruit reaches the packinghouse, it receives even more attention. A team of Sunkist inspectors monitors all steps to maintain rigorous quality standards. No shipment leaves the packinghouse until the fruit meets these standards.

First the fruit is carefully washed to remove orchard dust and dirt, and then a thin coat of water-soluble vegetable wax is applied. This is the same kind of wax used on other produce items, such as apples and tomatoes, and it replaces the natural oils lost in washing. But that's all that's added. No artificial color is ever used on Western citrus. The warm days and cool nights in growing areas cause the fruit to color naturally.

The fruit then journeys on long conveyor belts past inspection stations where premium fruit is carefully sorted from lower-grade fruit that is destined for processing. Only the best fruit receives the famous Sunkist stamp. First- or second-grade fruit is then packed in cardboard cartons and placed on pallets for shipping, often all in the same day. It's now ready for a salad in Seattle, a dessert in Des Moines, or a snack in Singapore.

CITRUS WORLDWIDE

Citrus production around the world has grown dramatically in recent decades. But the major producing regions remain the same as they have been through centuries of civilizations: the Orient, Africa, Mediterranean countries, South America, and the U.S. Sunbelt. Current world volume is over 61 million tons, with U.S. production accounting for 17 percent of the total.

While over 70 percent of Western citrus is sold fresh (largely due to the prominence of the navel orange, a superlative eating fruit), only 16 percent of Florida's production is sold fresh, the bulk being processed into frozen and packaged juices and citrus products.

Consumption of fresh citrus varies from country to country. Some places, such as Indonesia, have import restrictions and receive citrus infrequently. In the U.S., per capita consumption of oranges remains steady at about 15 pounds a year, while Hong Kong boasts the world-record orange consumption of 54 pounds per person per year.

The early history and romance of fresh citrus endures in the rolling green acres of groves throughout California and Arizona. It remains in the fragrance of orange blossoms on a warm evening, and in every fresh, sunny citrus salad or lemon pie—in our house, or yours.

The Sunkist Family of Products

Sunkist products make a world of difference, in other processed products and in any food prepared with them. That's because we grow *and* process citrus and we know everything about it, from the first leaves on a seedling to the essential oils in the peel.

PROCESSED PRODUCTS

Many Sunkist innovations actually pioneered the technology that helped to build today's multibillion dollar citrus-processing industry. Sunkist's two major processing plants in California annually convert over one million tons of fresh citrus into over 400 different products, from juices and concentrates to cattle feed. Some of these products, such as concentrated or single-strength juices and beverage bases, are marketed under our own Sunkist and Exchange brand labels. Others reach your household as the flavoring in orange cake mix, the lemon juice in dishwashing liquid or the fragrance in room fresheners.

Major manufacturers and marketers in over 60 countries around the world have been relying on Sunkist products for generations. Many of the finest flavor and perfume houses of Europe specify Sunkist products for their formulations.

Sunkist operations have expanded in recent years to include packaging of non-citrus flavor juices and beverage bases, including apple, grape, and tropical flavor blends.

LICENSED PRODUCTS

Products bearing the Sunkist name have been marketed overseas since the 1930s. These items have ranged from early citrus-flavored beverages to today's new innovations in nectars and fruit-flavored sauces and toppings. These products are manufactured and marketed by selected companies under license from Sunkist Growers, Inc. Sunkist monitors production and maintains strict quality control standards for all products.

Real growth in U.S. licensed products began in the 1970s. Today, several major companies market Sunkist soft drinks, juices, juice bars, juice drinks, fruit roll snacks, pectin candies, and vitamin C.

The Sunkist name on any item assures the consumer of a quality product that meets the highest standards for products in that category. Each new product that joins our family adds a new dimension to the Sunkist name and provides consumers with a reliable product they know they can trust.

Appetizers and Soups

Perhaps more than any other category, appetizers and soups reflect the range of ethnic cultures in which citrus has flourished and become part of the regional cuisine. From Asia and the Middle East, through sunny Mediterranean hillside groves, to our own neighbor, Mexico, citrus is a key ingredient in dishes like hummus, Greek lemon soup, and chilled seviche.

The best appetizers set the stage for the meal to come. They can reveal the theme for an entire dinner or provide an eclectic array of delicious foods. A richly varied assortment of hors d'oeuvres can even be the total fare for an evening of conversation and cocktails.

However they are served, these recipes are brightly flavored, colorful, and appetizing. And they're the best way to begin an evening for two or a dinner for twenty.

APPETIZERS AND SOUPS

HERBED CHEESE WITH GARLIC AND LEMON
SEVICHE OLÉ
SHRIMP PACIFICA
GRAPEFRUIT AND SHRIMP WITH ZIPPY COCKTAIL SAUCE
CITRUS ICE BOWL
STEAMED BUCKET OF CLAMS
DILLY GUACAMOLE
SALSA MEXICANA
LEMONY GOOD NACHOS
SLIMMERS' TUNA COCKTAIL
ZESTY CLAM DIP
EGGPLANT "CAVIAR"
HUMMUS BI TAHINA
EASY MARINATED MUSHROOMS
MARINATED MUSHROOMS ITALIANO
SALMON DIP FOR VEGETABLES
WESTERN SEAFOOD COCKTAIL
CREAMY HORSERADISH DIP FOR SEAFOOD AND VEGETABLES
DILLED MUSTARD DIP
ANTIPASTO PLATTER
SALMON PÂTÉ
LEMON FRESH BORSCHT
QUICK AND EASY LEMON FISH SOUP
HEARTY BEAN AND MACARONI SOUP
GREEK LEMON SOUP
CHILLED LEMON CUCUMBER SOUP
ORANGE-CARROT SOUP
WONTON SOUP
CALIFORNIA CIOPPINO
OLD-FASHIONED HOMEMADE CHICKEN STOCK

HERBED CHEESE WITH GARLIC AND LEMON

Pack this spread into a small crock. Or double the recipe and mold in a plastic wrap–lined 2-cup bowl. Chill; then unmold onto a serving plate.

- 1 package (8 ounces) cream cheese, softened
- 1 tablespoon finely chopped parsley
- 1 tablespoon finely chopped chives or green onion (scallion)
- 1 tablespoon finely chopped fresh tarragon, dill, or basil leaves
- ¼ teaspoon seasoned salt
- ⅛ teaspoon celery salt
- ⅛ teaspoon onion powder
- ⅛ teaspoon garlic powder
- Grated peel of ½ Sunkist lemon

Makes about 1 cup.

With an electric mixer, beat the cream cheese until light and fluffy. Add all the remaining ingredients *except* the grated peel and beat well. Stir in peel. Cover and chill to blend flavors. Serve as a spread with assorted crackers and/or fruit.

ORANGE VARIATION: Substitute 1 teaspoon fresh grated orange peel for the grated peel of ½ lemon.

SEVICHE OLÉ

The secret of any good seviche is to make it with good, fresh fish ... the fresher, the better!

1 pound fresh halibut, sea bass, or red snapper fillets	2 tablespoons chopped canned or fresh green chiles*
Grated peel of ½ Sunkist lemon	1 tablespoon salad or vegetable oil
¾ cup fresh squeezed lemon juice	1 tablespoon bottled taco sauce or a few drops of hot sauce, to taste
1 large tomato, diced and drained	1 tablespoon chopped cilantro
1 medium onion, chopped	½ teaspoon salt

Makes about 3½ cups.
About 103 calories per ½-cup serving.

With a sharp knife, cut fish on the diagonal into paper-thin slices. In a glass bowl, combine the fish, lemon peel, and lemon juice; cover. Marinate in refrigerator for 8 hours or overnight, until fish is opaque and has a "cooked" look; stir occasionally. (Or marinate in a tightly sealed plastic bag, turning occasionally.) Stir in remaining ingredients. Cover and chill for 30 minutes to blend flavors.

SERVE AS AN APPETIZER: In cocktail glasses, garnishing each as desired with lettuce, avocado slices, lemon slices or cartwheel twists, cilantro, or parsley.

SERVE AS A "DIP": With tortilla or corn chips.

*Reduce amount if using hot varieties, such as serrano or jalapeño chiles.

SHRIMP PACIFICA

1 pound medium shrimp, shelled, deveined, and cooked
3 Sunkist oranges, peeled and cut into bite-size pieces
2 medium onions, thinly sliced
¾ cup distilled white or wine vinegar
½ cup salad or vegetable oil
⅓ cup fresh squeezed lemon juice
¼ cup ketchup
1 medium clove garlic, minced
2 tablespoons sugar
1 tablespoon dehydrated sweet pepper flakes
1 teaspoon mustard seed
½ teaspoon celery seed
½ teaspoon salt
¼ teaspoon pepper
¼ teaspoon dried crushed red pepper
2 tablespoons chopped parsley

Makes about 8 cups.

In a large bowl, combine all the ingredients *except* the parsley; cover. Marinate in refrigerator for 8 hours or overnight; stir occasionally. (Or marinate in a tightly sealed plastic bag, turning occasionally.) To serve, stir in parsley.

TO SERVE AS INDIVIDUAL APPETIZERS: Drain; arrange in individual, lettuce-lined cocktail glasses or small dishes. Makes 6 to 8 servings.

GRAPEFRUIT AND SHRIMP WITH ZIPPY COCKTAIL SAUCE

½ cup chili sauce
½ cup ketchup
1 to 2 teaspoons fresh grated grapefruit peel
2 tablespoons fresh squeezed grapefruit juice
2 to 3 Sunkist grapefruit, peeled, sectioned, and chilled
1 pound medium-large shrimp, shelled, deveined, cooked, and chilled
Citrus Ice Bowl (page 20)

Makes about 1 cup sauce.

To make the sauce, in a small bowl, combine the chili sauce, ketchup, grapefruit peel, and grapefruit juice; cover and chill. Arrange chilled grapefruit sections and shrimp in Citrus Ice Bowl or serving bowl. Serve sauce as a dip for grapefruit sections and shrimp.

LEMON VARIATION: Substitute fresh grated peel of 1 lemon and juice of ½ lemon for grapefruit peel and juice.

CITRUS ICE BOWL

This citrus ice bowl proves that creative entertaining needn't be expensive. It's not only a serving bowl for any chilled appetizer, even if it's as simple as assorted raw vegetables, but a conversation piece as well.

YOU WILL NEED

1 (3-quart) metal bowl	Unpeeled Sunkist oranges and lemons, cut into thin cartwheel slices
1 (1½-quart) metal bowl	
Ice cubes	
2 (10-ounce) packages frozen vegetables to use as weights	Green leaves (mint, celery, dill, etc.)

TO ASSEMBLE

1. Line the bottom of the 3-quart bowl with ice cubes. Place the 1½-quart bowl on the ice cubes in the center of the larger bowl.
2. Holding the smaller bowl in place, fill the space between the bowls one third of the way up with ice cubes.
3. To prevent smaller bowl from sliding, weight it with 2 packages of frozen vegetables.
4. Pour 1 cup of cold water over ice cubes. Freeze until firm.
5. Arrange citrus slices against the sides of the outer bowl, holding them in place with additional ice cubes. Keep the citrus slices below the rim of the outer bowl. Arrange green leaves among the citrus slices.
6. Add water to fill one-third full; freeze until firm. Repeat twice. (The water should only come to within ¼ inch of rim of

larger bowl to allow for expansion during freezing.) Freeze until needed.

TO REMOVE RING FROM METAL BOWLS
1. Remove weights from small bowl; fill with warm water. Small bowl will lift out in about 1 minute.
2. Place larger bowl in warm water; remove Citrus Ice Bowl in about 1 minute.
3. Citrus Ice Bowl can be returned to freezer until ready to use.

TO SERVE
Place Citrus Ice Bowl on chilled serving dish with sloping sides to catch water as bowl melts.

STEAMED BUCKET OF CLAMS

Warm, crusty French or Italian bread is a go-along must for dipping into the zesty clam broth.

18 to 24 hard-shell clams
1 gallon cold water
⅓ cup cornmeal
⅓ cup salt
Grated peel of ½ Sunkist lemon

Juice of 1 Sunkist lemon
2 tablespoons olive or vegetable oil
2 tablespoons chopped parsley
Lemon wedges

Makes 2 to 4 servings.
About 148 calories per serving for 4.

Scrub clams well. To purge clams, combine water, cornmeal, and salt. Add clams and soak for 2 hours. Rinse well. In a 10-inch skillet, arrange clams in a single layer and drizzle them with lemon juice and oil. Bring the liquid to a boil over medium-high heat; cover tightly and cook for 5 minutes. Do not lift the lid of skillet during this cooking time. (If most clams have not opened, cook, covered, 1 to 2 minutes longer.) Remove clams to a serving bowl; discard any unopened clams. Stir lemon peel and parsley into clam juice in skillet. Pour over the clams. Serve with lemon wedges.

DILLY GUACAMOLE

Not a "true" guacamole because of the addition of sour cream and dill, but the zesty flavor is perfect for dipping assorted fresh vegetables.

1 large avocado
½ cup sour cream
Grated peel and juice of
    ½ Sunkist lemon
1 small clove garlic, minced

½ teaspoon dried dill weed
¼ teaspoon salt
⅛ teaspoon hot pepper sauce

Makes about 1 cup.

In a bowl, mash the avocado well; gradually blend in sour cream. Stir in lemon peel and juice, garlic, dill, salt, and hot pepper sauce; cover and chill. Serve as a dip with assorted raw vegetables.

SERVE WITH: Cauliflowerets, sweet green pepper strips or rings, zucchini slices, carrot curls, jícama sticks, cherry tomatoes, etc.

SALSA MEXICANA

Make this salsa as hot or as mild as you like. Serve as a dip with chips or as the salsa on Lemony Good Nachos (page 23).

1 medium clove garlic,
    minced
1 tablespoon salad or
    vegetable oil
1 can (8 ounces) tomato sauce
1 large tomato, chopped
⅓ cup water
¼ cup chopped onion
1 to 2 tablespoons chopped
    cilantro or parsley

Grated peel and juice of
    ½ Sunkist lemon
¼ teaspoon salt
1 or 2 small fresh serrano or
    jalapeño chiles *or* ½ to 1
    teaspoon dried crushed
    red pepper *or* ¼ cup
    chopped canned green
    chiles

Makes about 2 cups.
About 9 calories per tablespoon.

In a small saucepan, sauté the garlic in the oil until tender. Remove from heat and stir in remaining ingredients. Serve at room temperature as a dip with tortilla or corn chips.

Note: Omit water for a thicker salsa or to use with Lemony Good Nachos.

LEMONY GOOD NACHOS

8 (6-inch) corn tortillas*
Salad or vegetable oil
Grated peel of 1 Sunkist lemon
1 cup Salsa Mexicana (page 22)
1 cup (4 ounces) shredded Cheddar or Monterey Jack cheese
¼ cup sliced green onions (scallions)

Makes 4 servings.

Cut each tortilla into 6 or 8 wedges. Let stand, uncovered, to dry slightly. In small batches, fry in 1 inch of hot oil, about 1 minute, turning occasionally, until crisp and lightly browned. Drain the tortilla chips on paper toweling. Arrange chips in a 9- or 10-inch pie plate; sprinkle with grated lemon peel. Spoon Salsa Mexicana over chips; sprinkle with cheese and green onions. Serve as is *or* heat under a broiler for a few minutes to melt cheese.

*In place of the homemade chips, substitute 4 cups of packaged tortilla chips for corn tortillas and oil. Arrange the packaged tortilla chips in a pie plate and proceed as above.

SLIMMERS' TUNA COCKTAIL

1 can (8 ounces) tomato sauce
Grated peel and juice of 1 Sunkist lemon
2 tablespoons chopped parsley
2 teaspoons sugar
¼ teaspoon onion salt
Crisp salad greens
1 can (about 7 ounces) water-packed tuna, drained and chunked
1 cup sliced celery
Lemon cartwheel slices

Makes 4 servings.
About 103 calories per serving.

To make the sauce, combine tomato sauce, lemon peel and juice, parsley, sugar, and onion salt; chill. Arrange greens in 4 sherbet glasses or other small serving dishes. Divide tuna and celery equally on the greens; cover and chill. To serve, spoon the sauce over the tuna. Garnish with lemon cartwheel slices.

ZESTY CLAM DIP

1 package (3 ounces) cream cheese, softened
1 can (about 7 ounces) minced clams, drained
Juice of ½ Sunkist lemon
1 to 2 teaspoons chopped parsley or cilantro
¼ teaspoon soy sauce
1 small clove garlic, minced
Sunkist grapefruit, peeled and segmented and/or assorted raw vegetables

Makes about ⅔ cup.

In a small bowl, combine the cream cheese, clams, lemon juice, parsley, soy sauce, and garlic; blend well. Serve as a dip with grapefruit segments and/or raw vegetables.

EGGPLANT "CAVIAR"

Other sources have called this "poor man's caviar." Inexpensive to make, it is "rich" in flavor and a change from the usual dips and spreads.

1 medium eggplant (about 1½ pounds)
3 tablespoons finely chopped onion
1 small clove garlic, minced
2 tablespoons olive or vegetable oil
2 medium tomatoes, finely chopped
Grated peel and juice of ½ Sunkist lemon
1 teaspoon Worcestershire sauce
¼ teaspoon salt
Toast triangles or assorted crackers

Makes about 2½ cups.

Place the whole, unpeeled eggplant in a baking pan. Bake at 400° F. for 45 to 50 minutes (eggplant will soften and collapse). Cool slightly to handle. Peel and *finely* chop. In a small saucepan, sauté the onion and garlic in the oil until tender. In a bowl, combine eggplant, onion mixture, tomatoes, lemon peel and juice, Worcestershire sauce, and salt. Cover and chill. Serve as a spread on toast or crackers. Garnish with lemon cartwheel twists and parsley sprigs, if desired.

LOWER IN CALORIES VARIATION: Use only 1 tablespoon of oil. Serve as a dip with assorted raw vegetables (cucumber, zucchini, or jícama slices). About 8 calories and 2 mg. sodium per tablespoon.

HUMMUS BI TAHINA

A Middle Eastern menu staple that makes a tangy change-of-pace appetizer served with wedges of warm pita, "pocket," or Arab bread.

1 can (about 16 ounces) garbanzo beans (chick peas)	¼ cup toasted sesame seed
	1 large clove garlic, quartered
	¼ teaspoon salt
Grated peel and juice of 1 Sunkist lemon	

Makes about 1½ cups.

Drain the garbanzos, reserving ½ cup of the liquid. In a blender or food processor, combine garbanzos, ½ cup reserved liquid, and remaining ingredients; blend *well*. Cover and chill. Serve as a spread on crackers, pita bread, or toast triangles. Garnish with lemon cartwheel twists and parsley sprigs, if desired.

VARIATION: Stir in ¼ cup chopped ripe olives *or* canned pimientos after blending; chill.

SERVING SUGGESTION: Serve with warm wedges of Sesame-Citrus Pocket Bread (page 194).

Appetizers and Soups

EASY MARINATED MUSHROOMS

Fresh lemon juice and peel perk up any prepared salad dressing. In this recipe it's the base for a zesty easy-to-prepare mushroom appetizer.

1 bottle (8 ounces) Italian salad dressing
2 pounds medium-to-large mushrooms
Grated peel of ½ Sunkist lemon
Juice of 1 Sunkist lemon
2 tablespoons sliced pimiento (optional)
2 tablespoons chopped parsley

Makes about 4 cups.

In a large saucepan, combine the Italian dressing and mushrooms; bring to a boil. Cook, uncovered, for 2 to 3 minutes, stirring constantly. Add lemon peel, lemon juice, and pimiento. Cover and chill for 4 hours or more. Drain; reserve dressing.* Stir parsley into the mushrooms. Serve as an appetizer with toothpicks. Garnish with lemon cartwheel slices, if desired.

LOWER IN CALORIES VARIATION: Substitute 1 bottle (8 ounces) reduced calorie Italian salad dressing for regular Italian dressing. About 39 calories per ½-cup serving.

*Reserved dressing may be used on salads.

MARINATED MUSHROOMS ITALIANO

Turn this appetizer into a first-course salad by serving the chilled marinated mushroom slices on individual lettuce-lined plates. Garnish with sliced green onions (scallions).

1 pound mushrooms, thickly sliced
¾ cup salad or vegetable oil
Grated peel of ½ Sunkist lemon
Juice of 1 Sunkist lemon
1 teaspoon dried oregano leaves, crushed
1 teaspoon garlic salt
⅛ teaspoon pepper

Makes about 4 cups.

In a large bowl, combine all the ingredients; cover. Marinate in refrigerator for 4 hours or more; stir occasionally. (Or marinate in a tightly sealed plastic bag, turning occasionally.) Serve as an appetizer with toothpicks. Garnish with lemon cartwheel twists and parsley sprigs, if desired.

SALMON DIP FOR VEGETABLES

1 can (7¾ ounces) salmon, drained and flaked
½ cup sour cream
¼ cup finely chopped celery
2 tablespoons chopped green onion (scallion)
1 tablespoon chopped parsley
Grated peel and juice of ½ Sunkist lemon
¼ teaspoon seasoned salt

Makes about 1¼ cups.
About 32 calories per tablespoon.

In a bowl, combine all the ingredients; cover and chill. Serve as a dip with assorted raw vegetables such as cauliflowerets, sweet green pepper strips, carrot sticks, broccoli flowerets, etc.

WESTERN SEAFOOD COCKTAIL

1 can (4¼ ounces, dr. wt.) small shrimp, rinsed and drained
½ cup sliced celery
2 tablespoons salad or vegetable oil
Grated peel and juice of ½ Sunkist lemon
1 tablespoon toasted sesame seed
2 tablespoons sliced green onion (scallion)
1 avocado, cut into chunks*
Lettuce
Paprika
Lemon wedges

Makes 4 servings (about 2 cups).

*To prevent darkening, sprinkle additional lemon juice on the avocado chunks.

In a bowl, combine the shrimp, celery, oil, lemon peel, lemon juice, and sesame seed; cover and chill for 1 hour, stirring occasionally. Stir in green onion and avocado. To serve, spoon about ½ cup of the shrimp mixture into each of 4 lettuce-lined cocktail glasses; sprinkle with paprika and garnish with lemon wedges.

FRESH SHRIMP VARIATION: Substitute 1 cup (⅓ pound) tiny cooked shrimp for the canned shrimp. Add ¼ teaspoon salt, if desired.

TUNA VARIATION: Substitute 1 can (about 7 ounces) water-packed tuna, drained and chunked, for the shrimp.

Note: Can be prepared as 2 entrée servings.

CREAMY HORSERADISH DIP FOR SEAFOOD AND VEGETABLES

1 cup sour cream
Grated peel and juice of ½ Sunkist lemon
1 tablespoon prepared horseradish
1 tablespoon chopped green onion (scallion)
¼ teaspoon salt

Makes about 1 cup.

In a small bowl, combine all the ingredients, blending until smooth; cover and chill. Garnish with additional chopped green onion, if desired. Serve as a dip with cooked crab or shrimp or assorted raw vegetables.

DILLED MUSTARD DIP

1 package (3 ounces) cream cheese, softened
1 cup sour cream
2 to 3 tablespoons Dijon mustard
Grated peel and juice of ½ Sunkist lemon
1 teaspoon dried dill weed
½ teaspoon onion salt

Makes about 1¼ cups.

In a small bowl, combine all the ingredients, blending until smooth. Cover and chill. Serve as a dip with cooked crab or shrimp or assorted raw vegetables.

ANTIPASTO PLATTER

This colorful platter is perfect for a small buffet. Substitute chilled cooked shrimp or cracked crab for the tuna if the budget allows.

1 cup salad or vegetable oil
Juice of 2 Sunkist lemons
1 small clove garlic, minced
½ teaspoon salt
¼ teaspoon dried basil leaves, crushed
⅛ teaspoon pepper
1 cup ripe (black) olives
1 cup sliced mushrooms
1 can (about 8 ounces) artichoke hearts, drained and cut in half
1 small red onion, sliced and separated into rings
1 small cucumber, scored and sliced
Crisp salad greens
2 cans (about 7 ounces each) solid white tuna, drained and chunked
18 cherry tomatoes
3 hard-cooked eggs, cut into wedges
Lemon wedges

Makes 6 to 8 servings.

To make the dressing, combine oil, lemon juice, garlic, salt, basil, and pepper. In a large shallow dish, arrange olives, mushrooms, artichoke hearts, onion rings, and cucumber slices in rows; pour the dressing over the vegetables. Cover and chill for 2 hours. Drain, reserving the dressing. To serve, arrange the greens on a large serving platter and center tuna on greens. Then, in rows, arrange the marinated vegetables, cherry tomatoes, and eggs on both sides of tuna. Garnish with lemon wedges. Serve with reserved dressing.

SALMON PÂTÉ

Here's the perfect make-ahead appetizer . . . it looks good, tastes good, and is fun to prepare and serve.

FILLING
1 can (15½ ounces) salmon, *well drained* and flaked
4 ounces cream cheese, cubed
1 green onion (scallion), cut into 1-inch pieces
Grated peel of ½ Sunkist lemon
Juice of 1 Sunkist lemon
½ teaspoon dried dill weed
½ teaspoon seasoned salt

FROSTING
4 ounces cream cheese, softened
Grated peel of ½ Sunkist lemon
2 to 3 teaspoons milk or cream

Makes about 2 cups.

In a food processor,* using the metal blade, process all the filling ingredients until *well blended*. Line a small (2-cup) bowl with plastic wrap. Spoon salmon mixture into bowl, smoothing top. Cover; chill for 6 hours or overnight. For the frosting, combine the softened cream cheese and lemon peel. Stir in enough milk for a soft spreading consistency. Unmold salmon onto a serving dish; remove plastic wrap. Frost with cream cheese mixture. Sprinkle with additional fresh grated lemon peel and/or chopped parsley, if desired. Serve as an appetizer with assorted crackers or raw vegetables.

FRESH SALMON VARIATION: Substitute 1½ to 2 cups flaked, cooked fresh salmon for the canned salmon.

*To use blender, blend in two batches.

LEMON FRESH BORSCHT

2 cans (about 14 ounces each) beef broth*
2 cups water†
2 cups shredded fresh beets (about 2 medium)
1 cup shredded carrots
1 medium onion, chopped
1 teaspoon sugar
⅛ teaspoon pepper
1 cup shredded cabbage
Grated peel of ½ Sunkist lemon
Juice of 1 Sunkist lemon
Sour cream (optional)

Makes 6 servings (about 6½ cups).
About 49 calories per serving without sour cream.

In a large saucepan, combine the broth, water, beets, carrots, onion, sugar, and pepper; bring to a boil. Cook, covered, over medium heat for 15 minutes, or until vegetables are *just* tender. Add cabbage; cook, covered, 5 to 10 minutes longer. Stir in lemon peel and juice. Serve hot or cold, topped with sour cream and garnished with lemon cartwheel slices, if desired.

*Or substitute 5½ cups homemade beef stock for the broth and water.
†Or substitute 3½ cups homemade chicken stock (page 37) for the broth.

QUICK AND EASY LEMON FISH SOUP

When the fish is in the freezer and the family is hungry, this hearty soup comes to the rescue.

Two cans (about 14 ounces each) chicken broth†
1 medium onion, finely chopped
Grated peel and juice of ½ Sunkist lemon
1 bay leaf
¼ teaspoon dried basil leaves, crushed
1 package (12 ounces) frozen cod, sole, or haddock
1 can (about 15 ounces) whole tomatoes, undrained
1 can (8 ounces) tomato sauce
1½ cups curly or spiral macaroni
2 unpeeled medium zucchini, thinly sliced
¼ pound mushrooms, sliced
½ Sunkist lemon, cut into half-cartwheel slices

Makes 4 to 6 servings (about 8 cups).

In a large saucepot, combine the chicken broth, onion, lemon juice, bay leaf, and basil; bring to a boil. Add the *frozen* fish and reduce heat. Simmer, covered, for 15 minutes, or until fish flakes easily with a fork; remove fish. Cut or break cooked fish into bite-size pieces; reserve. Add the undrained tomatoes and tomato sauce to the stock; bring to a boil. Add the macaroni, stirring occasionally; boil for 5 minutes. Reduce heat. Add zucchini, mushrooms, and lemon peel; simmer for 4 to 5 minutes. Add cooked fish and lemon half-cartwheel slices; heat. Remove the bay leaf before serving.

HEARTY BEAN AND MACARONI SOUP

6 slices bacon
1 medium onion, sliced
1 medium clove garlic, minced
1 tablespoon butter or margarine
2 cans (10¾ ounces each) condensed chicken broth*
2 soup cans water*
1 can (about 16 ounces) garbanzo beans (chick peas), drained
1 can (about 15 ounces) red kidney beans, drained
1 can (about 15 ounces) stewed tomatoes
2 cups *cooked* large shell macaroni
Grated peel and juice of ½ Sunkist lemon

Makes 6 servings (about 10 cups).

In a saucepot, cook the bacon until crisp; remove and crumble. Pour off all but 2 tablespoons of the drippings. Sauté the onion and garlic in the drippings and butter until tender. Add chicken broth, water, beans, tomatoes, macaroni, lemon peel, and juice; heat to blend flavors. To serve, sprinkle individual servings of soup with crumbled bacon and cubed or shredded cheese, sliced green onions (scallions), and additional grated lemon peel, if desired.

*Or substitute 5½ cups homemade chicken stock (page 37) for the broth and water.

Appetizers and Soups   33

GREEK LEMON SOUP

The only secret to this classic lemon soup is to add the hot broth mixture gradually to the beaten eggs. If added too fast, a slight curdling can occur ... not as pretty, but it tastes just as good!

3 cans (about 14 ounces each) chicken broth*	Grated peel and juice of ½ Sunkist lemon
1 cup water*	2 eggs
⅓ cup raw regular rice	Lemon cartwheel slices
	Fresh parsley, chopped

*Makes 6 servings (about 6½ cups).
About 100 calories per serving.*

In a large saucepan, combine the chicken broth, water, and rice; bring to a boil. Cook, covered, over medium-low heat for 15 minutes, or until the rice is tender. In a bowl, combine lemon peel, lemon juice, and eggs, beating well. *Gradually* add 2 cups of the hot broth mixture, beating constantly. Stir back into remaining broth mixture in pan. Heat; do not boil. Garnish with lemon cartwheel slices and parsley.

*Or substitute 6½ cups homemade chicken stock (page 37) for the broth and water.

CHILLED LEMON CUCUMBER SOUP

Vary the richness of this chilled soup to suit your taste ... make it lower in calories with plain yogurt or splurge with heavy cream!

1 can (10¾ ounces) condensed chicken broth	½ teaspoon dried dill weed
2 cucumbers, peeled and chopped	⅛ teaspoon garlic powder
	1 cup sour cream
¼ cup finely chopped onion	1 carton (8 ounces) lowfat plain yogurt *or* heavy or whipping cream *or* 1 cup half-and-half
Grated peel and juice of ½ Sunkist lemon	
	White pepper to taste

Makes 4 to 6 servings (about 5 cups).

In a blender or food processor, combine the chicken broth, cucumbers, onion, lemon peel and juice, dill weed, and garlic powder. Blend until smooth. Stir in sour cream and yogurt; cover and chill about 4 hours. Season with pepper. Garnish with lemon or cucumber slices and fresh dill, if desired.

ORANGE-CARROT SOUP

2 cups water	1 tablespoon light brown sugar
2 cups shredded carrots	⅛ teaspoon pumpkin pie spice
1 small onion, finely chopped	
2 chicken bouillon cubes	Grated peel of ½ Sunkist orange
2 tablespoons butter or margarine	1⅓ cups fresh squeezed or Sunkist chilled orange juice
2 tablespoons all-purpose flour	

Makes 4 servings (about 3½ cups).
About 147 calories per serving.

In a large saucepan, combine the water, carrots, onion, and bouillon cubes; bring to a boil. Reduce heat; cover and simmer for 10 minutes, or until carrots are *very* tender. In a food processor or blender, purée carrot mixture (in two batches) until smooth. In the same saucepan, melt the butter; stir in the flour, sugar, pumpkin pie spice, and orange peel. Cook a few minutes, stirring constantly. Gradually blend in orange juice and puréed carrot mixture. Cook over low heat, stirring until slightly thickened and heated through.

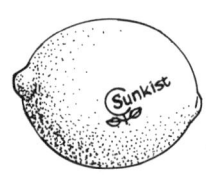

WONTON SOUP

1¼ cups finely chopped cooked chicken
¼ cup finely chopped celery
2 tablespoons finely chopped green onion (scallion)
Grated peel of ½ Sunkist lemon
1 package (12 ounces) wonton skins (about fifty 3½-inch squares)
3 cans (10¾ ounces each) condensed chicken broth*
4 soup cans water (5 cups)*
2 unpeeled medium zucchini, thinly sliced
¼ pound mushrooms, sliced
½ cup shredded carrots
½ Sunkist lemon, cut into cartwheel slices
1 tablespoon soy sauce (optional)

*Makes 8 to 12 servings (about 16 cups).
About 150 calories per serving for 12.*

To make the filling, in a small bowl, combine the chicken, celery, green onion, and lemon peel; mix well.

To make each wonton, lightly dampen the edges of the wonton skin with water. Place 1 teaspoon of filling in the center of wonton; fold in half to top edge (to form a rectangle). Fold again (toward top) to within ⅛ inch of top edge. Press sides to seal in filling; dampen ends with water. Laying rectangle on flat surface, form a horseshoe shape (top edge stretches as dampened ends form bottom of horseshoe). Overlap ends (one on top of the other). Press to seal.

To make the soup, in a large saucepot, combine the chicken broth and water; bring to a boil. Add the wontons; boil gently for 6 minutes, stirring occasionally. Reduce heat and add zucchini, mushrooms, and carrots. Simmer for 2 to 3 minutes; add lemon cartwheel slices and cook 2 minutes more, until vegetables and wontons are tender. Add the soy sauce.

SHRIMP VARIATION: Substitute 1 cup (⅓ pound) tiny cooked shrimp, finely chopped, for the chicken.

*Or substitute 9 cups homemade chicken stock (page 37, doubling the recipe) for the broth and water.

CALIFORNIA CIOPPINO

This is one of the Sunkist kitchen's favorite recipes. It may be called California Cioppino, but it's been served to friends from the West Coast to the shores of New Jersey. Feel free to substitute regional and seasonally available fish for that given, keeping the amount between 2½ to 3 pounds.

1 large onion, chopped
1 large sweet green pepper, chopped
½ cup sliced celery
2 medium cloves garlic, minced
2 teaspoons dried basil leaves, crushed
⅓ cup olive or vegetable oil
1 can (28 ounces) Italian style pear or plum tomatoes, undrained
2 cups dry white wine
1 bottle (8 ounces) clam juice
1 cup water
1 can (6 ounces) tomato paste
⅔ cup chopped parsley
1 teaspoon salt
1 bay leaf
1 Sunkist lemon, cut into cartwheel slices
1½ pounds sea bass, halibut, or other firm white fish, cut into 2-inch pieces
12 hard-shell clams, well scrubbed
½ pound bay scallops
½ pound medium-to-large shrimp, shelled and deveined
Juice of ½ Sunkist lemon
1 to 1½ pounds cooked crab legs, thawed if frozen, cut in 2- to 3-inch pieces and cracked (optional)

Makes 6 to 8 servings (about 16 cups).

In a 6- or 8-quart saucepot, sauté the onion, green pepper, celery, garlic, and basil in the oil until just tender. Add the undrained tomatoes and break up with the edge of a large spoon. Stir in wine, clam juice, water, tomato paste, ⅓ cup of the parsley, salt, and bay leaf; bring to a boil. Reduce heat; cover and simmer for 20 minutes. Add lemon cartwheel slices and sea bass; cook, covered, for 5 minutes. Add clams, scallops, shrimp, and lemon juice; bring to a boil. Reduce heat to medium-high. Cover; cook 5 minutes longer, or until fish is *just* cooked. Add crab and remaining ⅓ cup parsley; heat. Remove the bay leaf. Serve with sourdough bread, if desired.

OLD-FASHIONED HOMEMADE CHICKEN STOCK

Easy enough to make . . . it just needs time to simmer for a rich, full flavor. Freeze for use whenever homemade stock is needed in any recipe. The cooked, boneless chicken meat for use in salads or light entrees is the added bonus.

1 large broiler-fryer chicken (about 4 pounds)	1 to 2 chicken bouillon cubes (optional)
About 8 cups cool water	Spiral peel of 1 Sunkist lemon*
2 medium carrots, quartered	6 whole black peppercorns
1 large onion, quartered	3 sprigs parsley
1 celery stalk with leaves, cut in half	2 bay leaves
	1 teaspoon dried thyme leaves, crushed

Makes about 5 to 6 cups.

Remove the giblets from chicken; reserve the liver for another use or discard it. Cut the chicken into pieces. Arrange chicken pieces and giblets in a 6- to 8-quart saucepot; add enough water to just cover chicken. Bring to a boil and skim any foam from the surface. Add carrots, onion, celery, and bouillon cubes. Make a bouquet garni by wrapping the lemon peel, peppercorns, parsley, bay leaves, and thyme in a square of cheesecloth; tie bundle-fashion with string and add to saucepot. Reduce heat; cover and simmer 45 minutes. Remove the chicken pieces, *except* the wings and giblets, from the stock; cool chicken slightly. Remove and discard skin. Remove meat from bones and reserve for another use. Return the bones to the stock. Simmer briskly, with the cover slightly ajar, for 1½ hours. Strain stock (discarding solids) and chill. Remove solidified fat from surface. To use, heat to boiling.

---

*With vegetable parer, peel the lemon in a continuous spiral, removing the outer colored layer of peel only (save the fruit; squeeze juice for other uses).

Fish and Seafood

Not surprisingly, there is an abundance of excellent recipes for fish with citrus, especially fresh lemon. What makes this collection exciting and useful is the variety of fish and the versatility of many of the recipes.

In many recipes, we've noted several alternative varieties of fish. We've included some unique preparations, such as an oven-fried fish that's crispy but not greasy. A wine-poached fish starts with frozen fillets, a blessing on busy days. Many recipes enhance economical white fish with versatile sauces, such as spicy Italian, exotic curry, or tangy lemon-mustard.

Convenient canned salmon and tuna make a delicious tetrazzini or a baked casserole. More elegant shrimp, salmon, and scallops can be sautéed or grilled with lemon butter.

Some recipes recognize that most fish is naturally low in calories, and add little to dampen a dieter's enthusiasm. While other preparations throw caution to the wind, and splurge with butter and cheese.

Whether you live on a rocky coast, near mountain streams, or a city fish market, you'll find something here to match your catch. We know you'll find pleasure in preparing the harvest from sea or stream.

FISH AND SEAFOOD

COMPANY'S COMING FISH ROLL-UPS
POACHED FISH AND WINE SAUCE
FISH ITALIANO
SWEET AND SOUR FISH DELIGHT
BROILED LEMONY HALIBUT WITH QUICK HERBED HOLLANDAISE
OVEN-FRIED FISH WITH LEMON PONZU SAUCE
EASIEST EVER FISH STEAKS IN FOIL
CRISP-COATED FILLETS WITH TARRAGON TARTAR SAUCE
FISH STEAKS WITH ORANGE-CURRY SAUCE
AVOCADO AND CASHEW-TOPPED FILLETS
SAUTÉED LEMON CALAMARI
SAUCY APPLE FISH ROLLS
SCALLOP SAUTÉ WITH LEMON
SEAFOOD AND ORANGE KABOBS
SHRIMP ALFRESCO
ORIENTAL SHRIMP WITH ORANGES
BUFFET SALMON SUPREME
MUSHROOM-ALMOND BROILED SALMON STEAKS
SALMON BALLS WITH LEMON-MUSTARD SAUCE
QUICK SALMON BAKE FOR TWO
TUNA AND ASPARAGUS CRÊPE ROLL-UPS
BLENDER QUICK HOLLANDAISE SAUCE
LEMON TARTAR SAUCE
CREAMY CUCUMBER SAUCE

COMPANY'S COMING FISH ROLL-UPS

Elegance and ease in one dish. The zesty cheese sauce is excellent on these fish roll-ups as well as over cooked vegetable and egg dishes. Substitute any favorite cheese... caraway, Swiss, or Monterey Jack.

2 tablespoons butter or margarine
2 tablespoons all-purpose flour
¼ teaspoon salt
¼ teaspoon paprika
1¼ cups light cream, half-and-half, or milk
1 cup shredded Cheddar cheese
Grated peel and juice of ½ Sunkist lemon

1 package (10 ounces) frozen chopped spinach, cooked and *well drained*
2 tablespoons finely sliced green onion (scallion)
6 sole, haddock, or flounder fillets (about 1½ pounds)
Hot cooked rice
Lemon cartwheel twists

Makes 6 servings.

To make the sauce, in a saucepan, melt the butter. Remove from heat and stir in flour, salt, and paprika. Cook for a few minutes, stirring constantly. Gradually blend in cream. Cook over medium heat, stirring, until thickened. Add ½ cup of the cheese, lemon peel and juice; stir until cheese melts. In a bowl, combine ⅓ cup of the sauce, spinach, and green onion. Divide spinach mixture equally among fillets; roll up. Place, seam-side-down, in an 8-inch-square baking dish. Spoon remaining sauce over fish rolls. Bake at 350° F. for 30 to 35 minutes, or until fish flakes easily with a fork. Sprinkle with remaining ½ cup of cheese and, if desired, additional sliced green onion. Bake until cheese melts. Serve the fish on the rice. Stir sauce remaining in baking dish; serve over fish and rice. Garnish with lemon cartwheel twists.

POACHED FISH AND WINE SAUCE

This recipe was developed especially for the times "the fish is in the freezer," yet you want a tasty and elegant entrée that can be prepared quickly.

¾ cup water
¾ cup Chablis or other dry white wine
Juice of 1 Sunkist lemon
¼ teaspoon salt
¼ teaspoon pepper
1 bay leaf
2 packages (12 ounces each) frozen sole, cod, or haddock fillets
½ pound mushrooms, sliced
2 tablespoons sliced green onion (scallion)
¼ cup butter or margarine
¼ cup all-purpose flour
½ cup half-and-half
Grated peel of ½ Sunkist lemon
¼ teaspoon ground nutmeg

Makes 4 to 6 servings (about 5 cups).

In a 10-inch skillet, combine the water, wine, lemon juice, salt, pepper, and bay leaf; bring to a boil. Add the *frozen* fish; simmer, covered, for 15 minutes, or until fish flakes easily with a fork. Remove the fish from the skillet; reserve the poaching liquid. Discard the bay leaf. Cut or break cooked fish into bite-size pieces. In the same skillet, sauté the mushrooms and green onion in the butter until just tender. Remove from heat; stir in flour. Cook a few minutes, stirring constantly. Gradually blend in the reserved poaching liquid. Cook over medium heat, stirring, until thickened. Blend in half-and-half, poached fish, lemon peel, and nutmeg; heat. Sprinkle with additional sliced green onion and chopped pimiento, if desired.

SERVING SUGGESTION: Serve over Lemony Good Popovers (page 183).

FISH ITALIANO

SAUCE ITALIANO
1 medium onion, sliced
2 tablespoons butter or margarine
½ teaspoon dried oregano leaves, crushed
1 bay leaf
Generous dash of pepper
1 can (about 15 ounces) stewed tomatoes
1 can (8 ounces) tomato sauce
Grated peel of ½ Sunkist lemon

SAUTÉED FISH
Juice of 1 Sunkist lemon
1 pound sole, cod, or other whitefish fillets
⅓ cup all-purpose flour
½ teaspoon paprika
2 tablespoons butter or margarine
2 tablespoons salad or vegetable oil
Hot cooked spaghetti

Makes 4 servings.

To make the Sauce Italiano, in a large saucepan, sauté the onion in the butter with the oregano, bay leaf, and pepper until just tender. Add stewed tomatoes, tomato sauce, and lemon peel. Bring to a boil; reduce heat. Simmer for 10 minutes to blend the flavors. Remove the bay leaf.

To sauté the fish, sprinkle the lemon juice over the fillets. In a shallow dish, combine flour and paprika. Lightly coat fillets with flour mixture. In a large skillet, heat the butter and oil; sauté fillets for 3 to 4 minutes on each side, until lightly browned and fish flakes easily with a fork. To serve, arrange the fish on the cooked spaghetti. Spoon some sauce over the fish, and pass the rest separately.

FROZEN FRIED FISH VARIATION: Prepare the Sauce Italiano as above. Substitute 1 package (about 14 ounces) of frozen fried fish fillets (6 or 7 count) for the 1 pound of fillets. *Omit* the remaining sautéed fish ingredients. Prepare frozen fish fillets following package directions; sprinkle with the juice of ½ lemon. Serve as above with spaghetti and sauce.

SWEET AND SOUR FISH DELIGHT

½ pound halibut, swordfish, or other firm whitefish steak, cut into 1-inch cubes
Juice of 1 Sunkist lemon (3 tablespoons)
Water
1 small sweet green pepper, cut into strips
2 tablespoons finely chopped onion
1 tablespoon butter or margarine
¼ teaspoon ground ginger
1 can (8¾ ounces) apricot halves in heavy syrup
1 tablespoon soy sauce
¼ cup Chablis or other dry white wine
1 tablespoon cornstarch
1 teaspoon fresh grated lemon peel
Hot cooked rice and/or chow mein noodles

Makes 2 servings.

Place the fish cubes and 1 tablespoon of the lemon juice in a saucepan; add water to just cover fish. Bring to a boil; reduce heat. Simmer, covered, for 7 to 9 minutes, or until fish flakes easily with a fork. Drain. In a skillet, sauté the green pepper and onion in the butter with the ginger until just tender. Drain the apricots, reserving the syrup. Add apricot syrup, soy sauce, and remaining 2 tablespoons of lemon juice to skillet. Gradually blend the wine into the cornstarch; add to sautéed mixture. Cook over medium heat, stirring, until thickened. Add cooked fish, drained apricots, and lemon peel; heat. Serve with cooked rice and/or chow mein noodles. Garnish with lemon wedges, if desired.

BROILED LEMONY HALIBUT WITH QUICK HERBED HOLLANDAISE

Simple preparation brings out the best in good-quality fish. A quick-to-prepare herbed hollandaise sauce tops these simply prepared halibut steaks.

BROILED LEMONY HALIBUT

3 tablespoons salad or vegetable oil
Grated peel of ½ Sunkist lemon
Salt
Paprika
4 halibut steaks (1½ to 2 pounds)

QUICK HERBED HOLLANDAISE

½ cup butter or margarine
Juice of ½ Sunkist lemon (1½ tablespoons)
¼ teaspoon dried tarragon, dill, or basil leaves, crushed
Generous dash of white pepper (optional)
3 egg yolks*
1 tablespoon chopped parsley

Makes 4 servings (about ¾ cup sauce).

To prepare the broiled halibut, in a small bowl, combine the oil, lemon peel, salt, and paprika. Lightly brush the halibut with oil mixture; place fish on broiler pan. Broil 4 to 5 inches from heat for 5 to 6 minutes on each side, or until fish flakes easily with a fork. Brush occasionally with remaining oil mixture. Meanwhile, make the Quick Herbed Hollandaise. Serve the sauce over the fish. Garnish with lemon cartwheel twists and parsley sprigs, if desired.

To prepare the Quick Herbed Hollandaise, in a small saucepan, heat the butter with the lemon juice, tarragon, and pepper until bubbly. Add slowly to egg yolks, beating constantly with a wire whisk. Stir in the chopped parsley.

*Make sure the egg yolks are completely free of whites when separating the eggs.

OVEN-FRIED FISH WITH LEMON PONZU SAUCE

No deep-fat frying necessary for these crispy sesame-flavored "fish sticks."

Grated peel and juice of ½ Sunkist lemon
1½ pounds halibut, swordfish, or shark steaks (¾ to 1 inch thick), cut into 1-inch-wide strips
¼ cup yellow cornmeal
2 tablespoons all-purpose flour
2 tablespoons toasted sesame seed
½ teaspoon paprika
½ teaspoon onion salt
3 tablespoons salad or vegetable oil
Lemon Ponzu Sauce (below)

Makes 4 servings.

Preheat the oven to 500° F. Place a 13 × 9 × 2-inch baking dish in the oven to heat. Meanwhile, sprinkle the lemon peel and juice over the fish. In a shallow dish, combine the cornmeal, flour, sesame seed, paprika, and onion salt. Lightly coat fish with cornmeal mixture. Let stand for a few minutes for coating to set. Carefully remove the hot baking dish from the oven; coat the bottom of the dish with oil. Dip the fish in the oil, turning to coat all sides. Bake, uncovered, for 8 to 10 minutes, or until lightly browned and fish flakes easily with a fork. (It is not necessary to turn the fish.) Serve with Lemon Ponzu Sauce. Garnish with lemon wedges and parsley sprigs, if desired.

LEMON PONZU SAUCE

¼ cup water
2 tablespoons soy sauce
2 tablespoons dry sherry
Grated peel and juice of ½ Sunkist lemon

Makes about ½ cup.

In a small saucepan, combine all the ingredients; heat. Serve as a dipping sauce for the fish.

Fish and Seafood

EASIEST EVER FISH STEAKS IN FOIL

1 pound salmon, halibut, or swordfish steaks (1 inch thick)
Grated peel and juice of ½ Sunkist lemon
Salt
Paprika
1 tablespoon butter or margarine

Makes 4 servings.

Place the fish on a large piece of heavy-duty aluminum foil. Sprinkle with the lemon peel and juice, salt, and paprika; dot with butter. Wrap securely, place on a baking sheet, and bake at 450° F. for 10 to 13 minutes, or until fish flakes easily with a fork.

CRISP-COATED FILLETS WITH TARRAGON TARTAR SAUCE

Fresh lemon, fish, and tarragon make a 3-star flavor combination.

2 cups ice water
Juice of ½ Sunkist lemon
¼ teaspoon salt
1 pound halibut, sole, cod, or other whitefish fillets
½ cup corn flake crumbs
¼ cup grated Parmesan cheese
2 eggs, slightly beaten
¼ to ⅓ cup salad or vegetable oil
Lemon wedges
Parsley sprigs
Tarragon Tartar Sauce (page 48)

Makes 4 servings.

In a large shallow dish, combine the ice water, lemon juice, and salt. Add the fillets; let stand 5 minutes. Drain and pat dry with paper toweling. In a shallow dish, combine the corn flake crumbs and Parmesan cheese. Dip fillets into beaten eggs and then into crumb mixture. Dip and coat again. Let stand a few minutes for coating to set. In a large skillet, heat the oil and sauté the fillets for 3 to 4 minutes on each side until lightly browned and fish flakes easily with a fork. Garnish with lemon wedges and parsley sprigs. Serve with Tarragon Tartar Sauce.

Note: More corn flake crumbs and Parmesan cheese may be needed depending on the number of fillets per pound.

TARRAGON TARTAR SAUCE

½ cup mayonnaise or salad dressing
½ cup finely chopped dill pickle
3 tablespoons finely chopped onion
2 tablespoons chopped parsley
Grated peel and juice of ½ Sunkist lemon
½ to 1 teaspoon dried tarragon leaves, crushed
⅛ teaspoon pepper

Makes about 1 cup.

In a bowl, combine all the ingredients; chill.

FISH STEAKS WITH ORANGE-CURRY SAUCE

4 halibut, salmon, or other firm fish steaks (¾ inch thick)
Salad or vegetable oil
Salt and pepper
¾ cup mayonnaise or salad dressing
¼ cup ketchup
2 teaspoons fresh grated orange peel
2 tablespoons fresh squeezed orange juice
¼ teaspoon curry powder
1 Sunkist orange, cut into wedges or half-cartwheel slices
Cilantro sprigs (optional)

Makes 4 servings.

Brush the fish lightly with oil; then sprinkle with salt and pepper. Barbecue on a grill or broil 4 to 5 inches from heat for 5 to 7 minutes on each side, or until fish flakes easily with a fork. Brush occasionally with additional oil. Meanwhile, to make sauce, combine the mayonnaise, ketchup, orange peel, orange juice, and curry powder. Serve the sauce with the fish. Garnish with orange wedges and cilantro sprigs.

AVOCADO AND CASHEW-TOPPED FILLETS

This colorful fish entrée tastes as good as it looks.

4 sole or haddock fillets (about 1 pound)
Salt and pepper
2 tablespoons fresh squeezed lemon juice
Fine dry bread crumbs (seasoned or plain)
2 tablespoons butter or margarine
2 tablespoons salad or vegetable oil
1/3 cup light cream or half-and-half
1 teaspoon fresh grated lemon peel
1 avocado, sliced
Whole or chopped salted cashews
Lemon half-cartwheel slices
Parsley sprigs

Makes 4 servings.

Sprinkle the fillets with salt, pepper, and 1 tablespoon of the lemon juice; let stand for 5 to 10 minutes. Coat the fillets with bread crumbs. In a large skillet, heat the butter and oil; sauté the fillets for 3 to 4 minutes on each side, or until lightly browned and fish flakes easily with a fork. Remove the fish to a serving dish; sprinkle with the remaining 1 tablespoon of lemon juice. Keep warm. Add cream and lemon peel to the pan drippings. Bring to a boil, stirring constantly, until slightly thickened; spoon sauce over fish. Top with avocado slices and cashews. Garnish with lemon half-cartwheel slices and parsley sprigs.

SAUTÉED LEMON CALAMARI

Thin pieces of calamari cook in just minutes. The texture is somewhat like abalone with the flavor of sole, light and "unfishy."

3 tablespoons butter or margarine
1/4 teaspoon garlic salt
1 pound (4 thin pieces) calamari (giant squid)
Grated peel and juice of 1/2 Sunkist lemon
1 tablespoon chopped green onion (scallion)
1 tablespoon chopped parsley

Makes 4 servings.

In a large skillet, heat the butter with the garlic salt; sauté the calamari for 2 minutes on each side. (Calamari will remain white when fully cooked; do not brown.) Add lemon peel and juice, green onion, and parsley; sauté briefly. Garnish with lemon cartwheel slices, if desired.

SOLE VARIATION: If calamari is unavailable, substitute 1 pound sole fillets. Proceed as above, sautéing the fillets for 3 to 4 minutes on each side, or until lightly browned and fish flakes easily with a fork.

SAUCY APPLE FISH ROLLS

4 sole, cod, or perch fillets (about 1 pound)
¾ cup *plus* 2 tablespoons apple juice
Grated peel and juice of ½ Sunkist lemon
⅛ teaspoon salt
2 tablespoons butter or margarine
1 tablespoon all-purpose flour
1 tablespoon chopped parsley

Makes 4 servings.

Roll up fish fillets and place, seam-side-down, in a large saucepan. Add ¾ cup apple juice, lemon peel, lemon juice, and salt; dot fish with butter. Bring to a boil, reduce heat, cover, and simmer for 15 minutes, or until the fish flakes easily with a fork. Remove fish to a serving platter and keep warm. To make the sauce, gradually blend remaining 2 tablespoons apple juice into the flour; add to pan drippings. Cook over medium heat, stirring until thickened; add the parsley. To serve, spoon sauce over fish rolls.

MICROWAVE-HIGH POWER SETTING
Roll up fish fillets and place, seam-side-down, in an 8-inch-square glass baking dish. Add ¾ cup apple juice, lemon peel, lemon juice, and salt; dot fish with butter. Cook, covered with plastic wrap, for 3 minutes. Uncover and spoon cooking liquid over fish rolls. Cook, covered, for 3 to 4 minutes longer, or until fish flakes

easily with a fork. Remove fish to a serving platter; let stand, covered, for 2 minutes while making sauce. Reserve cooking liquid in baking dish. Gradually blend remaining 2 tablespoons apple juice into the flour; stir into reserved cooking liquid. Cook, covered, for 2 to 3 minutes (stirring once), until sauce boils and thickens; add the parsley. To serve, spoon sauce over fish.

SCALLOP SAUTÉ WITH LEMON

Try serving these bay or sea scallops, flavored with bacon, toasted sesame seed, and fresh lemon on cooked spinach pasta or parsleyed rice.

1 to 1½ pounds bay or sea scallops*
3 tablespoons toasted sesame seed
6 slices bacon

Grated peel and juice of 1 Sunkist lemon
2 teaspoons cornstarch
2 tablespoons chopped parsley

Makes 4 servings.

Rinse the scallops well; drain and pat dry with paper toweling. In a bowl, combine the scallops and sesame seed, stirring to coat evenly. In a large skillet, cook the bacon until crisp; remove, drain, and crumble. Pour off and reserve drippings. Wipe the skillet clean. Sauté the scallops (in two batches) in reserved drippings about 4 to 5 minutes. Return all the scallops to the skillet; stir in lemon peel and crumbled bacon. Gradually blend the lemon juice into the cornstarch; add to scallop mixture. Cook over medium heat, stirring, until slightly thickened. Sprinkle with parsley. Garnish with lemon wedges, if desired.

*Slice large sea scallops in half before coating them with the sesame seed.

SEAFOOD AND ORANGE KABOBS

Fresh oranges are the added dimension in these seafood kabobs.

Grated peel of ½ Sunkist orange
⅓ cup fresh squeezed orange juice
¼ cup salad or vegetable oil
¼ cup finely chopped onion
¼ teaspoon dried rosemary leaves, crushed
¼ teaspoon dried thyme leaves, crushed
¼ teaspoon salt
1 pound halibut or shark steak, cut into 1-inch cubes *or* 1 pound sea scallops (16 to 20)
1 unpeeled Sunkist orange, cut into 12 half-wedges*
12 medium mushrooms

Makes 4 servings.

To make the marinade, in a bowl, combine the orange peel, orange juice, oil, onion, rosemary, thyme, and salt; add the fish. Cover and marinate in refrigerator for 1 hour or longer, stirring occasionally. (Or marinate in a tightly sealed plastic bag, turning occasionally.) Drain marinade and reserve. Arrange the fish, orange half-wedges, and mushrooms alternately on 4 long metal or wooden skewers. Place the kabobs on a broiler pan. Brush with reserved marinade. Broil 4 inches from heat for 12 to 14 minutes, turning and brushing occasionally with remaining marinade.

*To make orange half-wedges, cut the orange in half crosswise; place cut-side-up. Cut 3 wedges from each half; cut the wedges in half.

SHRIMP ALFRESCO

⅔ cup salad or vegetable oil
Grated peel of ½ Sunkist lemon
⅓ cup fresh squeezed lemon juice
1 tablespoon minced onion
1 small clove garlic, minced
2 teaspoons sugar
½ teaspoon dried tarragon leaves, crushed
½ teaspoon salt
¼ teaspoon white pepper
¼ teaspoon paprika
1½ pounds medium shrimp, shelled and deveined
Lemon wedges

Makes 6 servings

To make the marinade, in a bowl, combine all the ingredients *except* the shrimp and lemon wedges; add the shrimp. Cover and marinate in refrigerator for 4 hours or overnight, stirring occasionally. (Or marinate in a tightly sealed plastic bag, turning occasionally.) Drain and reserve the marinade. Thread 6 to 8 shrimp on 6 long metal or wooden skewers. Barbecue on a grill 4 inches above glowing coals for 5 to 8 minutes, turning and brushing occasionally with the remaining marinade. Serve with lemon wedges.

TO BROIL THE SHRIMP: Place on a broiler pan 4 to 5 inches from heat and cook as above.

ORIENTAL SHRIMP WITH ORANGES

1 medium sweet green pepper, cut into thin strips
1 medium onion, chopped
2 tablespoons butter or margarine
Juice of 3 Sunkist oranges (1 cup)
3 tablespoons light brown sugar
1 tablespoon soy sauce
¼ teaspoon dry mustard
⅛ teaspoon pepper
¼ cup fresh squeezed lemon juice
2 tablespoons cornstarch
2 Sunkist oranges, peeled and cut into bite-size pieces
½ pound cooked small to medium shrimp *or* 2 cans (4¼ ounces dr. wt. each), rinsed and drained
Hot cooked rice

Makes 4 servings.

In a large saucepan, sauté the green pepper and onion in the butter until just tender. Add the orange juice, brown sugar, soy sauce, dry mustard, and pepper. Gradually blend the lemon juice into the cornstarch; add to vegetable mixture. Cook over medium heat, stirring, until thickened. Simmer for 5 minutes to blend the flavors. Add orange pieces and shrimp; heat. Serve on cooked rice.

BUFFET SALMON SUPREME

A perfect buffet dish or a colorful one-dish family meal.

1 can (15½ ounces) salmon
½ pound mushrooms, sliced
4 tablespoons butter or margarine
½ cup chopped green onions (scallions)
2 medium cloves garlic, minced
¼ cup all-purpose flour
½ teaspoon salt (optional)
⅛ teaspoon pepper
1 cup chicken broth
1 cup half-and-half
8 ounces spaghetti, cooked and drained
¼ cup grated Parmesan cheese
Grated peel of ½ Sunkist lemon
Juice of 1 Sunkist lemon
1 package (10 ounces) frozen broccoli, cooked and cut into bite-size pieces

Makes 6 servings (about 9 cups).

Drain and chunk the salmon, reserving the liquid. In a large saucepot, sauté the mushrooms in 2 tablespoons of the butter until just tender; remove. In the remaining 2 tablespoons of butter, sauté the green onions and garlic. Remove from heat; stir in flour, salt, and pepper. Cook for a few minutes, stirring constantly. Gradually blend in the chicken broth, half-and-half, and reserved salmon liquid. Cook over medium heat, stirring, until thickened. Add the cooked spaghetti, Parmesan cheese, lemon peel and juice; heat. Gently stir in mushrooms, broccoli, and salmon; heat. Arrange on a serving platter. Garnish with lemon cartwheel slices and parsley sprigs and serve with additional Parmesan cheese, if desired.

MUSHROOM-ALMOND BROILED SALMON STEAKS

4 salmon steaks (about 1¼ pounds), ¾ inch thick
Salad or vegetable oil
Grated peel and juice of ½ Sunkist lemon
2 tablespoons butter or margarine, softened
¼ pound mushrooms, chopped
2 tablespoons chopped parsley
2 tablespoons sliced almonds

Makes 4 servings.

Lightly brush the fish with oil. Place on a broiler pan and sprinkle with the lemon juice. Broil 4 to 5 inches from the heat for 4 to 6 minutes on each side, or until fish flakes easily with a fork. Meanwhile, in a bowl, combine the butter and lemon peel; stir in mushrooms, parsley, and almonds. Spoon mixture evenly over fish. Broil 1 to 2 minutes longer. Garnish with lemon wedges and parsley sprigs, if desired.

LOWER IN SODIUM VARIATION: Omit the oil; spray the broiler pan with non-stick cooking spray. Substitute 2 tablespoons *unsalted* butter or margarine for the regular butter or margarine. Proceed as above. Makes 4 servings. About 241 calories and 58 mg. sodium per serving.

SALMON BALLS WITH LEMON-MUSTARD SAUCE

This entrée is designed for two, but the recipe can easily be doubled.

SALMON BALLS
1 can (7¾ ounces) salmon
½ cup crushed cracker crumbs (soda, sesame, etc.)
2 tablespoons chopped green onion (scallion)
1 egg, slightly beaten
Juice of ½ Sunkist lemon
⅛ teaspoon pepper
3 tablespoons salad or vegetable oil
Hot cooked large shell or other macaroni *or* fettuccine

LEMON-MUSTARD SAUCE
Water
Reserved salmon liquid
1 tablespoon butter or margarine
1 tablespoon all-purpose flour
¼ teaspoon salt
Generous dash of pepper
¼ cup mayonnaise or salad dressing
Grated peel of ½ Sunkist lemon
½ teaspoon prepared mustard

Makes 2 servings (about 1 cup sauce).

To make the Salmon Balls, drain and flake the salmon, reserving the liquid for the sauce. In a bowl, combine the salmon, cracker crumbs, green onion, egg, lemon juice, and pepper. Shape firmly into 8 balls. In a skillet, brown the salmon balls well in oil. Serve on cooked macaroni with Lemon-Mustard Sauce. Garnish with lemon wedges and parsley, if desired.

To make the Lemon-Mustard Sauce, add water to the reserved salmon liquid to equal ¾ cup. In a small saucepan, melt the butter. Remove from heat and stir in the flour, salt, and pepper. Cook for a few minutes, stirring constantly. Gradually blend in the liquid. Cook over medium heat, stirring, until thickened. Remove from heat; blend in mayonnaise, lemon peel, and mustard.

QUICK SALMON BAKE FOR TWO

1½ cups *cooked* rice
1 can (7¾ ounces) salmon, drained and flaked
½ cup shredded Cheddar cheese
¼ cup chopped green onions (scallions)
2 eggs, slightly beaten
2 tablespoons butter or margarine, melted
Grated peel of 1 Sunkist lemon
Juice of ½ Sunkist lemon
¼ teaspoon seasoned salt

Makes 2 servings.

In a bowl, combine all the ingredients and mix well. Spoon into 2 small (about 1½-cup) ovenproof individual casseroles. Bake at 350° F. for 25 minutes. Sprinkle with additional cheese and garnish with lemon cartwheel twists and parsley sprigs, if desired.

TUNA VARIATION: Substitute 1 can (about 7 ounces) tuna for the salmon.

TUNA AND ASPARAGUS CRÊPE ROLL-UPS

With extra lemon crêpes on hand in the freezer, these tuna and asparagus roll-ups can be oven-ready in no time.

1 can (about 7 ounces) tuna, drained and flaked	Grated peel of ½ Sunkist lemon
1 cup shredded Cheddar cheese	10 Hint of Lemon Crêpes (page 189)
1 can (about 4 ounces) sliced mushrooms, drained	1 package (10 ounces) frozen asparagus spears, cooked and drained
2 tablespoons finely chopped green onion (scallion)	Blender Quick Hollandaise Sauce (below)

Makes 4 to 5 servings.

In a bowl, combine the tuna, cheese, mushrooms, green onion, and lemon peel. Spoon about 3 tablespoons of the tuna mixture onto each crêpe. Top each with 2 to 3 asparagus spears; roll up. Place, seam-side-down, on a baking sheet. Bake at 350° F. for 15 minutes, or until heated through. Serve with Blender Quick Hollandaise Sauce.

BLENDER QUICK HOLLANDAISE SAUCE

Serve with Tuna and Asparagus Crêpe Roll-ups (above), or any broiled, baked, or barbecued fish. For a "no blender" variation of this tangy hollandaise sauce see page 119.

½ cup butter or margarine	2 tablespoons fresh squeezed lemon juice
3 egg yolks*	⅛ teaspoon salt

Makes about 1 cup.

*Make sure the egg yolks are completely free of whites when separating the eggs.

In a small saucepan, heat the butter until bubbly. In a blender, process the egg yolks, lemon juice, and salt on "high" for 2 to 3 seconds. With the blender still running, remove the center cap of the cover; slowly add hot butter in a thin stream, blending just until the mixture thickens.

HERB VARIATION: Add ⅛ to ¼ teaspoon of any *one* of the following herbs to the butter: dried tarragon, oregano, basil, marjoram, or dill weed. Heat.

LEMON TARTAR SAUCE

Serve this traditional sauce with any fried, broiled, or poached fish.

½ cup Lemon Fresh
    Mayonnaise (page 142)
1 (2-inch) dill pickle, finely
    chopped
1 green onion (scallion),
    finely chopped

1 teaspoon fresh grated lemon
    peel
2 teaspoons fresh squeezed
    lemon juice

Makes about ½ cup.

In a bowl, combine all the ingredients; cover and chill.

CREAMY CUCUMBER SAUCE

Delicious on any poached, baked, or fried fish.

½ cup Lemon Fresh
    Mayonnaise (page 142)
½ medium cucumber, peeled,
    shredded, and drained
1 teaspoon fresh grated lemon
    peel

2 teaspoons fresh squeezed
    lemon juice
¼ teaspoon dried dill weed
Salt and pepper to taste

Makes about 1 cup.

In a bowl, combine all the ingredients; cover and chill.

Poultry

Richly delicious roast duck with orange sauce is a standard of elegance and a classic blend of flavors. From this heritage has grown a whole new family of contemporary citrus and poultry recipes. Chicken—inexpensive, light, nutritious, and easy to prepare—adapts well to sweet or savory seasoning. Poultry can be flavored in a grapefruit marinade and grilled; simmered in a skillet and garnished with orange slices; baked with a citrus sauce; or oven-roasted with a lemon and brandy glaze. For the easiest treatment of all, serve baked or broiled chicken with lemon wedges, as you would fish. It will become a standard, and a favorite.

Versatility of preparation and presentation makes poultry a favorite with busy and creative cooks. Citrus flavors make poultry a favorite with everyone. From easy to elegant, low calorie to extravagant, nothing beats poultry with citrus.

POULTRY

CRISPY BAKED CITRUS CHICKEN
LEMON CHICKEN AND ZUCCHINI
SLIM JIM BAKED CHICKEN LEGS
GRAPEFRUIT-TARRAGON CHICKEN
POULET WITH ORANGE SAUCE (GROWER RECIPE)
FAR EAST CHICKEN STRIPS AND FRUIT
SAVORY CHICKEN AND RICE
CURRIED BAKED CHICKEN
ORANGE BARBECUED CHICKEN
CITRUS BAKED CORNISH HENS
ROAST DUCKLING WITH HONEY-ORANGE SAUCE
FRUIT-AND-BRANDY-STUFFED GOOSE WITH LEMON SAUCE FLAMBÉ
BARBECUED TURKEY DRUMSTICKS
ROAST TURKEY WITH ALMOND DRESSING
AND LEMON-HONEY GLAZE

CRISPY BAKED CITRUS CHICKEN

Use any kind of cracker crumbs—sesame, wheat, or bacon—or substitute crushed regular or barbecued tortilla or corn chips. Cooking the chicken pieces on a rack makes it crunchy on all sides.

Grated peel and juice of ½ Sunkist orange or lemon
¼ cup butter or margarine, melted
1 cup *finely* crushed crackers *or* corn or tortilla chips
1 teaspoon paprika
½ teaspoon seasoned salt
2 pounds chicken drumsticks (10 to 12)

Makes 4 servings.

In a shallow dish, combine the peel, juice, and butter. In a second dish, combine crushed crackers, paprika, and seasoned salt. Dip the chicken in the butter mixture; then coat it with cracker mixture. Arrange chicken on a rack in a shallow baking pan; loosely cover with aluminum foil. Bake at 400° F. for 40 minutes. Remove the foil and bake, uncovered, 15 to 20 minutes longer, or until chicken is tender.

OLÉ VARIATION: With crushed corn or tortilla chips, try substituting 1 teaspoon chili powder for the paprika and ½ teaspoon garlic salt for the seasoned salt.

BROILER-FRYER VARIATION: Substitute 1 broiler-fryer (about 2½ pounds), cut into serving-size pieces, for the chicken drumsticks.

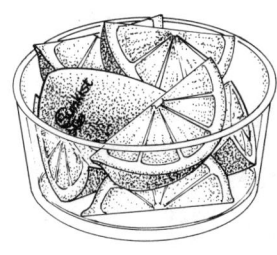

LEMON CHICKEN AND ZUCCHINI

1 broiler-fryer (about 2½ pounds), cut into serving-size pieces
2 tablespoons salad or vegetable oil
¾ cup water
1 medium onion, sliced
1 chicken bouillon cube
½ teaspoon dried basil leaves, crushed
2 unpeeled medium zucchini, thickly sliced
2 tablespoons cornstarch
Grated peel and juice of ½ Sunkist lemon
Sliced or chopped pimientos (optional)
½ Sunkist lemon, cut into half-cartwheel slices

Makes 4 servings.

In a 10-inch skillet, lightly brown the chicken in the oil; pour off the fat. Add ½ cup of the water, onion, bouillon cube, and basil. Cover and cook over low heat for 30 minutes. Add zucchini. Cover and cook 15 minutes longer, or until chicken and zucchini are tender. Remove chicken to a serving platter and keep warm. To make the sauce, gradually blend the remaining ¼ cup of water into the cornstarch; add to ingredients remaining in skillet. Cook over medium heat, stirring, until thickened. Add lemon peel and juice. Serve the sauce and vegetables over the chicken. Garnish with pimientos and lemon half-cartwheel slices.

SLIM JIM BAKED CHICKEN LEGS

As the name indicates, the calories have been cut by eliminating fat and oil. The chicken skin can be removed before cooking, but it helps to keep the chicken moist as it bakes. Other chicken parts can be substituted for the legs in this recipe.

Grated peel and juice of ½ Sunkist lemon
1 teaspoon paprika
½ teaspoon dried oregano or basil leaves, crushed
¼ teaspoon garlic salt
6 whole chicken legs with thighs (about 2½ pounds)

Makes 6 servings.
About 315 calories per serving.

Combine the lemon peel, paprika, oregano, and garlic salt; rub well into all sides of the chicken. Arrange the chicken on a rack in a shallow baking pan and loosely cover with aluminum foil. Bake at 400° F. for 40 minutes. Remove foil and sprinkle lemon juice over chicken. Bake, uncovered, 15 to 20 minutes longer, or until chicken is tender. Sprinkle with chopped parsley, if desired.

GRAPEFRUIT-TARRAGON CHICKEN

1 broiler-fryer (about 2½ pounds), cut into serving-size pieces
2 tablespoons salad or vegetable oil
2 cups thinly sliced carrots
1 medium onion, sliced
1 cup diagonally sliced celery
2 teaspoons fresh grated grapefruit peel
½ cup fresh squeezed grapefruit juice
¼ cup dry sherry
1 teaspoon dried tarragon leaves, crushed
¼ teaspoon salt
⅛ teaspoon pepper
¼ cup cold water
2 tablespoons all-purpose flour
1 Sunkist grapefruit, peeled, sectioned, and drained

Makes 4 servings.

In a 10-inch skillet, lightly brown the chicken in the oil; pour off the fat. Add all the remaining ingredients *except* the water, flour, and grapefruit sections. Cover and cook over low heat for 45 minutes, or until chicken is tender. Remove chicken and vegetables to a serving platter and keep warm. To make the sauce, gradually blend the water into the flour; add to the pan drippings. Cook over medium heat, stirring until thickened. Add grapefruit sections and heat. Serve the sauce over the chicken and vegetables.

POULET WITH ORANGE SAUCE
Eliza Poon, Mission Viejo, California
(Grower recipe contest winner)

As a child growing up in Hong Kong, Eliza loved Sunkist oranges from America. After living in China, studying in England, and finally moving to California, she fulfilled a lifelong dream by purchasing a 15-acre grove of orange trees. Today she uses fresh citrus in recipes for many Chinese and American dishes. This chicken with orange sauce is a family favorite—especially when the oranges are from her own ranch.

6 half chicken breasts (about 3 pounds)
Salt and pepper
2 tablespoons butter or margarine
½ cup fresh squeezed orange juice
¼ cup *plus* 2 tablespoons Chablis or other dry white wine
2 tablespoons chopped onion
1 tablespoon sugar
Hot cooked rice
1 tablespoon cornstarch
1 teaspoon fresh grated orange peel
2 Sunkist oranges, peeled and sectioned
1 Sunkist orange, cut into cartwheel slices
Parsley sprigs

Makes 6 servings.

Sprinkle the chicken with salt and pepper. In a large skillet, brown the chicken (in two batches) in the butter. Add orange juice, ¼ cup of the wine, onion, and sugar. Cover and cook over low heat for 20 to 25 minutes, or until chicken is tender. Arrange the chicken on the cooked rice on a serving platter and keep warm. Spoon off any excess fat from the pan drippings. To make the sauce, gradually blend the 2 tablespoons of wine into the cornstarch; add to pan drippings. Cook, stirring, until thickened. Stir in orange peel and sections and heat. Serve the sauce over the chicken. Garnish with orange cartwheel slices and parsley sprigs.

FAR EAST CHICKEN STRIPS AND FRUIT

A perfect prepare-ahead entrée for company. Fresh grapefruit juice adds liveliness to this Oriental-style marinade. The fruit and green pepper are skewered separately from the chicken, as they just need to be heated through on the barbecue.

6 half chicken breasts (about 3 pounds), skinned and boned
1 large sweet green pepper, cut into 12 pieces
6 canned pineapple slices, cut in half
1 Sunkist grapefruit, peeled and segmented

½ cup fresh squeezed grapefruit juice
¼ cup salad or vegetable oil
¼ cup soy sauce
¼ cup honey
¼ teaspoon ground ginger
¼ teaspoon garlic powder
Hot cooked rice

Makes 6 servings.

Cut each half chicken breast into 3 lengthwise strips. Thread 3 strips accordion-fashion on each of 6 long metal or wooden skewers. Parboil the green pepper in boiling water for 2 minutes; drain. On 6 additional skewers, alternately arrange the green pepper, pineapple, and grapefruit segments. Place all the skewers on a large platter or a 15½ × 10½ × 1-inch jellyroll pan. To make the marinade, combine the grapefruit juice, oil, soy sauce, honey, ginger, and garlic powder. Pour marinade over chicken and fruit. Cover with plastic wrap and marinate in refrigerator for 4 hours or overnight, turning occasionally. Remove chicken and barbecue on a grill 4 to 6 inches above glowing coals for 15 to 20 minutes, or until chicken is tender, turning and brushing often with marinade. Cook fruit and peppers 4 to 6 minutes, until just heated through, turning and brushing often with marinade. Serve with the cooked rice.

TO BROIL THE CHICKEN AND FRUIT: Place on a broiler pan. Broil 4 to 5 inches from heat and then cook as above.

SAVORY CHICKEN AND RICE

1 to 1¼ pounds skinless and boneless chicken thighs
1 tablespoon butter or margarine
1 medium onion, chopped
½ teaspoon poultry seasoning
1 cup raw regular rice
1½ cups apple juice
¼ cup water
Grated peel of 1 Sunkist lemon
Juice of ½ Sunkist lemon
2 tablespoons chopped parsley
Lemon cartwheel slices
Parsley sprigs

Makes 4 servings.

In a 10-inch non-stick skillet, lightly brown the chicken in butter. Remove the chicken and pour off all but 1 tablespoon of the pan drippings. In the same skillet, sauté the onion with poultry seasoning until just tender. Add rice, apple juice, water, lemon peel and juice; bring to a boil. Reduce heat and arrange the chicken over the rice. Cover and cook over low heat for 20 minutes, or until chicken is tender and liquid has been absorbed. Remove the chicken and stir chopped parsley into rice. Arrange the rice mixture and chicken on a serving platter. Garnish with lemon cartwheel slices and parsley sprigs.

CURRIED BAKED CHICKEN

2 tablespoons butter or margarine, softened
2 tablespoons honey
Grated peel of ½ Sunkist orange
1 teaspoon curry powder
1 broiler-fryer (about 2½ pounds), cut into serving-size pieces
¾ cup fresh squeezed orange juice
2 Sunkist oranges, peeled and cut into half-cartwheel slices
1 tablespoon cornstarch

Makes 4 servings.

Combine the butter, honey, orange peel, and curry powder; lightly spread the mixture on the chicken pieces. Arrange chicken, skin-side-down, in a 12 × 8 × 2-inch baking pan; add ½ cup of the orange juice. Cover with aluminum foil and bake at 400° F. for 40 minutes. Uncover, turn chicken, and bake, uncovered, 20 minutes longer, or until chicken is tender. Add the orange half-cartwheel slices and bake until the orange slices are heated through, about 5 minutes. Remove chicken and orange slices to a serving platter and keep warm. To make the sauce, gradually blend the remaining ¼ cup of orange juice into the cornstarch; add to the pan drippings. Cook over medium heat, stirring, until thickened. Serve the sauce over the chicken and orange slices.

ORANGE BARBECUED CHICKEN

Don't limit this citrus-flavored barbecue sauce to chicken only . . . it's excellent on pork ribs as well.

⅓ cup finely chopped onion
3 tablespoons butter or margarine
⅓ cup honey
Juice of 1 Sunkist lemon
3 tablespoons soy sauce
Grated peel of ½ Sunkist orange
¾ cup fresh squeezed orange juice
1½ tablespoons cornstarch
2 broiler-fryers (about 2½ pounds each), quartered
Salad or vegetable oil

Makes 6 to 8 servings.

To make the sauce, in a small saucepan, sauté the onion in the butter until tender. Add the honey, lemon juice, soy sauce, and orange peel. Gradually blend the orange juice into the cornstarch; add to the onion mixture. Cook over medium heat, stirring, until thickened. Lightly brush the chicken quarters with oil. Barbecue on a grill 6 inches above glowing coals for 20 minutes. Turn and cook 20 minutes longer. Brush with sauce. Continue cooking 20 minutes longer, or until the chicken is tender, turning and brushing occasionally with sauce.

To broil chicken: Lightly brush chicken quarters with oil. Place on a broiler pan. Broil 6 to 9 inches from heat for 15 minutes. Turn and cook 15 minutes longer. Brush with sauce. Continue cooking 15 minutes longer or until chicken is tender, turning and brushing occasionally with sauce.

ORANGE BARBECUED PORK RIBS VARIATION: Precook 4 to 6 pounds pork spareribs as follows: In a large heavy pan, cover the ribs with water and bring to a boil. Reduce heat and simmer for 45 to 50 minutes. Drain. To barbecue the ribs, brush with sauce. Cook on a grill 4 to 6 inches above glowing coals for 10 to 15 minutes on each side, brushing occasionally with sauce. Makes 4 to 6 servings.

To broil ribs: Precook ribs as above. Place on a broiler pan 5 to 6 inches from heat and cook as above.

CITRUS BAKED CORNISH HENS

Grated peel and juice of 1 Sunkist lemon
Grated peel of 1 Sunkist orange
¼ cup apricot preserves
2 tablespoons grated onion
1 tablespoon butter or margarine
1 tablespoon Dijon mustard
1 medium clove garlic, minced
4 Rock Cornish hens (about 1¼ pounds each), thawed if frozen (giblets and necks removed from body cavities)

Makes 4 servings.

To make the sauce, in a small saucepan, combine all the ingredients *except* the hens. Simmer for 5 minutes to blend the flavors and thicken sauce slightly. Tie the legs of each hen together with string and turn the wing tips under the back of each hen. Brush hens with sauce and arrange, breast-side-up, in a 13 × 9 × 2-inch baking dish. Bake at 350° F. for 60 minutes, or until hens are tender, brushing occasionally with the remaining sauce. Remove string. Garnish with lemon wedges and parsley sprigs, if desired.

ROAST DUCKLING WITH HONEY-ORANGE SAUCE

Quartering the duckling before cooking makes for easy serving with no carving necessary.

4-pound duckling, thawed if frozen, quartered*
⅓ cup sugar
1 tablespoon cornstarch
Grated peel of ½ Sunkist orange
1 cup fresh squeezed orange juice
Juice of ½ Sunkist lemon
3 tablespoons honey
2 tablespoons orange-flavored liqueur
1 Sunkist orange, peeled, cut into half-cartwheel slices

Makes 4 servings.

Arrange the duckling quarters, skin-side-up, on a rack in a roasting pan. Roast, uncovered, at 325° F. for 1¼ hours, or until internal temperature reaches 180 to 185° F. Meanwhile, to make the sauce, in small saucepan, combine the sugar and cornstarch. Gradually blend in all remaining ingredients *except* orange liqueur and orange half-cartwheel slices. Cook over medium heat, stirring, until thickened. Remove from heat. Add orange liqueur. Remove the duckling from the oven and spoon off the excess fat from the pan. Increase oven temperature to 400° F. Brush duckling quarters with ¼ cup of the sauce. Return to oven and continue roasting 15 minutes longer to glaze and crisp the skin. Add orange half-cartwheel slices to the remaining sauce and heat. Remove duckling to a serving platter and serve with the remaining sauce.

*To quarter a duckling: Remove the neck and giblets from the body cavity; rinse duckling well and drain. Remove the excess fat from the body cavity and neck skin. With poultry shears, remove tail and cut duckling in half lengthwise through the center of the breast and along both sides of the backbone, removing the backbone. Divide the halves into quarters, cutting just above the legs.

FRUIT-AND-BRANDY-STUFFED GOOSE WITH LEMON SAUCE FLAMBÉ

Garnish platter with parsley sprigs and lemon boats or shells (page 290) filled with cranberry sauce or other fruits, if desired.

¼ cup butter or margarine
¾ cup thinly sliced celery
½ cup sliced green onions (scallions)
1 teaspoon poultry seasoning
2 tablespoons brandy
Grated peel and juice of 1 Sunkist lemon
¾ cup coarsely chopped dried fruit (peaches, apricots, or pears *or* any combination)
½ teaspoon salt
4 cups day-old raisin-nut bread cubes (about 8 slices)
4 cups day-old white bread cubes (about 6 slices)
8- to 10-pound goose, thawed if frozen
Lemon Sauce Flambé (page 73)

Makes 6 to 8 servings.

To make stuffing, in a saucepan, melt the butter and sauté the celery and onions with the poultry seasoning until just tender. Remove from heat and stir in brandy, lemon peel, lemon juice, dried fruit, and salt. In a large bowl, toss the bread cubes with the sautéed mixture (stuffing will appear somewhat dry).

Remove the neck and giblets from the body cavity of the goose. Rinse the goose well and drain. Remove the excess fat from the body cavity and neck skin. Fill neck and body cavities loosely with the prepared stuffing. Fasten the neck skin to the back with a skewer. Tie the legs together with string. It is *not* necessary to close body cavity with skewers or string. Turn the wing tips under the back. Place the goose, breast-side-up, on a rack in a roasting pan. Insert a meat thermometer deep into the inside thigh muscle. Roast, uncovered, at 400° F. for 1 hour. (No need to baste.) Reduce temperature to 325° F. and roast 1½ to 2 hours longer, until internal temperature reaches 180 to 185° F. (Test the stuffing for 165° F.) The goose is done when the meaty part of the leg feels very soft and twists easily at the joint. During roasting, spoon or siphon off accumulated fat at 30-minute intervals so that the fat does not accumulate or brown excessively. Remove the goose from the oven and place on a large serving platter. Remove skewer and string. Serve with Lemon Sauce Flambé.

LEMON SAUCE FLAMBÉ

3 tablespoons butter or margarine
3 tablespoons sugar
Grated peel and juice of 1 Sunkist lemon
3 tablespoons brandy

In a small saucepan, melt the butter. Add sugar, lemon peel and juice; heat to boiling, stirring to dissolve sugar. Spoon over the goose. In a metal ladle or butter warmer, heat the brandy and ignite it. Slowly pour the flaming brandy over the goose.

BARBECUED TURKEY DRUMSTICKS

Double the sauce used to baste these tasty turkey drumsticks and there will be plenty left for dipping as well.

4 turkey drumsticks (about ½ pound each)
Salad or vegetable oil
1 tablespoon finely chopped onion
2 tablespoons butter or margarine
Grated peel of 1 Sunkist orange
½ cup fresh squeezed orange juice
¼ cup ketchup
2 teaspoons Worcestershire sauce
½ teaspoon seasoned salt
Juice of ½ Sunkist lemon
1 teaspoon cornstarch

Makes 4 servings.

Lightly brush the drumsticks with oil. Barbecue on a grill 4 to 6 inches above glowing coals for 1 hour, turning frequently. Meanwhile, to make the sauce, in a small saucepan, sauté the onion in the butter until tender. Add orange peel, orange juice, ketchup, Worcestershire sauce, and seasoned salt. Gradually blend the lemon juice into the cornstarch; add to onion mixture. Cook over medium heat, stirring, until thickened. After drumsticks have cooked for 1 hour, brush them with sauce. Continue cooking 15 minutes longer or until the turkey is tender, turning and brushing often with sauce.

VARIATION: For larger (about ¾-pound) turkey drumsticks, barbecue as above, cooking for 1 hour and 15 minutes, before brushing with sauce. Continue cooking 15 minutes longer, or until the turkey is tender, turning and brushing often with sauce.

TO OVEN-COOK TURKEY: Lightly brush drumsticks with oil and individually wrap each in aluminum foil. Place on a baking sheet. Bake ½-pound drumsticks at 400° F. for 1 hour. Remove from oven. Open foil and brush drumsticks with sauce. Return to oven and continue cooking 15 minutes longer, or until turkey is tender, turning and brushing often with sauce. If using ¾-pound drumsticks, bake for 1¼ hours; baste, and continue cooking for 15 minutes longer, or until turkey is tender, basting as above.

ROAST TURKEY WITH ALMOND DRESSING AND LEMON-HONEY GLAZE

Looking for a special presentation for your next turkey dinner? Look no further. Fresh orange juice and wine moisten the crunchy dressing. A lemon-honey glaze is spooned over the cooked turkey. Finish the presentation with whipped yams or cranberry sauce served in lemon boats or orange shells (page 290).

½ cup butter or margarine
1 cup chopped onions
1 cup chopped celery
2 chicken bouillon cubes
1 cup chopped whole natural almonds
⅓ cup chopped parsley
1 tablespoon poultry seasoning
¼ teaspoon pepper
8 cups day-old bread cubes (½ whole wheat, ½ raisin, *or* any combination)
½ cup fresh squeezed orange juice
½ cup Chablis or other dry white wine
2 eggs, slightly beaten
12- to 14-pound turkey, thawed if frozen
Butter or margarine, melted
Parsley sprigs
Lemon-Honey Glaze (page 75)

Makes 8 to 12 servings.

To make dressing, melt the ½ cup butter in a large saucepot; sauté the onions and celery with the bouillon cubes until just tender. Stir in almonds, parsley, poultry seasoning, and pepper. Add bread cubes and toss lightly. Add orange juice, wine, and eggs; toss until just mixed.

Remove the neck and giblets from the body cavity of the turkey; rinse the turkey well and drain. Fill the neck cavity with a small amount of dressing; fasten the skin back with skewers. Fill the body cavity loosely with the remaining dressing. Tie the legs together with string. It is *not* necessary to close the body cavity with skewers or string. Turn the wing tips under the back. Place turkey, breast-side-up, on a rack in a roasting pan. Insert a meat thermometer deep into inside thigh muscle. Brush the turkey well with melted butter. Protect the skin of the neck cavity, wing tips, and leg bones from overbrowning by covering with small pieces of aluminum foil. Roast, uncovered, at 325° F. As turkey becomes lightly golden brown (after about 1½ to 2 hours), cover loosely with a "tent" of foil. Continue roasting for a total of 20 to 22 minutes per pound or until internal temperature reaches 180 to 185° F. (A 12-pound turkey will take about 4 to 4½ hours; 14-pound about 4½ to 5 hours.) The turkey is done when the meaty part of the leg feels very soft and twists easily at the joint. As turkey roasts, brush occasionally with melted butter and accumulated pan drippings. Remove the skewers and string. Let cooked turkey rest for 20 minutes before carving. Place on large serving platter. Garnish with parsley sprigs and serve with Lemon-Honey Glaze.

LEMON-HONEY GLAZE

1 Sunkist lemon	2 tablespoons honey
¼ cup butter or margarine	2 tablespoons brandy (optional)

With a vegetable parer, peel the lemon in a continuous spiral, removing the outer colored layer of peel only; cut into thin slivers. Cut lemon in half and ream out juice. In a small saucepan, melt the butter. Add lemon peel, juice, and honey; simmer for 5 minutes to blend the flavors. Add brandy and spoon over the cooked turkey.

Beef, Lamb, and Pork

With rare exceptions, like Greek lamb with lemon or pork chops with orange sauce, citrus is seldom associated with meats. But orange, lemon, grapefruit, and even tangerine flavors are wonderful complements to a variety of meats.

Citrus juice and peel are important ingredients in marinades; they add bright, fresh flavor. The best barbecue sauces include orange or lemon juice, and are as good on pork chops as they are on beef ribs.

But often the best discoveries are the more subtle ones — like the zest lemon adds to meat loaf or the zip from a touch of grapefruit in chili. You'll be surprised by the delicious flavors, and you'll know it was just a bit of citrus that made the difference.

BEEF, LAMB, AND PORK

FILLMORE MARINATED FLANK STEAK
LEMON BARBECUED CHUCK ROAST
BEEF TANGABOBS
GERMAN-STYLE POT ROAST
ORANGE SWISS STEAK
SHIRLEE K'S GRAPEFRUIT CHILI
"BEST EVER" MEAT LOAF
TWO-WAY TANGERINE MEATBALLS AND MEAT LOAF
VEAL PICCATA
BARBECUED BUTTERFLIED LEG OF LAMB
LEMONY LAMB SHANKS
HERBED LAMB KABOBS
BR'S LICKIN' GOOD COUNTRY-STYLE RIBS
PORK CHOPS WITH ORANGE-RICE PILAF
SKILLET PORK CHOPS WITH CITRUS RICE
LEMON BARBECUED PORK CHOPS
TIPTON ORANGE-BARBECUED PORK CHOPS
CROWN ROAST OF PORK
FAVORITE ORANGE DRESSING FOR PORK
ORANGE-GLAZED HAM
GOLDEN ORANGE SAUCE FOR PORK
RABBIT AU VIN

FILLMORE MARINATED FLANK STEAK

If the family likes steak and onions—try this marinade on any of the less tender cuts of steak, such as round or chuck.

1½-pound beef flank steak	1 medium onion, thinly sliced
6 tablespoons salad or vegetable oil	2 tablespoons sugar
Grated peel of ½ Sunkist lemon	2 tablespoons soy sauce
Juice of 3 Sunkist lemons (½ cup)	½ teaspoon dried oregano leaves, crushed
	⅛ teaspoon pepper
	1 tablespoon butter

Makes 4 to 6 servings.

Score the steak lightly on both sides. To make the marinade, in a shallow baking dish, combine all the remaining ingredients *except* the butter; add the steak and turn to coat it with the marinade. Cover and marinate in refrigerator for 2 hours or longer, turning occasionally. (Or marinate in a tightly sealed plastic bag.) Remove steak and broil 4 inches from heat for 5 minutes. Turn and broil 4 minutes longer (for rare) or until desired doneness. Or barbecue on a grill 4 inches above glowing coals for 5 minutes on each side (for medium-rare) or until desired doneness. Meanwhile, drain the onion from the marinade and discard marinade. In a small skillet, sauté the onion in the butter until tender. To serve, slice the steak thinly on the diagonal and top with the sautéed onion. Garnish with lemon cartwheel slices and parsley sprigs, if desired.

LEMON BARBECUED CHUCK ROAST

4-pound beef chuck blade roast (about 2 inches thick)
Grated peel of ½ Sunkist lemon
⅔ cup fresh squeezed lemon juice
⅓ cup salad or vegetable oil
1 green onion (scallion), chopped
1 teaspoon prepared mustard
1 teaspoon Worcestershire sauce
½ teaspoon salt
⅛ teaspoon pepper

Makes 6 to 8 servings.

Trim any excess fat from the roast. To make the marinade, in a shallow baking dish, combine the remaining ingredients; add the roast and turn to coat with the marinade. Cover and marinate in refrigerator for 6 hours or overnight, turning occasionally. (Or marinate in a tightly sealed plastic bag.) Remove the roast and barbecue on a grill 4 to 6 inches above glowing coals for 20 minutes on each side (for medium-rare) or until desired doneness, brushing occasionally with marinade.

TO BROIL CHUCK ROAST: Marinate roast as above. Place on a broiler pan 6 to 9 inches from heat and cook as above.

BEEF TANGABOBS

Grated peel of 1 Sunkist tangerine
¼ cup fresh squeezed tangerine juice
¼ cup salad or vegetable oil
1 tablespoon soy sauce
1 small clove garlic, minced
¼ teaspoon ground ginger
1½ pounds beef top sirloin (about 1¼ inch thick), cut into cubes
1 large sweet green pepper, cut into 1-inch pieces
2 Sunkist tangerines, peeled, segmented, and seeded
Hot cooked rice (optional)

Makes 4 servings.

To make the marinade, in a bowl, combine tangerine peel and juice, oil, soy sauce, garlic, and ginger; add the beef. Cover and marinate in refrigerator for 3 hours or longer, stirring occasionally. (Or marinate in a tightly sealed plastic bag, turning occasionally.) Drain and reserve the marinade. Arrange beef, green pepper, and tangerine segments alternately on 4 long metal or wooden skewers. Place the kabobs on a broiler pan. Brush with marinade. Broil 4 inches from heat for 10 minutes (for medium-rare) or until desired doneness, turning and brushing occasionally with marinade. Or barbecue on a grill 4 inches above glowing coals for 10 minutes (for medium-rare) or until desired doneness. Serve with cooked rice, if you wish.

ORANGE VARIATION: Substitute fresh grated peel of ½ valencia orange for the tangerine peel and 2 small valencia oranges, peeled and segmented, for the tangerines.

GERMAN-STYLE POT ROAST

The flavor of fresh squeezed orange juice subtly flavors this pot roast and also highlights the smooth, rich gravy that is excellent over noodles or mashed potatoes.

4- to 5-pound boneless beef chuck pot roast	Juice of 1 Sunkist lemon
3 tablespoons salad or vegetable oil	1 large onion, sliced
	2 tablespoons light brown sugar
Grated peel of ½ Sunkist orange	½ teaspoon pepper
	2 bay leaves
1½ cups fresh squeezed orange juice	¼ cup cold water
	¼ cup all-purpose flour

Makes 6 to 8 servings (about 2½ cups gravy).

In a large saucepot, brown the meat on all sides in the oil. Add all the remaining ingredients *except* the water and flour; bring to a boil. Reduce heat; cover, and simmer for 2½ hours, or until the beef is tender. Remove roast to a serving platter and keep warm. Remove and discard the bay leaves. Spoon off the excess fat from the pan drippings. To make the gravy, gradually blend the water into the flour; add to pan drippings and cook over medium heat, stirring, until thickened. Serve with the roast. Garnish the roast with orange cartwheel slices and parsley sprigs, if desired.

ORANGE SWISS STEAK

Home cooking at its best!

- 2 pounds beef round steak (about ¾ inch thick), cut into serving-size pieces
- 2 tablespoons salad or vegetable oil
- ½ pound mushrooms, thickly sliced
- 1 medium onion, chopped
- ½ cup Chablis or other dry white wine
- 2 tablespoons ketchup
- 2 teaspoons soy sauce
- ½ teaspoon dried thyme leaves, crushed
- Grated peel of ½ Sunkist orange
- ½ cup fresh squeezed orange juice
- 1 tablespoon all-purpose flour
- 2 Sunkist oranges, peeled and cut into half-cartwheel slices

Makes 6 servings.

In a large skillet, brown the steak on both sides in the oil. Add all the remaining ingredients *except* the orange juice, flour, and orange half-cartwheel slices; bring to a boil. Reduce heat; cover, and simmer for 1½ hours or until the beef is tender. Remove steak to a serving platter and keep warm. Spoon off any excess fat from the pan drippings. To make the gravy, gradually blend the orange juice into the flour; add to pan drippings and cook over medium heat, stirring, until thickened. Return the steak to the skillet. Add orange half-cartwheel slices and heat.

SHIRLEE K'S GRAPEFRUIT CHILI

Grapefruit in chili? Unusual? . . . Yes. Good tasting? . . . Yes. Trying is believing!

1½ pounds ground beef
1 medium onion, chopped
½ cup thinly sliced celery
2 cans (about 15 ounces each) stewed tomatoes
1 can (about 15 ounces) tomato sauce
1 can (about 15 ounces) red kidney beans, drained
2 to 4 tablespoons chili powder
1 tablespoon fresh grated grapefruit peel
½ teaspoon garlic salt
¼ teaspoon pepper
2 Sunkist grapefruit, peeled and sectioned
Tortilla chips or 6 grapefruit shells (page 290)
Shredded Cheddar or Monterey Jack cheese

Makes 6 servings (about 7 cups).

In a large skillet, brown the beef and cook the onion and celery until tender. Pour off any excess fat. Add stewed tomatoes, tomato sauce, beans, chili powder, grapefruit peel, garlic salt, and pepper. Cover and simmer for 30 minutes. Add grapefruit sections and heat. Serve over tortilla chips or in grapefruit shells topped with cheese. Garnish with avocado slices and additional grapefruit sections, if desired.

"BEST EVER" MEAT LOAF

1 pound lean ground beef
½ pound bulk pork sausage
1 egg, slightly beaten
4 slices day-old bread, finely crumbled
1 small onion, finely chopped
Grated peel and juice of 1 Sunkist lemon
1 teaspoon salt
¼ teaspoon dried oregano leaves, crushed
¼ teaspoon dried thyme leaves, crushed
½ cup ketchup
¼ cup packed light brown sugar
1 teaspoon dry mustard
½ Sunkist lemon, cut into half-cartwheel slices

Makes 4 to 6 servings.

Thoroughly combine the beef, sausage, egg, bread crumbs, onion, half the lemon peel and juice, salt, oregano, and thyme; shape into an 8 × 4 × 2-inch loaf. Place in an aluminum foil–lined 12 × 8 × 2-inch baking dish and bake at 350° F. for 1 hour. Meanwhile, to make the sauce, combine the ketchup, brown sugar, mustard, and remaining lemon peel and juice. Remove meat loaf from oven. Spoon one third of the sauce over the meat loaf; top with lemon half-cartwheel slices. Return to the oven and bake 15 minutes longer. Serve with the remaining sauce.

TWO-WAY TANGERINE MEATBALLS AND MEAT LOAF

In a hurry? Shape this savory meat mixture into a loaf and bake. Or take the time to form it into meatballs. When tangerines are out of season, substitute orange peel, juice, and segments.

1 pound ground beef	1 cup fresh squeezed
½ pound bulk pork sausage	tangerine juice
¼ cup fine dry bread crumbs	Juice of ½ Sunkist lemon
1 egg, slightly beaten	2 tablespoons sugar
2 teaspoons fresh grated	1 tablespoon cornstarch
tangerine peel	2 medium Sunkist tangerines,
¼ teaspoon ground nutmeg	peeled, segmented, and
1 tablespoon salad or	seeded
vegetable oil	Hot cooked rice

Makes 6 servings.

Thoroughly combine the beef, sausage, bread crumbs, egg, 1 teaspoon of tangerine peel, and nutmeg. Shape firmly into 24 small balls. In a large skillet, brown the meatballs well in the oil. Remove meatballs from skillet and pour off all but 2 tablespoons of the pan drippings. To make the sauce, gradually blend the tangerine and lemon juice into the sugar and cornstarch. Add to the drippings in the pan and cook over medium heat, stirring, until thickened. Add meatballs and cook, covered, over low heat for 5 minutes. Uncover and add tangerine segments and remaining 1 teaspoon of peel; heat. Serve over hot cooked rice.

MEAT LOAF VARIATION: Increase ground beef to 1½ pounds. Omit salad oil. Thoroughly combine beef, sausage, bread crumbs, egg, 1 teaspoon of tangerine peel, and nutmeg. Shape into a 9 × 4 × 2-inch loaf. Place in an aluminum foil–lined 12 × 8 × 2-inch baking dish. Bake at 350° F. for 1 to 1¼ hours. Remove to a serving platter and keep warm. Reserve 2 tablespoons of the pan drippings. To make the sauce, in a small saucepan, combine the sugar and cornstarch. Gradually blend in tangerine juice, lemon juice, and reserved pan drippings; cook over medium heat, stirring, until thickened. Add tangerine segments and remaining 1 teaspoon of peel and heat. To serve, arrange a few tangerine segments and a small amount of sauce on top of the meat loaf. Serve with the remaining tangerine sauce. Makes 6 servings.

VEAL PICCATA

1 pound veal cutlets
1 egg
⅓ cup all-purpose flour
½ teaspoon dried oregano leaves, crushed
2 tablespoons butter or margarine
2 tablespoons salad or vegetable oil
Grated peel and juice of ½ Sunkist lemon
½ Sunkist lemon, cut into half-cartwheel slices
1 to 2 teaspoons drained capers (optional)

Makes 4 servings.

With a meat mallet or rolling pin, flatten the cutlets between two sheets of plastic wrap to a ¼-inch thickness. In a shallow dish, slightly beat the egg. In a second dish, combine the flour and oregano. Dip cutlets into egg; then lightly coat with flour mixture. In a 10-inch skillet, heat the butter and oil. Over medium heat, sauté 3 to 4 cutlets at a time for 2 to 3 minutes on each side, until lightly browned. Remove to a serving dish and keep warm. Add lemon peel and juice, lemon half-cartwheel slices, and capers to the pan drippings in the skillet. Heat and spoon over the cutlets. Garnish with parsley sprigs, if desired.

BARBECUED BUTTERFLIED LEG OF LAMB

Lamb served at its BEST!

5-to-6 pound leg of lamb, boned and butterflied, with excess fat removed	1 to 2 cloves garlic, minced
Grated peel and juice of 1 Sunkist lemon	1 teaspoon dried rosemary leaves
3 tablespoons salad or vegetable oil	1 teaspoon dried tarragon leaves
1 tablespoon grated onion	¼ teaspoon coarse black pepper

Makes 8 to 10 servings.

If necessary, to even the thickness of the butterflied lamb, slash the thicker muscles vertically, about ½ inch. Insert 3 to 4 long metal skewers lengthwise to prevent the lamb from curling when cooking. Place the lamb on a large platter or 15½ × 10½ × 1-inch jellyroll pan. To make the marinade, combine the remaining ingredients. Spoon half the marinade over the lamb; turn lamb over and spoon on the remaining marinade. Cover with plastic wrap and marinate in refrigerator for 4 hours or overnight. Remove the lamb and barbecue on a grill 6 inches above glowing coals for 20 minutes on each side (for medium-rare) or until desired doneness, brushing occasionally with any remaining marinade.

TO BROIL LAMB: Prepare and marinate butterflied lamb as above. Place on a large broiler pan 6 to 9 inches from heat and cook as above.

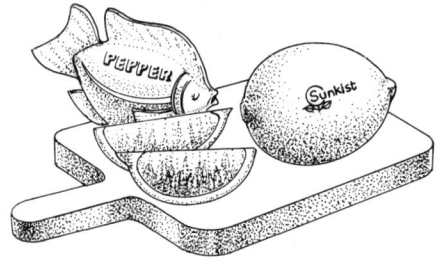

LEMONY LAMB SHANKS

1 teaspoon salt
1 teaspoon paprika
½ teaspoon dried thyme leaves, crushed
½ teaspoon pepper
4 lamb shanks (¾ to 1 pound each)
All-purpose flour
Salad or vegetable oil
4 whole black peppercorns
2 parsley sprigs
1 bay leaf, crumbled
¾ cup *plus* 2 tablespoons water
Grated peel and juice of 1 Sunkist lemon
1 medium onion, sliced
2 medium cloves garlic, minced
1 tablespoon all-purpose flour
½ unpeeled Sunkist lemon, cut into cartwheel slices
1 tablespoon drained capers

Makes 4 servings (about 2 cups sauce).

Combine the salt, paprika, thyme, and pepper; rub well into all sides of the shanks. Lightly coat with flour. In a large saucepot, slowly brown shanks in oil; pour off the fat. Make a bouquet garni of the peppercorns, parsley, and bay leaf in a square of cheesecloth; tie bundle-fashion with string. Add bouquet garni, ¾ cup of water, lemon peel and juice, onion, and garlic to the lamb shanks. Cover and cook over low heat for 2 hours, or until lamb is tender. Turn and baste the shanks occasionally with the pan drippings while cooking. Remove and discard bouquet garni. Remove shanks to a serving platter and keep warm. To make the sauce, gradually blend 2 tablespoons of water into 1 tablespoon of flour. Add to the pan drippings and cook over medium heat, stirring, until thickened. Add lemon cartwheel slices and capers. Heat and pour the sauce over the shanks. Serve with cooked noodles and garnish with additional parsley sprigs, if desired.

HERBED LAMB KABOBS

There's no oil in this flavorful marinade, and only 2 teaspoons are used to baste the lamb kabobs.

¼ cup water
Grated peel of ½ Sunkist lemon
Juice of 1 Sunkist lemon
2 teaspoons Worcestershire sauce
1 small clove garlic, minced
½ teaspoon salt
¼ teaspoon dried thyme leaves, crushed
¼ teaspoon dried rosemary leaves, crushed
⅛ teaspoon pepper
1 pound lean boneless lamb, cut into 1-inch cubes
8 boiling onions (about ½ pound)
Boiling water
1 medium sweet green pepper, cut into 8 pieces
2 teaspoons salad or vegetable oil

Makes 4 servings.
About 246 calories per serving.

To make the marinade, in a bowl, combine the water, lemon peel, lemon juice, Worcestershire sauce, garlic, salt, thyme, rosemary, and pepper. Add the lamb, cover, and marinate in refrigerator for 2 hours or longer, stirring occasionally. (Or marinate in a tightly sealed plastic bag, turning occasionally.) Parboil the onions in boiling water for 4 minutes; add green pepper and parboil 1 minute longer. Remove the lamb from the marinade and discard marinade. Arrange lamb, onions, and green pepper alternately on 4 long metal or wooden skewers. Place kabobs on a broiler pan, brush lightly with oil, and broil 4 to 5 inches from heat for 4 to 5 minutes. Turn and broil 4 to 5 minutes longer (for medium-rare) or until desired doneness.

BR'S LICKIN' GOOD COUNTRY-STYLE RIBS

If most barbecue sauces are too sweet for your taste, you'll enjoy the well-rounded flavor of this all-purpose sauce for pork. Oven-cooked or grilled over coals, these ribs are finger-lickin' good.

4 pounds country-style pork ribs	1 tablespoon Worcestershire sauce
1½ cups ketchup	1 medium clove garlic, minced
1 can (about 14 ounces) beef broth	2 teaspoons curry powder
Grated peel and juice of 1 Sunkist lemon	2 teaspoons chili powder
3 tablespoons sugar	2 teaspoons paprika
	⅛ teaspoon pepper

Makes 6 servings (about 2⅔ cups sauce).

Trim any excess fat from the ribs and arrange them in a shallow roasting pan or pans. Cover with aluminum foil and bake at 350° F. for 1¼ hours. Meanwhile, to make the sauce, in a large saucepan, combine remaining ingredients and bring to a boil. Reduce heat and simmer briskly, uncovered, for 10 minutes to blend the flavors. Remove the ribs from the oven and spoon off the excess fat from the pan. Cover the ribs with half the sauce and continue baking, uncovered, 1 hour longer, or until the pork is tender, basting occasionally with the sauce in the roasting pan. Serve with the remaining sauce.

TO BARBECUE PORK SPARERIBS: Precook 4 to 6 pounds of pork spareribs as follows: In a large saucepot, cover ribs with water and bring to a boil. Reduce heat and simmer for 45 to 50 minutes. Drain. To barbecue the ribs, brush with the sauce and barbecue on a grill 4 to 6 inches above glowing coals for 10 to 15 minutes on each side, brushing often with sauce. Serve with the remaining sauce. Makes 6 servings.

PORK CHOPS WITH ORANGE-RICE PILAF

A skillet pork chop and rice/noodle meal that's both family and company fare.

4 pork chops (about 1½ pounds) cut ¾ to 1 inch thick
2 tablespoons salad or vegetable oil
2½ cups chicken broth
⅓ cup chopped onion
Grated peel of ½ Sunkist orange
½ teaspoon celery salt
⅛ teaspoon pepper
¾ cup raw regular rice
½ cup fine egg noodles, broken in pieces
2 Sunkist oranges, peeled and sectioned

Makes 4 servings.

In a large skillet, thoroughly brown the chops in the oil. Remove chops and pour off the fat. In the same skillet, combine the broth, onion, orange peel, celery salt, and pepper. Stir in the rice and noodles and bring to a boil. Reduce heat; arrange chops over rice and noodles. Cover, and cook over low heat for 25 minutes, or until pork is tender and liquid has been absorbed. Remove chops and keep warm. Add the orange sections to the rice mixture and heat. Arrange the chops and rice mixture on a serving platter.

VARIATION: Substitute 2½ cups water and 2 chicken bouillon cubes for the chicken broth.

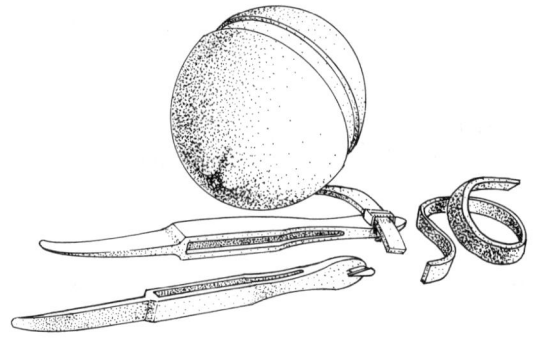

SKILLET PORK CHOPS WITH CITRUS RICE

For a dash of color and flavor, add a bit of chopped fresh basil or parsley to the cooked rice before serving.

6 pork chops (about 2 pounds) cut ½ to ¾ inch thick	1 cup raw regular rice
	1 can (10¾ ounces) condensed chicken broth
2 tablespoons salad or vegetable oil	⅓ cup water
	Grated peel of 1 Sunkist tangerine
1 medium onion, chopped	
1 tablespoon butter or margarine	3 Sunkist tangerines, peeled, segmented, and seeded
½ teaspoon poultry seasoning	⅓ cup walnut halves

Makes 6 servings.

In a large skillet, thoroughly brown the chops in the oil. Remove chops and pour off the fat. In the same skillet, sauté the onion in the butter with the poultry seasoning. Add the rice, chicken broth, and water; bring to a boil. Reduce heat; arrange chops over the rice. Cover, and cook over low heat for 25 minutes, or until pork is tender and liquid has been absorbed. Remove chops and keep warm. Add the tangerine peel, segments, and nuts to the rice mixture and heat. Arrange the chops and rice mixture on a serving platter. Garnish with parsley sprigs, if desired.

ORANGE VARIATION: Substitute fresh grated peel of ½ orange for the tangerine peel and 2 medium oranges, peeled and sectioned, for the tangerines.

LEMON BARBECUED PORK CHOPS

Favorite recipes are best when served year 'round. So, barbecue or broil these zesty lemon-enhanced pork chops in any season.

2 tablespoons chopped green onion (scallion)	2 tablespoons light brown sugar
1 tablespoon butter or margarine	2 tablespoons Chablis or other dry white wine
½ cup ketchup	6 pork chops (about 2½ pounds) cut ¾ to 1 inch thick
¼ cup soy sauce	
Grated peel and juice of 1 Sunkist lemon	
	Salad or vegetable oil

Makes 6 servings (about 1 cup sauce).

In a small saucepan, sauté the green onion in the butter. Stir in all the remaining ingredients *except* the pork chops and oil. Bring to a boil, reduce heat, and simmer for a few minutes to blend flavors.

To barbecue pork chops: Lightly brush both sides of chops with oil. Barbecue on a grill 6 inches above glowing coals for 10 minutes. Turn and cook 10 minutes longer. Brush with the sauce. Continue cooking for 10 minutes, or until pork is tender, turning and brushing often with sauce. Serve with any remaining sauce.

To broil pork chops: Lightly brush both sides of chops with oil. Place on a broiler pan about 5 inches from heat and broil for 8 minutes. Turn and broil 8 minutes longer. Brush with the sauce and continue cooking for 8 to 10 minutes, or until pork is tender, turning and brushing often with the sauce. Serve with any remaining sauce.

TIPTON ORANGE-BARBECUED PORK CHOPS

¼ cup chopped onion
1 medium clove garlic, minced
2 tablespoons butter or margarine
½ teaspoon dried rosemary leaves, crushed
Grated peel of ½ Sunkist orange
½ cup fresh squeezed orange juice
½ cup ketchup
2 tablespoons honey or light brown sugar
6 pork chops (about 2½ pounds) cut ¾ to 1 inch thick
Salad or vegetable oil

Makes 6 servings (about 1¼ cups sauce).

In a small saucepan, sauté the onion and garlic in the butter with the rosemary. Stir in all the remaining ingredients *except* the pork chops and oil. Bring to a boil, reduce heat, and simmer for a few minutes to blend flavors.

To barbecue or broil pork chops: Follow the directions for Lemon Barbecued Pork Chops (page 92).

CROWN ROAST OF PORK

Definitely for entertaining! . . . whether it's a family gathering or dinner for friends. Prepare the dressing and bake it with the pork during the last hour of cooking.

6- to 7-pound pork crown roast (about 16 ribs)
½ cup apple jelly
Grated peel of ½ Sunkist orange
¼ cup cold water
2 tablespoons all-purpose flour
Brown cooking sauce (optional)
Pepper to taste
Favorite Orange Dressing for Pork (page 94)
6 to 8 orange shells (page 290), optional
Parsley sprigs

Makes 8 to 12 servings (about 1½ cups gravy).

Have the butcher remove the backbone, French-cut the rib bones, and securely tie the roast. Cover rib ends with aluminum foil to prevent overbrowning. Place roast on a rack in a large shallow baking pan. Roast, uncovered, at 325° F. for 2 hours. Meanwhile, make the glaze: In a small saucepan, combine the apple jelly and orange peel; simmer for a few minutes to blend flavors and melt the jelly. Remove roast from oven after 2 hours and brush with half the glaze. Return to the oven and continue to roast, brushing occasionally with the remaining glaze, for 45 to 60 minutes longer, or until the internal temperature reaches 170° F. and pork is tender. Remove roast to a serving platter and let rest for 15 minutes before carving. Remove foil. Spoon off the excess fat from the pan drippings. To make the gravy, gradually blend the water into the flour; add to the pan drippings and cook over medium heat, stirring, until thickened. Stir in a few drops of brown cooking sauce (to color the gravy to desired brownness) and pepper to taste. Serve a couple of tablespoons of gravy over each serving of pork. For a spectacular presentation, lightly spoon Favorite Orange Dressing into the center of the roast. Fill orange shells with remaining dressing and serve with roast. Garnish the platter with parsley sprigs. Tie citrus peel strips around the ribs, if desired.

FAVORITE ORANGE DRESSING FOR PORK

- ⅔ cup chopped celery
- ½ cup chopped onion
- 1 medium apple, peeled and diced
- ¼ cup butter or margarine
- 4 cups prepared seasoned dressing or stuffing mix
- ⅓ cup raisins
- 1 can (8 ounces) whole berry cranberry sauce
- Grated peel of ½ Sunkist orange
- ¾ cup fresh squeezed orange juice
- 3 tablespoons light brown sugar
- 1 beef or chicken bouillon cube
- 2 tablespoons butter, melted, *or* pan drippings (pork chop or bacon)

Makes 6 servings (about 5½ cups).

In a skillet, sauté the celery, onion, and apple in the ¼ cup of butter until tender. In a large bowl, combine the celery mixture, dressing mix, and raisins. In the same skillet, combine the cranberry sauce, orange peel, orange juice, brown sugar, and bouillon cube; cook over medium-low heat for 10 minutes, stirring occasionally. Add to dressing mixture and toss well. Lightly pack into a 1½-quart casserole and sprinkle with the 2 tablespoons of melted butter or pan drippings. Bake, covered, at 350° F. for 45 minutes.

BAKED PORK CHOPS AND STUFFING: Prepare the dressing as above and spoon into a 13 × 9 × 2-inch baking dish. In a large skillet, thoroughly brown 6 (½ to ¾ inch thick) pork chops in hot oil for about 8 to 10 minutes. Arrange chops on top of dressing and bake, covered with aluminum foil, at 350° F. for 45 minutes, or until pork is tender. Garnish with orange half-cartwheel slices, if desired. Makes 6 servings.

ORANGE-GLAZED HAM

4- to 6-pound ready-to-eat boneless smoked ham	¼ cup fresh squeezed orange juice
½ cup apricot preserves	¼ teaspoon ground ginger
Grated peel of ½ Sunkist orange	Orange Peel Poinsettia Flower (page 297)

Makes 12 to 18 servings.

Place the ham on a rack in a shallow baking pan. Bake ham according to package directions for temperature and timing. Meanwhile, to make the glaze, in a small saucepan, combine the apricot preserves, orange peel, orange juice, and ginger. Bring to a boil and reduce heat. Simmer for a few minutes to blend the flavors, stirring occasionally. About 30 to 45 minutes before ham is done, remove it from the oven. Arrange the Orange Peel Poinsettia Flower on ham and secure with toothpick halves. Brush or spoon on glaze. Return ham to the oven and continue baking 30 to 45 minutes longer, or until the internal temperature reaches 130° F., brushing occasionally with remaining glaze. Remove the toothpicks before serving. The poinsettia garnish will cling to the ham.

GOLDEN ORANGE SAUCE FOR PORK

Grated peel of ½ Sunkist orange
Juice of 3 Sunkist oranges (1 cup)
¼ cup sugar
1 tablespoon cornstarch
⅛ teaspoon ground nutmeg or allspice (optional)

Makes about 1 cup.

In a small saucepan, combine all the ingredients. Cook over medium heat, stirring constantly, until the mixture thickens.

SERVING SUGGESTION: Serve as a sauce over cooked roast pork, ham slices, or steaks.

RABBIT AU VIN

Rabbit is a succulent, moist alternative to chicken and, like chicken, can be found, either fresh or frozen, at your supermarket.

3 slices bacon
1 fryer rabbit (about 2½ pounds), cut into serving-size pieces
⅔ cup Chablis or other dry white wine
Juice of ½ Sunkist lemon
12 boiling onions (about ¾ pound)
2 medium carrots, sliced on the diagonal
1 medium clove garlic, minced
2 chicken bouillon cubes
½ teaspoon dried thyme leaves, crushed
¼ pound mushrooms, sliced
½ Sunkist lemon, cut into cartwheel slices
⅓ cup cold water
2 tablespoons all-purpose flour
2 tablespoons chopped parsley
Hot cooked rice or noodles

Makes 4 servings (about 1¼ cups sauce).

In a large skillet, cook the bacon until crisp; remove, drain, and crumble. In the same skillet, lightly brown the rabbit in the drippings. Add wine, lemon juice, onions, carrots, garlic, bouillon cubes, and thyme. Cover and cook over low heat for 1 hour, or until rabbit is tender. Add mushrooms and lemon cartwheel slices 5 minutes before the end of the cooking time. Remove the rabbit and vegetables to a serving platter and keep warm. To make the sauce, gradually blend the water into the flour; add to the pan drippings and cook over medium heat, stirring, until thickened. Spoon a portion of the sauce over the rabbit and vegetables. Sprinkle with parsley and reserved crumbled bacon. Serve with cooked rice or noodles and remaining sauce.

Vegetables, Pasta, and Rice

Once considered only an "accompaniment" to meat, vegetables are now more prominent and popular in our cooking than ever before. High in nutritional value, low in calories, excitingly different in color, flavor, and texture, vegetables are often the star of the show.

The potato is much more than a basic companion to the entrée, especially when dressed up with lemon and dill or herb butter patties. Steamed rice is nice, but with the flavors of orange and sesame or in a carrot-rice bake, it's special and superlative. And pasta with lemon, herbs, and fresh vegetables becomes a new entrée or a tempting side dish with veal or chicken.

From simple to simply elegant, vegetables accented with citrus flavors and a sprinkling of herbs and spices bring pleasant surprises and unexpected compliments.

VEGETABLES, PASTA, AND RICE

EAST-WEST SAUTÉED ASPARAGUS
BARBECUED ORANGE BAKED BEANS
SWEET AND SOUR BEETS
FRESH BROCCOLI AND PASTA COMBO
GOLDEN TREASURE BRUSSELS SPROUTS
STIR-FRIED BRUSSELS SPROUTS AND TANGERINES
LEMON BUTTERED CABBAGE
CALIFORNIA CARROTS
CAULIFLOWER ALLA PARMESAN
SAVORY CORN ON THE COB
MUSHROOM CAPS ROYALE
SCANDINAVIAN DILLED POTATOES
SKINNY-MINNY'S BAKED POTATO WEDGES
ORANGE-SWEET POTATO BAKE
ORIENTAL ORANGE SPINACH
CREAMED SPINACH À LA LEMON
LEMON-GLAZED ACORN SQUASH
WINTER SQUASH À L'ORANGE
SOUTHWEST STUFFED ZUCCHINI OR GREEN PEPPERS
STIR-FRIED ZUCCHINI AND MUSHROOMS
CHEESY VEGETABLE ENTRÉE FOR TWO
ORANGE VEGETABLE MEDLEY
VEGETABLE TEMPURA
THREE "Cs" RICE BAKE
"OPEN SESAME" RICE PILAF
TANGY PASTA WITH BASIL AND PARMESAN
HERBED LEMON-BUTTER PATTIES
PARSLEY-DILL BUTTER
TANGY LEMON-SESAME BUTTER
"EASIEST EVER" HOLLANDAISE SAUCE
VERSATILE VEGETABLE RELISH SAUCE

EAST-WEST SAUTEÉD ASPARAGUS

1½ pounds asparagus, thinly sliced on the diagonal
1 cup diagonally sliced celery
1 medium clove garlic, minced
2 tablespoons salad or vegetable oil
1 chicken bouillon cube
⅔ cup cold water
1 tablespoon cornstarch
½ cup sliced water chestnuts
2 green onions (scallions), cut into thin strips
Grated peel and juice of ½ Sunkist lemon
1 to 2 teaspoons soy sauce

Makes six ½-cup servings (about 3 cups).
About 99 calories per serving.

In a skillet, sauté the asparagus, celery, and garlic in oil with the bouillon cube until just tender, about 5 minutes. Gradually blend the water into the cornstarch. Add to asparagus. Cook over medium heat, stirring, until thickened. Add remaining ingredients and heat.

BARBECUED ORANGE BAKED BEANS

This is the perfect "bake-a-long" with oven-prepared chicken, ribs, or pork chops.

¼ cup finely chopped onion
1 tablespoon salad or vegetable oil
¼ cup bottled barbecue sauce of your choice
2 tablespoons light brown sugar
Grated peel of ½ Sunkist orange
2 cans (16 ounces each) baked beans
1 Sunkist orange, peeled, cut into bite-size pieces and drained

Makes 4 to 6 servings (about 4 cups).

In a small pan, sauté the onion in oil until just tender; stir in the barbecue sauce, brown sugar, and orange peel. In a 1½-quart casserole, combine baked beans and onion mixture, blending well. Bake, uncovered, at 350° F. for 40 minutes; stir occasionally. Stir in orange pieces; bake, uncovered, for 5 minutes longer.

SWEET AND SOUR BEETS

Fresh beets are great, but canned beets are certainly a work-saver. This adaptation of an old-time favorite is enlivened with fresh lemon, caraway, and cloves for a spicy, sweet and sour flavor.

1 can (16 ounces) sliced beets
3 tablespoons sugar
Grated peel and juice of 1 Sunkist lemon
½ teaspoon caraway seed
¼ teaspoon salt
⅛ teaspoon ground cloves
2 tablespoons cold water
1 tablespoon cornstarch

Makes four ½-cup servings (about 2 cups).

Drain the liquid from the beets into a saucepan, reserving beets. Add sugar, lemon juice, caraway seed, salt, and cloves; bring to a boil. Reduce heat and simmer for a few minutes to blend the flavors. Gradually blend the water into the cornstarch; add to hot liquid. Cook over medium heat, stirring until thickened. Add beets and lemon peel and heat.

FRESH BROCCOLI AND PASTA COMBO

A macaroni and vegetable dish in one! The full-flavored cheese sauce complements both the pasta and the fresh broccoli.

1 small onion, chopped
1 medium clove garlic, minced
2 tablespoons butter or margarine
2 teaspoons instant chicken bouillon
¼ teaspoon dried marjoram leaves, crushed
1 tablespoon all-purpose flour
1 cup milk
1 cup shredded Swiss or caraway cheese
1 pound broccoli, separated into flowerets, cooked, and drained
1½ cups curly or spiral macaroni, cooked, and drained
Grated peel and juice of ½ Sunkist lemon

Makes 4 servings (about 5½ cups).

In a 10-inch skillet, sauté the onion and garlic in the butter with the bouillon and marjoram until just tender. Remove from heat and stir in flour. Cook for a few minutes, stirring constantly. Gradually blend in milk. Cook over medium heat, stirring, until thickened. Add cheese and stir until melted. Add broccoli, macaroni, lemon peel and juice and heat.

GOLDEN TREASURE BRUSSELS SPROUTS

1 pound Brussels sprouts, trimmed and cut in half lengthwise
1 pound carrots, quartered
Boiling water
¼ cup butter or margarine
Grated peel and juice of ½ Sunkist lemon
1 teaspoon toasted sesame seed
1 small clove garlic, minced

Makes 6 servings (about 4 cups).
About 122 calories and 111 mg. sodium per serving.

In a large covered saucepan, cook Brussels sprouts and carrots in 1 inch of boiling water until tender, about 10 minutes; drain well. In the same saucepan, melt the butter with the lemon peel and juice, sesame seed, and garlic. Add cooked vegetables and heat.

STIR-FRIED BRUSSELS SPROUTS AND TANGERINES

This might seem like an unusual combination, but the Brussels sprouts and tangerines are seasonally compatible, and their combined colors and flavors delightful to both the eye and the palate.

1 pound Brussels sprouts, trimmed and cut in half lengthwise
Boiling water
1 small onion, thickly sliced
2 tablespoons butter or margarine
1 teaspoon caraway seed
1 chicken bouillon cube
½ pound mushrooms, thickly sliced
Grated peel of 1 Sunkist tangerine
2 medium or 3 small Sunkist tangerines, peeled, segmented and seeded

Makes 4 to 6 servings (about 5½ cups).

Parboil the Brussels sprouts in boiling water for 5 minutes; drain well. In a large skillet, stir-fry Brussels sprouts and onion in butter with caraway seed and bouillon until *just* tender, 3 to 5 minutes. Add mushrooms and stir-fry for a few minutes longer. Stir in tangerine peel and segments and heat.

ORANGE VARIATION: Substitute the fresh grated peel of ½ orange for the tangerine peel and 2 small oranges for the tangerines.

LEMON BUTTERED CABBAGE

3 tablespoons butter or margarine
½ to 1 teaspoon caraway or celery seed
1 medium head cabbage (about 1½ pounds), coarsely chopped

Grated peel and juice of ½ Sunkist lemon
Salt and pepper to taste

Makes 4 servings (about 4 cups).

In a large skillet, melt the butter with caraway seed; add the cabbage. Cook over high heat for 3 to 4 minutes, stirring constantly. Reduce heat and cover. Simmer for 2 to 3 minutes, or until *just* tender. Stir in lemon peel and juice. Season with salt and pepper.

LOWER IN SODIUM CABBAGE VARIATION: Use *unsalted* butter or margarine. Omit the salt. About 121 calories and 35 mg. sodium per serving.

LIMA BEAN VARIATION: Substitute 2 packages (10 ounces each) frozen baby lima beans for the cabbage. In a saucepan, cook the lima beans following the package directions. Drain and return to saucepan. Stir in butter, caraway seed, lemon peel and juice and heat. Season with salt and pepper. Makes 4 to 6 servings (about 4 cups).

CALIFORNIA CARROTS

1 pound carrots, cut into ¼-inch-thick slices (about 3 cups)
Boiling water
Grated peel of ½ Sunkist orange
1 Sunkist orange, peeled and cut into bite-size pieces
2 tablespoons butter or margarine, softened
1 tablespoon chopped green onion (scallion)

Makes 3 to 4 servings (about 2 cups).

In a covered saucepan, cook the carrots in 1 inch of boiling water until *just* tender, 10 to 15 minutes. Drain and return the carrots to the saucepan. Add the remaining ingredients and heat.

BROWN SUGAR OR HONEY VARIATION: Omit green onion; stir in 2 tablespoons of light brown sugar *or* 1 tablespoon honey with the remaining ingredients.

CAULIFLOWER ALLA PARMESAN

Such a simple way to prepare cauliflower . . . but such flavor!

1 medium head cauliflower
Boiling water
Juice of 1 Sunkist lemon
2 to 3 tablespoons butter or margarine, melted
2 to 3 tablespoons grated Parmesan cheese
¼ teaspoon paprika
Salt and pepper to taste

Makes 4 to 6 servings.

In a large covered saucepan, cook the cauliflower in 1 inch of boiling water with half the lemon juice until tender (flowerets 5 to 10 minutes; whole 15 to 20 minutes); drain. To serve, sprinkle cauliflower with remaining lemon juice and butter. Combine Parmesan cheese and paprika; sprinkle the mixture over the cauliflower. Season with salt and pepper. Garnish with lemon cartwheel twists and parsley sprigs, if desired.

SAVORY CORN ON THE COB

4 to 8 fresh ears of corn,
    husks and silk removed
Boiling water
Lemon wedges
Butter or margarine, softened
Seasoned salt (optional)

Makes 4 to 8 servings.

In a large saucepot, cook the corn in rapidly boiling water for 4 to 8 minutes, or until tender; drain. To serve, rub corn with lemon wedges. Spread with butter and sprinkle with seasoned salt.

MICROWAVE—HIGH POWER SETTING
Omit water. Individually wrap 2 to 4 ears of corn in wax paper. Cook just until tender (approximately 3 to 5 minutes for 2 ears, *or* 7 to 8 minutes for 4 ears). Let stand for 2 to 4 minutes. Serve as above. Makes 2 to 4 servings.

MUSHROOM CAPS ROYALE

Lemon butter and Parmesan cheese add zest to these broccoli-filled mushroom caps. Serve either as an attractive side dish or as a savory bite-size appetizer.

1 pound large mushrooms (12 to 14)
1 tablespoon fresh squeezed lemon juice
2 tablespoons butter or margarine, melted
1 cup cooked chopped broccoli, drained
¼ cup mayonnaise or salad dressing
¼ cup grated Parmesan cheese
Grated peel of ½ Sunkist lemon
Paprika

Makes 4 to 6 servings.

Remove the stems from the mushrooms; chop stems and reserve them. Combine the lemon juice and 1 tablespoon of the butter. Brush mushroom caps with lemon-butter mixture; arrange, cavity-side-up, in a 12 × 8 × 2-inch baking dish. In a small skillet, sauté chopped mushroom stems in remaining 1 tablespoon of butter until just tender. Add broccoli, mayonnaise, Parmesan cheese, and lemon peel; blend well. Spoon about 1½ tablespoons of the broccoli mixture into each mushroom cap. Sprinkle with paprika. Bake at 350° F. for 13 to 15 minutes, or until heated through.

APPETIZER VARIATION: Substitute 1 pound medium mushrooms (24 to 28) for the large mushrooms. Spoon about 1 teaspoon of the broccoli mixture into each mushroom cap. Bake as above.

SCANDINAVIAN DILLED POTATOES

5 unpeeled medium potatoes (about 1½ pounds), cut lengthwise into 6 wedges each
Boiling salted water
Juice of 1 Sunkist lemon (3 tablespoons)
1 medium clove garlic, minced
¼ cup sliced green onions (scallions)
2 tablespoons butter or margarine
Grated peel of ½ Sunkist lemon
½ teaspoon dried dill weed
¼ teaspoon seasoned salt

Makes 4 to 6 servings.

In a covered skillet, cook the potatoes in boiling salted water with 2 tablespoons of the lemon juice and garlic for 20 minutes, or until tender; drain well. In the same skillet, sauté the green onions in the butter with lemon peel, dill, and seasoned salt. Add potatoes and remaining 1 tablespoon of lemon juice and heat.

SKINNY-MINNY'S BAKED POTATO WEDGES

If you love the taste and crispiness of French-fried potatoes, but not the calories, try these oven-crisped potato wedges. Cooked with a minimum of oil, they have a hint of lemon and a lot fewer calories. *

4 unpeeled large baking potatoes (about 2 pounds), cut lengthwise into thick wedges	2 tablespoons salad or vegetable oil
	Paprika
	Salt to taste (optional)
Juice of 1 Sunkist lemon	Lemon wedges

Makes 6 servings.
About 139 calories and 4 mg. sodium per serving without salt added.

In a large bowl, toss the potato wedges with the lemon juice and oil; let stand for 30 minutes or longer. Arrange potato wedges in a single layer on a 15½ × 10½ × 1-inch non-stick jelly-roll pan or baking sheet and drizzle any remaining lemon-oil mixture over them. Sprinkle with paprika. Bake at 400° F. for 45 minutes; turn the potato wedges and sprinkle with additional paprika. Bake 15 minutes longer, or until tender and well browned. Season with salt. Serve with lemon wedges.

*An equivalent serving of homemade potatoes deep-fried in vegetable oil would total about 400 calories.

ORANGE–SWEET POTATO BAKE

1½ pounds (about 4) yams (sweet potatoes), cooked, peeled and cut into ¼-inch-thick slices	2 teaspoons cornstarch
	¼ cup butter or margarine
	¼ cup packed light brown sugar
2 Sunkist valencia oranges, peeled and cut into cartwheel slices	¼ teaspoon pumpkin pie spice
	¼ cup walnut or pecan halves
Grated peel and juice of ½ Sunkist orange	¼ cup shredded or flaked coconut (optional)

Makes 6 servings.

In an 8-inch-square baking dish, arrange the yams and orange cartwheel slices overlapping. In a small saucepan, gradually blend the orange juice into the cornstarch; add the butter, brown sugar, orange peel, and pumpkin pie spice. Cook over medium heat, stirring, until thickened. Pour over yams and oranges. Sprinkle with nuts and coconut. Bake at 375° F. for 15 minutes, or until heated through.

ORIENTAL ORANGE SPINACH

2 large bunches *or* 2 packages (10 ounces each) fresh spinach
⅓ cup chicken broth
1 tablespoon soy sauce
½ teaspoon sugar
2 Sunkist oranges, peeled and cut into bite-size pieces
1 tablespoon toasted sesame seed

Makes 6 servings (about 3 cups). About 48 calories per serving.

Remove the stems and wash the spinach. Place the spinach (with the water that clings to the leaves) in a large saucepot. Cook, covered, over medium-high heat for 4 to 5 minutes, stirring occasionally until leaves are *just* wilted; drain well. In same saucepot, combine chicken broth, soy sauce, and sugar; bring to a boil. Stir in spinach and orange pieces and heat. Serve in individual bowls; sprinkle with the sesame seed. Serve with additional soy sauce, if desired.

FROZEN SPINACH VARIATION: Substitute 2 packages (10 ounces each) frozen leaf spinach for the fresh spinach. Prepare the frozen spinach following package directions; drain well. Proceed as above.

CREAMED SPINACH À LA LEMON

Many people associate creamed spinach with a dinner of prime ribs and Yorkshire pudding . . . popular restaurant fare. Here's a real homespun recipe flavored with bacon and fresh lemon.

4 slices bacon
1 medium onion, finely chopped
1 small clove garlic, minced
2 tablespoons butter or margarine
3 tablespoons all-purpose flour
1¾ cups milk

2 packages (10 ounces each) frozen chopped spinach, cooked and *well drained*
2 tablespoons grated Parmesan cheese
Grated peel of 1 Sunkist lemon
Juice of ½ Sunkist lemon
Generous dash of pepper

Makes 6 servings (about 5 cups).

In a skillet, cook the bacon until crisp; remove, drain, and crumble. Pour off all but 1 tablespoon of the drippings. In the same skillet, sauté the onion and garlic in the drippings and butter until tender. Remove from heat and stir in the flour. Cook for a few minutes, stirring constantly. Gradually blend in the milk. Cook over medium heat, stirring, until thickened. Add the spinach, Parmesan cheese, lemon peel, lemon juice, crumbled bacon, and pepper; heat.

LEMON-GLAZED ACORN SQUASH

1 unpeeled acorn squash (about 2 pounds)
2 tablespoons butter or margarine
Grated peel and juice of ½ Sunkist lemon

1 tablespoon sugar
1 tablespoon honey
¼ teaspoon ground ginger
1 tablespoon cold water
1 teaspoon cornstarch

Makes 4 to 6 servings.

Cut the squash crosswise into ½-inch slices; remove and discard seeds. In a covered 2-quart casserole, bake squash at 350° F. for 1 hour, or until tender. Meanwhile, to make the glaze, in a saucepan, melt the butter and stir in the lemon peel, lemon juice, sugar, honey, and ginger. Gradually stir the water into the cornstarch; add to glaze mixture. Cook, stirring, until thickened. Remove squash from oven and drain any excess liquid from casserole. Pour glaze over squash.

MICROWAVE—HIGH POWER SETTING

Cut squash crosswise into ½-inch slices; remove and discard seeds. In a covered 2-quart glass casserole, cook squash for 8 to 10 minutes; let stand, covered, while preparing glaze. To make glaze, in a 1-cup glass measure, melt butter (approximately 30 seconds). Stir in lemon peel, lemon juice, sugar, honey, and ginger; cook 1 minute. Gradually blend water into cornstarch; add to glaze mixture. Cook until thickened (approximately 1 minute), stirring once. Pour glaze over squash. Cook, covered, until heated through (approximately 2 minutes).

WINTER SQUASH À L'ORANGE

2½ pounds butternut squash, cut in half and seeds removed, *or* a 2½-pound piece Hubbard or banana squash
¼ cup butter or margarine
¼ cup packed light brown sugar *or* honey

Grated peel and juice of ½ Sunkist orange
¼ teaspoon ground cinnamon or nutmeg
¼ cup slivered almonds, toasted

Makes 4 to 6 servings (about 3 cups).

Place the squash, cut-side-down, in a shallow baking pan; bake at 350° F. for 1 to 1½ hours, or until tender. Scoop the squash from the shell. In a bowl, mash squash with electric mixer or potato masher. In a saucepan, melt the butter with the brown sugar, orange peel, orange juice, and cinnamon. Gradually add hot butter mixture to squash, beating until well blended. Sprinkle with almonds.

SOUTHWEST STUFFED ZUCCHINI OR GREEN PEPPERS

4 unpeeled large zucchini (about 2 pounds), cut in half lengthwise
Boiling water
2 eggs, slightly beaten
1 can (12 ounces) vacuum packed whole-kernel corn with peppers, drained
1 cup shredded Swiss cheese
⅓ cup coarsely crushed crackers (soda, sesame, etc.)
Grated peel and juice of ½ Sunkist lemon
½ teaspoon dry mustard
Chopped parsley

Makes 8 servings.

Parboil the zucchini in boiling water for 5 to 7 minutes; drain well and cool slightly. With the tip of a spoon carefully scoop out the centers and discard, leaving ¼-inch shells; drain, cut-side-down, on paper toweling. To make the filling, in a bowl combine all the remaining ingredients *except* the parsley. Spoon the filling into zucchini shells. Arrange in a shallow baking dish. Bake at 350° F. for 25 minutes. Sprinkle with parsley.

GREEN PEPPER VARIATION: Substitute 4 medium-to-large sweet green peppers for the zucchini. Cut a slice from the stem end of each pepper; remove the seeds and membranes. Parboil the peppers in boiling water for 2 minutes; drain. Make the filling as above. Spoon the filling into the green pepper shells. Arrange in a shallow baking dish. Bake at 350° F. for 30 minutes. Sprinkle with parsley. Makes 4 servings.

STIR-FRIED ZUCCHINI AND MUSHROOMS

Using a large non-stick skillet for stir-frying lessens the amount of oil needed to cook any vegetable combination. The small amount of butter is for additional flavor.

1 tablespoon butter or margarine	½ pound mushrooms, sliced
1 tablespoon salad or vegetable oil	4 green onions (scallions), cut in 2-inch pieces
1 chicken bouillon cube	1 small sweet red or green pepper, cut into ½-inch squares
1 medium clove garlic, minced	Grated peel and juice of ½ Sunkist lemon
4 unpeeled medium zucchini (about 1 pound) thinly sliced	

Makes 4 to 6 servings (about 4 cups).

In a large non-stick skillet, heat the butter with the oil, bouillon cube, and garlic. Add zucchini and mushrooms and stir-fry over medium-high heat for 3 minutes. Add green onions and pepper; cook 2 minutes longer, or until vegetables are *just* tender. Stir in lemon peel and juice.

Vegetables, Pasta, and Rice

CHEESY VEGETABLE ENTRÉE FOR TWO

More restaurants are featuring vegetable platters on their lunch and dinner menus. Here's a stay-at-home version for two.

1 unpeeled medium zucchini, cut into ½-inch-thick slices	1 to 2 tablespoons butter or margarine, melted
1 medium carrot, thinly sliced on the diagonal	Grated peel of ½ Sunkist lemon
1 medium onion, quartered	1½ cups (6 ounces) shredded American process cheese, Swiss, or caraway cheese
Boiling water	
¼ pound small mushrooms	Lemon wedges
1 package (10 ounces) frozen broccoli spears, cooked and drained	

Makes 2 servings.

In a covered saucepan, cook the zucchini, carrot, and onion in 1 inch of boiling water for 5 minutes, or until *just* tender. Add the mushrooms and cook for 1 minute longer. Drain and divide the vegetables between 2 shallow 12-ounce ovenproof serving dishes. Brush with butter. Sprinkle lemon peel and cheese over vegetables. Bake at 400° F. for 5 minutes, or until vegetables are heated through and cheese melts. Serve with lemon wedges.

ORANGE VEGETABLE MEDLEY

2 cups cauliflowerets	½ teaspoon ground ginger
2 cups broccoli flowerets	¼ cup fresh squeezed orange juice
Boiling water	
2 tablespoons butter or margarine	1 teaspoon cornstarch
Grated peel of ½ Sunkist orange	2 Sunkist oranges, peeled and cut into half-cartwheel slices
1 teaspoon instant chicken bouillon	2 green onions (scallions), cut into thin strips

Makes 4 servings (about 4 cups).
About 130 calories per serving.

In a large covered saucepan, cook the cauliflower and broccoli in 1 inch of boiling water until *just* tender, 6 to 8 minutes; drain. In the same saucepan, melt the butter with the orange peel, bouillon, and ginger. Gradually blend the orange juice into the cornstarch; add to butter mixture. Cook over medium heat, stirring, until thickened. Add cooked vegetables, orange half-cartwheel slices, and green onions and heat.

VEGETABLE TEMPURA

1 egg
1 cup water
2 tablespoons fresh squeezed lemon juice
1 cup *plus* 2 tablespoons all-purpose flour
1 tablespoon cornstarch
½ teaspoon baking powder
Salad or vegetable oil
8 cups assorted prepared vegetables*
Ponzu Sauce (page 116)
Lemon wedges

Makes 4 to 8 servings.

In a bowl, beat the egg well with the water and lemon juice. Blend in flour, cornstarch, and baking powder (batter should still be lumpy). In a wok or electric skillet, heat 1 to 2 inches of oil to 350 to 375° F. Dip a few vegetables at a time in the batter; shake off excess batter. Cook vegetables in small batches in hot oil for 1 to 2 minutes, turning as necessary. Drain on paper toweling and keep warm. Serve with Ponzu Sauce and/or lemon wedges.

---

*Prepare any of the following vegetables (Clean, cut and wipe vegetables *completely* dry.):
    Sweet green pepper, cut into rings
    Broccoli and/or cauliflower, cut into flowerets
    Carrots and/or zucchini, thinly sliced on the diagonal
    Eggplant, French-fry cut
    Green beans and/or Chinese pea pods (snow peas), whole
    Mushrooms, whole or sliced
    Onions, sliced
    Sweet potatoes, thinly sliced rounds

PONZU SAUCE

¼ cup soy sauce
½ teaspoon fresh grated lemon peel
¼ cup fresh squeezed lemon juice

Makes about ½ cup.

Combine all the ingredients. Serve as a dipping sauce for tempura.

THREE "Cs" RICE BAKE

Carrots, cheese, and curry team up in this tasty rice bake.

2¼ cups water
1 cup raw regular rice
¼ cup finely chopped onion
1 tablespoon butter or margarine
½ teaspoon curry powder
½ teaspoon salt
⅛ teaspoon pepper
3 cups shredded carrots (about 6 medium)
1½ cups shredded Cheddar cheese (about 6 ounces)
¾ cup milk
3 eggs, well beaten
Grated peel and juice of 1 Sunkist lemon

Makes 4 to 6 servings (about 5½ cups).

In a large saucepan, bring the water to a boil. Stir in rice, onion, butter, curry powder, salt, and pepper. Cover and cook over low heat for 10 minutes. Stir in carrots. Cover and cook 15 minutes longer, or until liquid has been absorbed. Stir in cheese, milk, eggs, and lemon peel and juice. Pour into a shallow 1½-quart baking dish. Bake at 350° F. for 30 minutes, or until set. Garnish with lemon cartwheel slices and parsley sprigs, if desired.

"OPEN SESAME" RICE PILAF

¼ cup sesame seed
2 tablespoons salad or vegetable oil
1 cup raw regular rice
1 medium onion, chopped
2 chicken bouillon cubes
2 cups hot water
Grated peel of ½ Sunkist orange

Makes 4 to 6 servings (about 4 cups).

In a saucepan, *lightly* brown the sesame seed in the oil, stirring constantly. Add rice, onion, and bouillon cubes; sauté for a few minutes. Add hot water and bring to a boil. Reduce heat, cover, and simmer for 20 minutes, or until rice is tender and the liquid has been absorbed. Stir in the orange peel.

TANGY PASTA WITH BASIL AND PARMESAN

Tangy Pasta (below)
1 large clove garlic, minced
¼ cup chopped fresh basil *or* 2 teaspoons dried basil leaves, crushed
2 tablespoons butter or margarine
2 tablespoons olive or vegetable oil
Grated peel and juice of ½ Sunkist lemon
¼ cup chopped parsley
⅔ cup grated Parmesan cheese
Fresh ground pepper to taste

Makes 4 servings (about 4 cups).

Prepare the Tangy Pasta. In a large skillet, sauté the garlic with the basil in the butter and oil; stir in lemon peel and juice. Reduce heat and add Tangy Pasta, parsley, and ⅓ cup of the Parmesan cheese; toss well. To serve, sprinkle with remaining ⅓ cup cheese and season with pepper.

Note: Increase butter and oil, as desired, for more sauce (but also more calories!).

TANGY PASTA
About 2 quarts water
Juice of 1 Sunkist lemon
8 ounces dry pasta: egg noodles, fettuccine, linguine, spaghetti, spaghettini, or vermicelli

Makes 4 servings (about 4 cups).

In a large saucepot, bring the water and lemon juice to a boil; add the pasta. Cook for 8 to 10 minutes, or until tender. Drain well.

HERBED LEMON-BUTTER PATTIES

No molds are needed, just roll the herbed butter mixture in wax paper, chill, and slice. Serve it with cooked asparagus, broccoli, carrots, corn, or spinach.

½ cup butter or margarine, softened	1 to 2 teaspoons of *one* of the following finely chopped fresh herbs: basil, marjoram, mint, oregano, parsley, or tarragon leaves*
Grated peel and juice of ½ Sunkist lemon	

Makes about ½ cup.

In a small bowl, combine all the ingredients. On wax paper, shape butter mixture into a 1 × 7-inch roll or rectangle; chill. Slice into patties.

HOT HERBED BUTTER VARIATION: In a small saucepan, melt the butter. Add the remaining ingredients and heat. Pour over cooked vegetables.

*Or substitute ½ teaspoon dried herbs, crushed.

PARSLEY-DILL BUTTER

Serve over cooked zucchini, Brussels sprouts, green beans, or potatoes.

¼ cup butter or margarine	1 tablespoon chopped parsley
Grated peel and juice of ½ Sunkist lemon	½ teaspoon dried dill weed

Makes about ⅓ cup sauce.

In a small saucepan, melt the butter. Add the remaining ingredients and heat.

TANGY LEMON-SESAME BUTTER

Serve over cooked asparagus, broccoli, cauliflower, lima beans, spinach, or zucchini.

¼ cup butter or margarine	1 tablespoon toasted sesame seed
Grated peel and juice of ½ Sunkist lemon	1 teaspoon sugar
	¼ teaspoon garlic salt

Makes about ⅓ cup.

In a small saucepan, melt the butter. Add the remaining ingredients and heat.

VARIATION: Omit the sugar and substitute onion salt for the garlic salt.

"EASIEST EVER" HOLLANDAISE SAUCE

The secret to this easy Hollandaise Sauce is in separating the egg yolks. Remove all the egg whites, as they can thin the sauce. Add the bubbly lemon-butter mixture slowly to the egg yolks and presto . . . a delicious sauce that is ready in minutes. For a blender variation see page 57. Serve over cooked asparagus, broccoli, or broiled tomatoes.

½ cup butter or margarine	⅛ teaspoon salt
Juice of ½ Sunkist lemon (1½ tablespoons)	3 egg yolks

Makes about ¾ cup.

In a small saucepan, heat the butter with the lemon juice and salt until bubbly. Add slowly to egg yolks, beating constantly with a wire whisk.

VERSATILE VEGETABLE RELISH SAUCE

Serve this tasty sauce over cooked fresh, frozen, or drained canned green beans and sliced mushrooms, chilled; assorted cooked vegetables, chilled; or sliced tomatoes on crisp salad greens.

⅔ cup salad or vegetable oil
Grated peel of ½ Sunkist lemon
Juice of 2 Sunkist lemons (⅓ cup)
¼ cup sweet pickle relish
2 tablespoons finely chopped green onion (scallion)
2 tablespoons finely chopped sweet green pepper
2 tablespoons chopped parsley
2 tablespoons chopped pimiento
1 teaspoon sugar
½ teaspoon salt

Makes about 1 cup.

In a jar with a lid, combine all the ingredients and shake well.

APPETIZER VARIATION: Spoon sauce over assorted raw vegetables (cauliflowerets, cherry tomatoes, and cucumber and/or zucchini slices, and sweet green pepper squares).

Salads and Salad Dressings

Nowhere is citrus a more natural ingredient than with the abundant array of crisp, fresh produce in salads. Lemon's natural tang gives a lift to any bowl of crisp greens and vegetables. Oranges are a luscious complement to chicken or tuna, and grapefruit blends deliciously with broccoli or spinach.

Consider salads for a first course: tender Boston lettuce with a tangy lemon-sesame dressing. Or as a light entrée: chicken with rice and fresh oranges. Or for a light weekend brunch: a salad of the freshest fruits.

Remember that fresh lemon juice prevents many cut fruits from discoloring. It's a natural with avocados, peaches, pears, apples, and bananas.

Experiment with contrasts in color, flavor, and texture. Then top your creation with a light and bright or thick and rich citrus dressing. Or squeeze on all the flavor of a fresh lemon wedge for only 4 calories, with virtually no sodium. The options are yours, and all the choices are delicious.

SALADS AND SALAD DRESSINGS

ZESTY MOLDED POTATO SALAD
FRESH ORANGE-PASTA SALAD
LEMON GREEK SALAD
SPINACH SALAD FLAMBÉ
CINDY'S GARDEN FETTUCCINE SALAD
FRESH FRUIT SALAD WITH PINEAPPLE DRESSING
CHILLED GRAPEFRUIT AND BROCCOLI SALAD
GRAPEFRUIT AND SPINACH SALAD
BEST-EVER CAESAR SALAD
GERMAN-STYLE HOT POTATO SALAD
FALLBROOK'S FAVORITE SALAD
GREEN AND ORANGE SALAD WITH BLUE CHEESE DRESSING
SUNNY FRESH GRAPEFRUIT AND PINEAPPLE MOLD
CHICKEN AND ORANGE RICE SALAD
WESTERN CHICKEN SALAD IN GRAPEFRUIT SHELLS
SHOW-OFF SALMON MOLD
EASY THREE-BEAN SALAD
ORANGE WALDORF SALAD
MARINER'S FRUIT SALAD
WILD RICE–FILLED TOMATOES
GARDEN FRESH COLESLAW
TANGERINE SPINACH SALAD WITH CALORIE-CONSCIOUS DRESSING
TUNA-MAC STUFFED AVOCADO
GRAPEFRUIT-MINT DRESSING
LEMON-SESAME DRESSING
JUNIOR-SIZE LEMON-SESAME DRESSING
CITRUS-HONEY DRESSING
LEMON-FRESH MAYONNAISE
LEMONY LOW SODIUM MAYONNAISE
LEMON-AVOCADO DRESSING
ROSY'S HONEYED FRUIT SALAD DRESSING
YOGURT–BLUE CHEESE DRESSING
LOW CALORIE LEMON FRENCH DRESSING
LEMON HERBED VINEGAR

ZESTY MOLDED POTATO SALAD

6 unpeeled medium potatoes (about 2 pounds), cooked and chilled
4 hard-cooked eggs, chopped
1 small sweet green pepper, cut into thin strips
1 small onion, finely chopped
⅓ cup chopped sweet pickles
⅓ cup mayonnaise or salad dressing
⅓ cup sour cream
Grated peel and juice of 1 Sunkist lemon
2 tablespoons chopped pimiento or sweet red pepper
1 tablespoon sugar
½ teaspoon salt
½ teaspoon celery seed
¼ teaspoon white pepper

Makes 6 to 8 servings (about 6 cups).

Peel and cube the potatoes. In a large bowl, combine the potatoes and remaining ingredients. Press the mixture firmly into an oiled 6-cup ring mold; chill. Run a knife around the inside of the mold; invert onto a serving plate. Garnish with lemon cartwheel twists, carrot curls, and parsley sprigs, if desired.

FRESH ORANGE-PASTA SALAD

Grated peel of ½ Sunkist orange
Juice of 1 Sunkist orange
3 tablespoons salad or vegetable oil
½ teaspoon seasoned salt
½ teaspoon dried dill weed
2 cups curly or spiral macaroni, cooked and drained
2 Sunkist oranges, peeled and cut into half-cartwheel slices
2 cups broccoli flowerets, cooked and drained
½ cup sliced celery
¼ cup sliced green onions (scallions)

Makes 4 servings (about 5 cups). About 214 calories per serving.

In a large bowl, combine the orange peel, orange juice, oil, seasoned salt, and dill. Add the remaining ingredients and toss gently. Cover and chill.

LEMON GREEK SALAD

⅓ cup salad or vegetable oil
Grated peel and juice of 1 Sunkist lemon
½ teaspoon dried oregano leaves, crushed
¼ teaspoon garlic salt
¼ teaspoon pepper
1 can (6 ounces, dr. wt.) pitted ripe (black) olives, drained
1 medium cucumber, scored and sliced
1 medium sweet green pepper, cut into 1-inch pieces
12 cherry tomatoes, cut in half
4 ounces feta cheese, cubed or crumbled
1 small head iceberg lettuce, torn into bite-size pieces

Makes 4 to 6 servings (about 8 cups)

In a bowl, combine the oil, lemon peel and juice, oregano, garlic salt, and pepper. Add the olives, cucumber, green pepper, tomatoes, and cheese; mix well. Cover and chill. To serve, arrange the lettuce in a salad bowl; top with marinated vegetable mixture. Toss gently, if desired.

SPINACH SALAD FLAMBÉ

An eye- and palate-pleaser for entertaining. Flambé tableside for a very impressive first course.

1 large bunch *or* 1 package (10 ounces) fresh spinach, washed and torn into bite-size pieces
1 small head Bibb or Boston lettuce, torn into bite-size pieces
½ pound mushrooms, sliced
6 slices bacon, cut into 1-inch pieces
Juice of 2 Sunkist lemons (6 tablespoons)
3 tablespoons sugar
2 teaspoons Worcestershire sauce
3 tablespoons brandy

Makes 6 servings (about 10 cups).

In a large bowl, combine the spinach, lettuce, and mushrooms. In a skillet, cook the bacon until crisp. Do not drain. Add lemon juice, sugar, and Worcestershire sauce; heat to boiling. Pour the dressing over salad mixture, leaving the bacon in the skillet; toss well. Divide the salad mixture among 6 individual salad plates. Add brandy to bacon in the skillet and heat. Ignite and spoon over the salads. Serve immediately.

CINDY'S GARDEN FETTUCCINE SALAD

For an even more colorful salad, half spinach fettuccine and half egg fettuccine can be used in this great make-ahead salad.

½ cup salad or vegetable oil
Grated peel of 1 Sunkist lemon
Juice of 1½ Sunkist lemons (4½ tablespoons)
2 tablespoons white wine vinegar
2 tablespoons toasted sesame seed
1 large clove garlic, minced
½ teaspoon onion salt
8 ounces fettuccine noodles, cooked and drained (about 5 cups, cooked)
½ pound tiny cooked shrimp
1 bunch *or* 1 package (10 ounces) fresh spinach, washed and cut into thin strips
2 medium carrots, shredded
1 unpeeled medium zucchini, shredded
2 green onions (scallions), cut in thin strips
2 to 4 tablespoons chopped cilantro
Fresh ground black pepper to taste

Makes 8 servings (about 12 cups).

In a large bowl, combine the oil, lemon peel, lemon juice, vinegar, sesame seed, garlic, and onion salt. Add noodles and shrimp; toss well. Cover and chill for 2 hours or longer; stir occasionally. To serve, add remaining ingredients and toss well.

FRESH FRUIT SALAD WITH PINEAPPLE DRESSING

1 can (8 ounces) crushed pineapple, drained
⅔ cup sour cream
2 tablespoons honey
Grated peel of ½ Sunkist orange
¼ cup chopped pecans or walnuts

3 Sunkist oranges, peeled and cut into cartwheel slices
2 unpeeled red apples, sliced
2 bananas, sliced
Green and red grape clusters
Salad greens

Makes 4 servings.

To make the salad dressing, combine the drained pineapple, sour cream, honey, and orange peel; chill. To serve, stir the nuts into the dressing. On 4 individual serving plates, arrange the fruit on the salad greens. Serve with the salad dressing.

YOGURT DRESSING VARIATIONS: Substitute 1 can (8 ounces) crushed pineapple in unsweetened pineapple juice, *well drained*, for the regular pineapple. Substitute 1 carton (8 ounces) lowfat vanilla yogurt for the sour cream. Omit the honey.

CHILLED GRAPEFRUIT AND BROCCOLI SALAD

2 Sunkist grapefruit
⅓ cup salad or vegetable oil
1 tablespoon Dijon mustard
½ teaspoon dried dill weed
¼ teaspoon onion salt (optional)

1 pound broccoli, separated into flowerets, cooked, drained, and chilled
¼ pound mushrooms, sliced

Makes 6 servings (about 5½ cups).
About 169 calories and 48 mg. sodium per serving without onion salt.

Over a bowl, peel and section the grapefruit; drain and reserve about ¼ cup of the grapefruit juice. In a shallow dish, combine the oil, reserved grapefruit juice, mustard, dill, and onion salt. Add chilled broccoli, mushrooms, and grapefruit sections.

Chill for 30 minutes, stirring occasionally. (Or marinate in a tightly sealed plastic bag, turning occasionally.)

GRAPEFRUIT AND SPINACH SALAD

⅔ cup salad or vegetable oil
¼ cup white wine vinegar
2 teaspoons fresh grated grapefruit peel
½ teaspoon garlic salt
⅛ teaspoon dried tarragon leaves, crushed
1 large bunch *or* 1 package (10 ounces) fresh spinach, washed and torn into bite-size pieces

2 Sunkist grapefruit, peeled and cut into half-cartwheel slices
1 small red onion, sliced and separated into rings
½ cup (about 2 ounces) crumbled blue cheese (optional)

Makes 6 servings (about 9 cups).

In a jar with a lid, combine the oil, vinegar, grapefruit peel, garlic salt, and tarragon; chill. In a large bowl, combine the spinach, grapefruit half-cartwheel slices, onion, and cheese; cover and chill. To serve, shake the dressing well. Lightly toss spinach mixture with as much dressing as desired.

BEST-EVER CAESAR SALAD

Probably no "authentic" Caesar Salad has ever been made without the tangy juice of fresh lemons.

1 small clove garlic, minced
½ cup olive or salad oil
2 medium heads romaine lettuce, torn into bite-size pieces and chilled
½ teaspoon salt
Fresh ground black pepper to taste

1 egg, coddled 1 minute*
Juice of 2 Sunkist lemons
1 tablespoon Worcestershire sauce
6 whole anchovy fillets (optional)
1 cup croutons
⅓ cup grated Parmesan cheese

*To coddle an egg, cook it for 1 minute in gently boiling water.

Makes 6 to 8 servings (about 12 cups).

Add the garlic to the oil; let stand for several hours, or as long as time permits. In a large salad bowl, toss the romaine with the garlic-oil, salt, and pepper. Break the egg into the middle of the salad. Squeeze or pour lemon juice over the romaine. Add Worcestershire sauce and anchovies; toss well. Add croutons and Parmesan cheese; toss lightly.

GERMAN-STYLE HOT POTATO SALAD

5 slices bacon	Grated peel and juice of 1 Sunkist lemon
1 medium onion, chopped	1 teaspoon celery seed
2 teaspoons instant chicken bouillon	2½ pounds potatoes, cooked, peeled, and cubed or sliced
½ cup water	
1 tablespoon sugar	¼ cup grated Parmesan cheese (optional)
1 tablespoon Dijon mustard	2 tablespoons chopped parsley

Makes 6 servings (about 6 cups).

In a skillet, cook the bacon until crisp; remove, drain, and crumble. In the drippings, sauté the onion with the bouillon until tender. Add water, sugar, mustard, lemon peel, lemon juice, and celery seed. Stir in potatoes and heat. Sprinkle with Parmesan cheese, parsley, and crumbled bacon.

FALLBROOK'S FAVORITE SALAD

½ cup salad or vegetable oil
Grated peel of ½ Sunkist orange
⅓ cup fresh squeezed orange juice
Juice of ½ Sunkist lemon
2 tablespoons honey
1 teaspoon paprika
1 to 2 teaspoons milder soy sauce

2 Sunkist oranges, peeled and cut into half-cartwheel slices
1 small to medium avocado, sliced
1 kiwifruit, peeled, thinly sliced
12 to 16 walnut halves
1 small-to-medium head iceberg lettuce, cut into 4 thick slices

Makes 4 servings.

To make the dressing, in a jar with a lid, combine the oil, orange peel, orange juice, lemon juice, honey, paprika, and soy sauce; shake well. Cover and chill. On 4 individual salad plates, arrange orange half-cartwheel slices, avocado, kiwifruit, and walnut halves on lettuce slices. Serve with the dressing.

GREEN AND ORANGE SALAD WITH BLUE CHEESE DRESSING

The secret to this dressing is to stir the oil into the sour cream gradually before *adding the remaining ingredients.*

8 cups assorted salad greens torn into bite-size pieces
3 Sunkist oranges, peeled and cut into bite-size pieces
⅓ cup salad or vegetable oil
½ cup sour cream

Grated peel and juice of ½ Sunkist lemon
2 ounces (about ½ cup) crumbled blue cheese
1 small clove garlic, minced
½ teaspoon dried dill weed
¼ teaspoon seasoned salt

Makes 6 to 8 servings (about 10 cups).

In a large bowl, combine the salad greens and oranges; cover and chill. In a small bowl, *gradually* add the oil to the sour cream, stirring constantly with a wire whisk. Stir in remaining ingredients; cover and chill. To serve, pour the dressing over the salad mixture and toss well.

SUNNY FRESH GRAPEFRUIT AND PINEAPPLE MOLD

1 can (about 8 ounces) crushed pineapple
2 envelopes unflavored gelatine
3 tablespoons sugar
2 cups boiling water
Juice of 1 Sunkist grapefruit (¾ cup)
½ cup shredded carrots
1 teaspoon fresh grated grapefruit peel
1 Sunkist grapefruit, peeled and cut into bite-size pieces

Makes 6 servings (about 4 cups).
About 95 calories and 6 mg. sodium per serving.

Drain the pineapple well; reserve the juice. In a bowl, combine the gelatine and sugar. Add boiling water and stir to dissolve gelatine. Add grapefruit and reserved pineapple juices. To chill quickly, place the bowl of gelatine mixture inside a large bowl filled with ice; stir the mixture occasionally until very thick, but not set, about 30 to 35 minutes. Stir in drained pineapple, carrots, grapefruit peel and grapefruit pieces. Pour into a lightly oiled 5-cup mold; chill until firm, about 1½ hours or longer. To serve, unmold onto a serving dish.

CHICKEN AND ORANGE RICE SALAD

A refreshing main-dish salad for warm weather eating.

2 cups water
1 chicken bouillon cube
Grated peel of ½ Sunkist orange
1 cup raw regular rice
1½ cups cubed cooked chicken
1 can (about 2 ounces, dr. wt.) sliced ripe (black) olives, drained
¼ cup sliced green onions (scallions)
2 Sunkist oranges, peeled and cut into half-cartwheel slices
Fresh Orange Dressing (below)
Salad greens

Makes 4 main-dish salads (about 5 cups).

In a saucepan, bring the water to a boil with the bouillon cube and orange peel. Add rice and return to a boil. Reduce heat; cover, and simmer for 20 minutes, or until liquid has been absorbed. Cool slightly. In a bowl, combine rice, chicken, olives, green onions, and orange half-cartwheel slices. Toss gently with the Fresh Orange Dressing; cover and chill. To serve, arrange on salad greens on individual serving plates. Garnish with parsley sprigs, if desired.

FRESH ORANGE DRESSING:

Juice of 1 Sunkist orange (⅓ cup)
3 tablespoons salad or vegetable oil
½ teaspoon celery salt
½ teaspoon dried tarragon leaves, crushed
⅛ teaspoon paprika

Makes about ½ cup.

In a jar with a lid, combine all the ingredients and shake well.

WESTERN CHICKEN SALAD IN GRAPEFRUIT SHELLS

The secret flavoring is pumpkin pie spice. Serving the salad in hollowed-out grapefruit shells adds to the presentation.

2 Sunkist grapefruit	1½ cups cubed cooked chicken
¼ cup salad or vegetable oil	
2 teaspoons sugar	1 small avocado, sliced
¼ teaspoon salt (optional)	2 tablespoons sliced green onion (scallion)
⅛ teaspoon pumpkin pie spice	

Makes 4 main-dish salads.
About 342 calories and 50 mg. sodium per serving without the salt.

Cut the grapefruit in half. With a grapefruit knife, cut around each section to loosen the "meat" from the membrane; reserve the sections. Squeeze the juice from the shells to equal ⅓ cup. With a spoon, scrape the grapefruit shells clean. Scallop or notch the edges, if desired (see page 290). Chill. Combine the ⅓ cup grapefruit juice, oil, sugar, salt, and pumpkin pie spice. Pour over the reserved grapefruit sections, chicken, avocado, and green onion; mix lightly. Cover and chill. To serve, spoon the chicken mixture into the shells. Serve in icers and garnish with additional grapefruit sections and avocado slices, if desired.

SHOW-OFF SALMON MOLD

A 4-cup fish-shaped mold makes this a buffet pleaser.

1 envelope unflavored gelatine	1 can (15½ ounces) salmon, drained and flaked
¼ cup fresh squeezed lemon juice	½ cup *cooked* peas
1 cup boiling water	2 hard-cooked eggs, chopped
¾ cup mayonnaise or salad dressing	1 tablespoon finely chopped fresh dill weed, *or* 1 teaspoon dried dill weed
1 teaspoon prepared mustard	
¼ teaspoon salt	Grated peel of 1 Sunkist lemon

Makes 6 servings (about 4 cups).

In a large bowl, soften the gelatine in the lemon juice for 5 minutes. Add boiling water and stir to dissolve the gelatine. Add the mayonnaise, mustard, and salt; beat until smooth. Chill the mixture until slightly thickened, about 1 hour, stirring occasionally. Gently stir in remaining ingredients. Pour into a lightly oiled 4-cup mold. Chill until firm, about 1½ hours. To serve, unmold onto a serving plate and garnish with additional fresh dill weed and lemon half-cartwheel slices, if desired.

EASY THREE-BEAN SALAD

For a picnic take-along or a barbecue side dish, this easy salad is a winner.

DRESSING
Grated peel of ½ Sunkist lemon
¼ cup fresh squeezed lemon juice
2 tablespoons water
1 package (about 0.6 ounce) Italian salad dressing mix
⅔ cup salad or vegetable oil

SALAD
1 can (16 ounces) cut green beans, drained
1 can (about 15 ounces) red kidney beans, drained
1 can (about 16 ounces) garbanzo beans (chick peas), drained
1 small onion, sliced and separated into rings
Salad greens

Makes 6 servings (about 5 cups).

In a jar with a lid, combine the lemon peel, lemon juice, and water with the dressing mix; shake well. Add oil and shake well again. In a large bowl, combine the beans and onion; pour dressing over and mix well. Cover and chill. Serve on salad greens.

ORANGE WALDORF SALAD

Grated peel of ½ Sunkist orange
4 Sunkist oranges, peeled and cut into bite-size pieces
1 unpeeled medium red apple, cut into bite-size pieces
1 cup miniature marshmallows
½ cup sliced celery
½ cup mayonnaise or salad dressing
⅓ cup chopped walnuts
⅛ teaspoon ground cinnamon

Makes 4 to 6 servings (about 4½ cups).

In a bowl, combine all the ingredients; cover and chill. Serve on salad greens, if desired.

MARINER'S FRUIT SALAD

½ to ¾ cup mayonnaise or salad dressing
Grated peel and juice of ½ Sunkist lemon
2 cans (about 7 ounces each) tuna, drained and chunked
2 Sunkist oranges, peeled, cut into bite-size pieces, and drained
1 unpeeled red apple, cut into bite-size pieces
1 cup grapes, cut in half and seeded
½ cup chopped walnuts
Salt to taste (optional)
Salad greens
Paprika
Lemon wedges

Makes 6 servings (about 5 cups).

In a bowl, combine the mayonnaise, lemon peel and juice. Stir in the tuna, orange pieces, apple, grapes, and walnuts; season with salt. Cover and chill. To serve, spoon tuna mixture onto salad greens; sprinkle with paprika and garnish with lemon wedges.

WILD RICE–FILLED TOMATOES

½ cup raw wild rice
1½ cups water
⅛ teaspoon salt
1 cup frozen peas, *cooked* and drained
½ cup mayonnaise or salad dressing
2 hard-cooked eggs, chopped
¼ cup sliced green onions (scallions)
Grated peel and juice of 1 Sunkist lemon
½ teaspoon seasoned salt
6 medium tomatoes
Salad greens or lettuce cups

Makes 6 servings.

Put the wild rice in a strainer and run cold water over it until the water runs clear. In a saucepan, bring the 1½ cups water to a boil. Add rice and salt; return to a boil. Reduce heat, cover, and cook over low heat for about 35 minutes, or until the rice puffs open and reveals the white interior. Drain and cool. Combine cooled rice with all the remaining ingredients *except* the tomatoes and salad greens. Cover and chill. Place tomatoes stem-side-down. Cut lengthwise to stem, but not quite through, to make 6 wedges; arrange on the greens. Spoon about ½ cup of the rice mixture into each tomato. Garnish each with a lemon cartwheel twist, if desired.

GARDEN FRESH COLESLAW

For a special presentation, serve this coleslaw in a large bowl lined with the outer leaves of a head of cabbage or in orange shells (page 290).

½ cup mayonnaise or salad dressing
Grated peel of 1 Sunkist orange
2 tablespoons fresh squeezed orange juice
1 tablespoon sugar
¼ teaspoon salt
¼ teaspoon white pepper
3 Sunkist oranges, peeled, cut into bite-size pieces, and well drained
1 small head cabbage, cut into long thin shreds (9 to 10 cups)
1 carrot, shredded
1 small sweet green pepper, shredded
¼ cup thinly sliced green onions (scallions)

Makes 6 to 8 servings (about 9 cups).

To make the dressing, combine the mayonnaise, orange peel, orange juice, sugar, salt, and pepper; cover and chill. In a large bowl, combine the remaining ingredients; cover and chill. To serve, toss the salad with the dressing. Garnish with green pepper rings and orange cartwheel slices, if desired.

HERB VARIATIONS: Add ¼ to ½ teaspoon celery seed, dried dill weed, or dried tarragon leaves, crushed.

TANGERINE SPINACH SALAD WITH CALORIE-CONSCIOUS DRESSING

When tangerines are not in season, substitute orange peel, juice, and segments.

- 1 large bunch *or* 1 package (10 ounces) fresh spinach, washed and torn into bite-size pieces
- 1 small head Bibb or Boston lettuce, torn into bite-size pieces
- 2 to 3 Sunkist tangerines, peeled, segmented, and seeded
- ¼ pound mushrooms, sliced
- 4 ounces cooked ham, cut into julienne strips
- Calorie-Conscious Dressing (page 139)
- 2 hard-cooked eggs, sliced

Makes 6 entrée servings (about 9 cups).
About 126 calories per serving with dressing.

In a large bowl, combine the spinach, lettuce, tangerine segments, mushrooms, and ham; cover and chill. To serve, pour the Calorie-Conscious Dressing over the salad mixture and toss well. Garnish with sliced eggs.

CALORIE-CONSCIOUS DRESSING

Grated peel of ½ Sunkist tangerine
½ cup fresh squeezed tangerine juice
Juice of ½ Sunkist lemon
1 tablespoon salad or vegetable oil
Low calorie sugar substitute to equal 2 teaspoons sugar
½ teaspoon chili powder
½ teaspoon dried thyme leaves, crushed
¼ teaspoon salt

Makes about ¾ cup.
About 16 calories per tablespoon.

In a jar with a lid, combine all the ingredients; chill. Shake well before serving.

TUNA-MAC STUFFED AVOCADO

1 can (about 7 ounces) tuna, drained and chunked
1½ cups *cooked* small shell or elbow macaroni
⅓ to ½ cup mayonnaise or salad dressing
¼ cup chopped sweet green pepper
¼ cup sliced green onions (scallions)
Grated peel of ½ Sunkist orange
¼ teaspoon seasoned salt
2 large avocados, halved
Fresh lemon juice
Salad greens
2 Sunkist oranges, peeled and cut into cartwheel slices
Lemon wedges (optional)

Makes 4 servings.

In a bowl, combine the tuna, macaroni, mayonnaise, green pepper, green onions, orange peel, and seasoned salt. Cover and chill. To serve, brush avocado halves (peeled or unpeeled) with fresh lemon juice; place on salad greens arranged on 4 individual serving plates. Fill each avocado half with about ⅔ cup of the tuna mixture. Arrange orange cartwheel slices on salad greens and garnish with lemon wedges.

GRAPEFRUIT-MINT DRESSING

Serve over salads of summer or winter fruits with fresh grapefruit sections or grapefruit half-cartwheel slices.

1 cup sour cream or lowfat plain yogurt
2 tablespoons honey
2 teaspoons fresh grated grapefruit peel
2 tablespoons fresh squeezed grapefruit juice
1 tablespoon chopped fresh mint, *or* 1 teaspoon dried mint leaves, crushed

Makes about 1 cup.
About 40 calories and 8 mg. sodium per tablespoon (sour cream); about 18 calories and 10 mg. sodium per tablespoon (yogurt).

In a small bowl, combine all the ingredients; cover and chill.

LEMON-SESAME DRESSING

This versatile dressing will be a repeat favorite. It's one of Sunkist's best. Serve it with a tossed salad of assorted greens, avocado, tomato, and cashew nuts or *iceberg lettuce, cooked chicken, green onion (scallion), and orange half-cartwheel slices.*

⅔ cup salad or vegetable oil
Grated peel of ½ Sunkist lemon
Juice of 1 Sunkist lemon
2 tablespoons distilled white vinegar
2 tablespoons toasted sesame seed
1 tablespoon sugar
½ teaspoon onion salt
½ teaspoon salt (optional)

Makes about 1 cup.

In a jar with a lid, combine all the ingredients and shake well.

POPPY SEED VARIATION: Substitute 2 teaspoons of poppy seed for the 2 tablespoons of sesame seed. Serve over crisp salad greens.

JUNIOR-SIZE LEMON-SESAME DRESSING

⅓ cup salad or vegetable oil
Grated peel of ½ Sunkist lemon
Juice of 1 Sunkist lemon

1 tablespoon toasted sesame seed
2 teaspoons sugar
½ teaspoon onion salt

Makes about ½ cup.

In a jar with a lid, combine all the ingredients and shake well.

CITRUS-HONEY DRESSING

Serve this over a fruit salad with orange half-cartwheel slices or bite-size pieces.

½ cup salad or vegetable oil
Grated peel of ½ Sunkist orange
Juice of 1 Sunkist orange
Juice of 1 Sunkist lemon

2 tablespoons honey
1 tablespoon poppy seed *or* toasted sesame seed
¼ teaspoon salt
¼ teaspoon paprika

Makes about 1 cup.

In a jar with a lid, combine all the ingredients; chill. Shake well before serving.

LEMON FRESH MAYONNAISE

There's nothing like fresh mayonnaise! This recipe is also the base for Creamy Cucumber Sauce (page 58) and Lemon Tartar Sauce (page 58).

2 egg yolks	1 teaspoon dry mustard
2 tablespoons fresh squeezed lemon juice	½ teaspoon salt
	1¼ cups salad or vegetable oil

Makes about 1¼ cups.

In a food processor, using the metal blade, process the egg yolks, lemon juice, mustard, and salt for 2 to 3 seconds. Continue processing, adding the oil through the feed tube in a steady stream just until mixture thickens, about 1 minute.

Note: To make in a blender, follow the method in Lemony Low Sodium Mayonnaise (below).

LEMONY LOW SODIUM MAYONNAISE

Make your own low sodium mayonnaise . . . it's as easy as leaving out the salt!

2 egg yolks	1 teaspoon dry mustard
2 tablespoons fresh squeezed lemon juice	Dash of cayenne pepper
	1¼ cups salad or vegetable oil

Makes about 1¼ cups.
Less than 1 mg. sodium and about 127 calories per tablespoon.

In a blender, blend the egg yolks, lemon juice, mustard, and cayenne pepper on "high" for 2 to 3 seconds. With the blender still running, remove the center cap of the cover and slowly add the oil in a steady stream just until the mixture thickens, about 1 minute.

Note: To make in a food processor, follow method in Lemon Fresh Mayonnaise (page 142).

LEMON-AVOCADO DRESSING

Serve this over individual salads of grapefruit sections, crabmeat, cooked asparagus spears, and leafy red lettuce.

1 large avocado	½ teaspoon garlic salt
1 cup sour cream	Grated peel and juice of ½
¼ cup finely chopped green onions (scallions)	Sunkist lemon

Makes about 2 cups.

In a bowl, mash the avocado pulp well; gradually blend in the sour cream. Stir in remaining ingredients; cover and chill.

Note: Add milk if a thinner consistency is desired.

ROSY'S HONEYED FRUIT SALAD DRESSING

A delicious quick and easy pink dressing... it's low in sodium. Serve this over a fruit salad of orange cartwheel slices, melon slices or balls, banana slices, grapes, and/or strawberries.

Grated peel of ½ Sunkist lemon	⅓ cup salad or vegetable oil
Juice of 1 Sunkist lemon	¼ cup cranberry juice cocktail
	3 tablespoons honey

Makes about 1 cup.
Less than 1 mg. sodium and about 55 calories per tablespoon.

In a jar with a lid, combine all the ingredients; chill. Shake well before using.

YOGURT–BLUE CHEESE DRESSING

Serve this over any favorite green salad or as a zesty dip with assorted raw vegetables. Lowfat yogurt decreases the calories; sour cream increases the flavor.

1 cup lowfat plain yogurt or sour cream	Grated peel and juice of ½ Sunkist lemon
⅓ cup (1¼ ounces) crumbled blue cheese	1 small clove garlic, minced
	¼ teaspoon seasoned salt
	⅛ teaspoon pepper

Makes about 1 cup.

Combine all the ingredients; cover and chill.

LOW CALORIE LEMON FRENCH DRESSING

It would be hard to make a lower-in-calorie salad dressing... especially one that tastes so good! Serve it over crisp greens.

1 envelope unflavored gelatine	Low calorie sugar substitute to equal 2 to 4 teaspoons sugar
¼ cup cold water	
½ cup boiling water	1 teaspoon finely minced onion
¼ cup fresh squeezed lemon juice	¼ teaspoon curry powder
	¼ teaspoon paprika

Makes about 1 cup.
About 3 calories per tablespoon (negligible sodium, depending on sugar substitute used).

In a jar with a lid, soften the gelatine in cold water. Add boiling water; cover and shake to dissolve gelatine. Add remaining ingredients and shake well. Chill for about 1¼ hours, or until dressing begins to thicken; shake well.

Note: If the salad dressing solidifies, immerse the jar in warm water for a few minutes to reliquefy the gelatine.

LEMON HERBED VINEGAR

This delightful citrus vinegar adds a hint of fresh herbs and lemon to any homemade salad dressing. A bottle of this vinegar tied with a bow makes a perfect hostess gift!

4 Sunkist lemons
4 small sprigs fresh dill, basil, or tarragon

32 to 40 ounces white wine vinegar

Makes four 8- to 10-ounce bottles.

With a vegetable parer, peel each lemon in a continuous spiral, removing the outer colored layer of peel only. In each of four 8- to 10-ounce bottles with lids, place the peel of 1 lemon and 1 herb sprig; fill with vinegar. Refrigerate for at least 2 days to blend the flavors.

LEMON VINEGAR VARIATION: Omit the fresh herbs. Proceed as above.

LEMON-GARLIC VINEGAR VARIATION: Omit the fresh herbs; add 1 or 2 cloves garlic, cut in half, to each bottle. Proceed as above.

ORANGE VINEGAR AND ORANGE HERB VINEGAR VARIATIONS: Substitute the peel of 4 oranges for the lemons in above recipes. Proceed as above.

Note: Cut the peeled lemons in half crosswise; then ream out the juice. Use the lemon juice in beverages, on fish or poultry, or freeze for later use.

Eggs and Breakfast or Brunch Ideas

Citrus juice and fruit compotes have long been considered among the brightest flavors of the morning. But citrus is also delicious in a variety of egg and brunch dishes.

You'll be surprised how well a bit of fresh grated peel or a slice of orange blends with the delicate and versatile egg. When you have the time for a leisurely breakfast, try the salmon omelet with lemon and dill sauce. And you'll have the kids coming back for more, with delicious pigs *on* a blanket.

Deviled eggs and pickled eggs with beets, tart and tangy with lemon, make nutritious snacks, beautiful buffet offerings, and a good start for a light and cool summer supper.

So think of eggs for any meal of the day, and add citrus to make them distinctive and memorable.

EGGS AND BREAKFAST OR BRUNCH IDEAS

CRÊPES HUEVOS RANCHEROS
B. J.'s OMELETTE À L'ORANGE
SALMON OMELET WITH DILL AND LEMON SAUCE
CHEESY VEGETABLE FRITTATA
DILLY ORANGE SCRAMBLE
SPRINGTIME ASPARAGUS QUICHE
DEVILISH EGGS
PICKLED EGGS AND BEETS
ORANGE "PUFF" PANCAKE
SUNRISE FRENCH TOAST
PIGS ON A BLANKET
BROILED ORANGE OR GRAPEFRUIT TOPPERS

CRÊPES HUEVOS RANCHEROS

For brunch, lunch, or dinner, this crêpe and egg dish has a lively south-of-the-border flavor.

TOPPING
1 medium avocado
⅓ cup sour cream
½ teaspoon fresh grated lemon peel
1 tablespoon fresh squeezed lemon juice
¼ teaspoon onion salt
Generous dash of hot pepper sauce

FILLING
1 can (4 ounces) whole green chiles
6 eggs, slightly beaten
2 tablespoons milk
¼ teaspoon salt
⅛ teaspoon pepper
2 tablespoons butter or margarine
8 Hint of Lemon Crêpes (page 189)
1 cup shredded Monterey Jack or Cheddar cheese

Makes 4 servings.

To make the topping, in a small bowl, mash the avocado; stir in the remaining ingredients and set aside. Drain the chiles; seed and cut them into 8 lengthwise pieces. Combine eggs, milk, salt, and pepper. In a 10-inch skillet, melt the butter; pour in the egg mixture. Cook over medium-low heat, stirring occasionally, until the eggs are set but still moist. Spoon cooked eggs down the center of the crêpes; top with the chiles. Sprinkle with cheese and roll up. Arrange crêpes, seam-side-down, on baking sheet. Bake at 400° F. for 7 to 9 minutes, or until heated through. To serve, spoon the topping over crêpes.

B. J.'S OMELETTE À L'ORANGE

1 cup sour cream
1 tablespoon light brown sugar
Grated peel of 1 Sunkist orange
6 eggs, separated

¼ teaspoon salt
2 tablespoons butter or margarine
2 Sunkist oranges, peeled and sectioned

Makes 3 to 4 servings.

To make sauce, in a small bowl, combine the sour cream, brown sugar, and half the orange peel. In a bowl, with an electric mixer, beat the egg yolks and salt until thick and light in color; stir in remaining orange peel. With clean beaters, beat the egg whites until soft peaks form. Fold in egg yolks. In an ovenproof 10-inch skillet, melt the butter; pour in the egg mixture. Cook over medium-low heat for about 5 minutes, or until the underside is *lightly* browned. Place in oven. Bake at 325° F. for 10 minutes, or until top is set. Loosen around the edges with a spatula. Make a slit across the center; fold in half. Carefully turn out onto a serving platter. Top with a small amount of sauce; garnish with a few orange sections. Serve with the remaining sauce and orange sections.

SALMON OMELET WITH DILL AND LEMON SAUCE

This extra special egg entrée is picture-perfect when served with asparagus bundles tied in lemon rings.

SALMON OMELET
6 eggs, separated
Grated peel and juice of 1 Sunkist lemon

1 can (7¾ ounces) salmon, drained and flaked
2 tablespoons butter or margarine

DILL AND LEMON SAUCE

2 tablespoons butter or margarine	Grated peel of ½ Sunkist lemon
2 tablespoons all-purpose flour	¼ teaspoon dried dill weed
1 tablespoon sliced green onion (scallion)	¼ teaspoon salt (optional)
	Dash of pepper
	1 cup milk

Makes 3 to 4 servings (about 1⅓ cups sauce).

To make the Salmon Omelet, in a bowl, with an electric mixer, beat the egg yolks until thick and light in color; stir in the lemon peel and juice. With clean beaters, beat the egg whites until soft peaks form. Fold in egg yolks and salmon. In an ovenproof 10-inch skillet, melt the butter; pour in the egg mixture. Cook over medium-low heat for about 5 minutes or until the underside is *lightly* browned. Place in oven. Bake at 325° F. for 10 minutes, or until the top is set. Loosen around the edges with a spatula. Make a slit across the center; fold in half. Carefully turn out onto a serving platter. Serve with Dill and Lemon Sauce.

To make the Dill and Lemon Sauce, in saucepan, melt the butter. Remove from the heat and stir in the flour, green onion, lemon peel, dill, salt, and pepper. Cook for a few minutes, stirring constantly. Gradually blend in the milk. Cook over medium heat, stirring, until thickened.

SERVING SUGGESTION: Cook 1 pound fresh or 1 package (10 ounces) frozen asparagus; drain. Divide the asparagus into 3 or 4 bundles. Slip 2 lemon rings (page 293) around each bundle. Arrange on a serving platter around the Salmon Omelet.

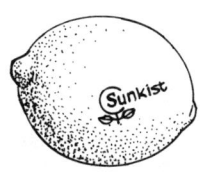

CHEESY VEGETABLE FRITTATA

3 slices bacon, cut in half
1 unpeeled medium zucchini, shredded and *well drained*
2 tablespoons chopped onion
¼ teaspoon seasoned salt
⅛ teaspoon dried dill weed
1 small tomato, chopped and *well drained*
6 eggs
3 tablespoons grated Parmesan cheese
2 tablespoons milk or sour cream
Grated peel of 1 Sunkist lemon
½ cup shredded Cheddar cheese
Lemon cartwheel twists
Parsley sprigs

Makes 4 to 6 servings.

In an ovenproof 10-inch skillet, cook the bacon until crisp; remove and drain. In the drippings, sauté the zucchini and onion with the seasoned salt and dill until just tender. Stir in the tomato. In a bowl, slightly beat the eggs, Parmesan cheese, and milk; stir in the lemon peel. Pour the egg mixture over the zucchini mixture in the skillet. Cook over low heat (do not stir) until eggs set around the edges but are moist on top. Arrange bacon spoke-wheel-fashion on egg mixture and sprinkle with Cheddar cheese. Bake at 450° F. for 4 to 5 minutes, or until eggs are set and cheese melts. Sprinkle with additional dill, if desired. Garnish with lemon cartwheel twists and parsley sprigs.

DILLY ORANGE SCRAMBLE

8 eggs, slightly beaten
1 package (3 ounces) cream cheese, cut into small pieces
2 tablespoons milk
Grated peel of ½ Sunkist orange
¼ teaspoon dried dill weed
¼ teaspoon salt
⅛ teaspoon pepper
2 tablespoons butter or margarine
2 Sunkist oranges, peeled, cut into bite-size pieces, and drained

Makes 4 servings.

In a bowl, combine all the ingredients *except* the butter and orange pieces. In a 10-inch skillet, melt the butter; pour in the egg mixture. Cook over medium-low heat until the eggs are almost set, stirring occasionally. Add orange pieces and continue to cook, until eggs are set but still moist.

MICROWAVE—HIGH POWER SETTING
Combine all the ingredients *except* the butter. In a large glass bowl, cook the butter until melted (approximately 30 seconds). Pour in the egg-orange mixture. Cook, covered with wax paper, for 3 minutes; stir cooked eggs to center of bowl. Cook, covered, until eggs are almost set (approximately 3 minutes), stirring three times. Let stand, covered, for 1 to 2 minutes before serving.

TANGERINE VARIATION: Substitute the fresh grated peel of ½ tangerine and 2 medium tangerines, peeled, segmented, seeded, and cut in half for the orange peel and pieces.

SPRINGTIME ASPARAGUS QUICHE

1 (9-inch) unbaked pie shell (page 260)
1 cup (4 ounces) shredded caraway, provolone, or Monterey Jack cheese
1 can (4 ounces) sliced mushrooms, *well drained*
6 to 8 (4-inch) partially cooked fresh asparagus spears, or defrosted frozen asparagus spears, *well drained*

3 eggs
1¼ cups half-and-half
Grated peel and juice of ½ Sunkist lemon
¼ teaspoon seasoned salt
Generous dash of ground nutmeg

Makes 4 to 6 entrée or 8 appetizer servings.

Prick the bottom and sides of the pie shell with a fork. Bake at 375° F. for 10 minutes to partially cook but not brown the crust.

Sprinkle ¾ cup of the cheese and mushrooms over the bottom of the crust. Arrange the asparagus spears, spoke-wheel-fashion, over the mushrooms. In a bowl, slightly beat the eggs with the half-and-half, lemon juice, seasoned salt, and nutmeg; stir in lemon peel. Pour the egg mixture over the asparagus. Sprinkle with the remaining ¼ cup of cheese. Bake at 375° F. for 50 minutes,* or until a knife inserted in the center comes out clean. Garnish with lemon cartwheel twists and parsley sprigs, if desired.

*If excess browning occurs during baking, cover edges of crust with thin strips of aluminum foil.

DEVILISH EGGS

No mayonnaise in these deviled eggs! The recipe can be doubled or tripled for picnic or buffet parties.

6 hard-cooked eggs, shelled and cut in half lengthwise
¼ cup sour cream
1 teaspoon fresh grated lemon peel

1 teaspoon Dijon mustard
¼ teaspoon dried dill weed
⅛ teaspoon salt (optional)
⅛ teaspoon white pepper

Makes 6 servings.

Carefully remove the egg yolks. In a bowl, mash the yolks (or push them through a sieve); blend in the remaining ingredients. Fill the egg whites with the yolk mixture; cover and chill. Garnish with chopped parsley or sprinkle with paprika, if desired.

LOWER IN CALORIES VARIATION: Substitute 3 tablespoons lowfat plain yogurt for the sour cream. About 87 calories and 86 mg. sodium per serving without adding salt.

PICKLED EGGS AND BEETS

1 cup water
1 cup cider vinegar
1 large onion, thickly sliced
2 large cloves garlic, halved
2 tablespoons whole mixed pickling spice
1 tablespoon sugar
1 can (16 ounces) sliced beets, undrained
Juice of 6 Sunkist lemons (1 cup)
12 hard-cooked eggs, shelled
1 Sunkist lemon, cut into cartwheel slices

Makes 6 to 12 servings.

In a large saucepan, combine the water, vinegar, onion, garlic, pickling spice, and sugar; bring to a boil. Reduce heat and simmer for 10 minutes to blend the flavors. Remove from heat. Add the undrained beets and lemon juice. In a 2½-quart or larger glass jar with a tight-fitting lid, combine the cooked shelled eggs and lemon cartwheel slices. Spoon beet mixture and liquid over eggs; refrigerate for 24 hours or longer.

Note: Refrigerate longer (up to 1 week) for more color and flavor.

ORANGE "PUFF" PANCAKE

Somewhat like a popover in texture and taste, this large puffed shell can be filled with any combination of fresh fruit. Also try serving it filled with Dilly Orange Scramble (page 152) for an extra-special brunch entrée.

3 eggs
½ cup buttermilk biscuit or pancake mix
½ cup milk
2 tablespoons butter or margarine
Grated peel of 1 Sunkist orange
4 Sunkist oranges, peeled, cut into bite-size pieces, and drained
⅓ cup light brown sugar
Sour cream
Nutmeg

Makes 4 servings.

Preheat the oven to 425° F. In a bowl, beat the eggs with an electric mixer until foamy. Gradually add the biscuit mix alternately with the milk; beat until smooth. In a 9-inch glass pie plate or a 9- or 10-inch ovenproof skillet, melt the butter in the preheated oven. Meanwhile, continue beating the egg mixture at high speed for 3 minutes more; stir in orange peel. Carefully remove hot pie plate from oven; pour in batter. Bake for 17 to 20 minutes, or until pancake is puffed and browned. Meanwhile, combine orange pieces and brown sugar. Spoon fruit into warm pancake; top with sour cream and sprinkle with nutmeg.

SUNRISE FRENCH TOAST

Fresh grapefruit and canned apricots make a delicious topping for this thick, golden brown French toast.

3 eggs, slightly beaten	6 (1-inch-thick)* slices French bread
½ cup milk	Vegetable shortening or butter
1 tablespoon fresh grated grapefruit peel	Sifted confectioners' sugar
¼ teaspoon salt (optional)	Grapefruit-Apricot Syrup (below)

Makes 2 to 3 servings.

In a shallow dish, combine the eggs, milk, grapefruit peel, and salt. Dip the bread in the egg mixture, turning to coat both sides. In a large skillet, in two batches, brown the bread on both sides in the shortening. Remove to a serving platter. Sprinkle with confectioners' sugar and serve with Grapefruit-Apricot Syrup.

GRAPEFRUIT-APRICOT SYRUP

1 can (8¾ ounces) unpeeled apricot halves	½ cup light corn syrup
1 tablespoon cornstarch	1 Sunkist grapefruit, peeled and sectioned
¼ teaspoon ground cinnamon	

*Unsliced loaf bread (white, egg twist, etc.) may be substituted for French bread. Cut 3 slices (1 inch thick) in half diagonally.

Makes about 1½ cups.

Drain the apricots, reserving the syrup. In a small saucepan, combine the cornstarch and cinnamon. Gradually blend in reserved apricot syrup and corn syrup. Cook, over medium heat, stirring constantly, until thickened. Add grapefruit sections and apricots and heat.

MAPLE VARIATION: Substitute maple-flavored syrup for the corn syrup.

PIGS ON A BLANKET

2 Sunkist oranges, peeled
1 pound link sausages (about 16)
½ cup maple-flavored syrup
Waffles or pancakes

Makes 4 to 6 servings.

Cut the oranges in half lengthwise and, with a shallow "V" shape cut, remove the white center core. Place halves cut-side-down; cut lengthwise and crosswise into bite-size pieces. In a large skillet, fry the sausage links; pour off the fat. Add syrup and heat, stirring occasionally. Stir in orange pieces and heat. Serve over waffles or pancakes.

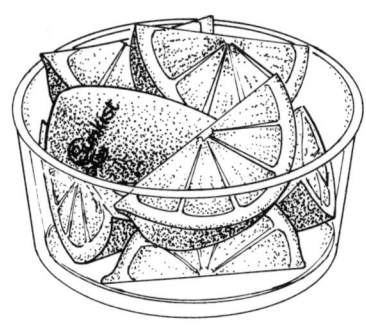

BROILED ORANGE OR GRAPEFRUIT TOPPERS

2 Sunkist oranges *or* grapefruit, peeled and each one cut into 6 cartwheel slices
1 tablespoon maple-flavored syrup
1 tablespoon honey
1 teaspoon fresh grated orange *or* grapefruit peel
Generous dash of ground cinnamon and nutmeg
Chopped nuts, diced apple, *or* granola
Pancakes, waffles, *or* French toast

Makes 4 servings.

Arrange the orange cartwheel slices on a baking sheet. Combine the syrup, honey, orange peel, and spices. Brush each orange slice lightly with the syrup mixture; sprinkle with chopped nuts. Broil 4 to 5 inches from heat for 2 to 3 minutes, or until hot. Top pancakes with orange cartwheel slices, and serve with additional maple-flavored syrup, if desired.

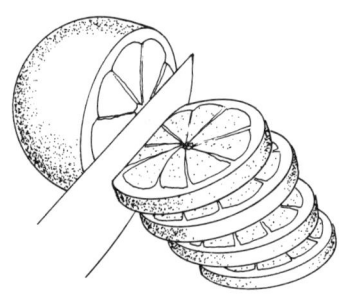

Sandwiches

We're not sure just what makes sandwiches so much fun. But everyone seems to become creative and adventurous when putting favorite ingredients together for a wholesome and satisfying sandwich.

It's easy to include fresh citrus. Keep a flavored butter spread on hand. Butter or margarine blended with a bit of grated orange or lemon peel is wonderful on bread or toast. Include fresh orange slices with tuna, cheese, poultry, or ham fillings.

Try citrus flavors in a hearty triple-decker, or a lighter sandwich with tuna. Enjoy oranges in a hot grilled cheese with avocado or a cold and crunchy chicken salad. In every one, savor the flavor that citrus adds. Then let your imagination take over, and create your own citrus sandwich favorites.

SANDWICHES

**EVERYONE'S FAVORITE TRIPLE DECKER
SUBMARINE SUPREME
CRUNCHY CHICKEN SALAD SANDWICHES
NEPTUNE POCKET SANDWICHES
BAGELS AND ORANGE-CREAM CHEESE
MONTEREY ENGLISH MUFFINS
HUNGRYMAN'S GRILLED SANDWICHES
CALIFORNIA QUESADILLAS**

EVERYONE'S FAVORITE TRIPLE DECKER

Tasting is believing. The flavors combined in this sandwich are sure to make it a favorite.

¼ cup butter or margarine, softened
Grated peel of ½ Sunkist orange
12 slices white, whole wheat, or rye bread, toasted

4 slices (about 4 ounces) Monterey Jack or Muenster cheese
1 large avocado, sliced
4 slices (about 4 ounces) cooked ham
2 Sunkist oranges, peeled and cut into cartwheel slices

Makes 4 sandwiches.

In a small bowl, combine the butter and orange peel. Lightly spread one side of each slice of bread with the butter mixture. Assemble 4 triple-decker sandwiches with layers of cheese and avocado slices, and ham and orange cartwheel slices. Secure with toothpicks and cut into triangles.

SUBMARINE SUPREME

2 teaspoons prepared mustard
1 teaspoon fresh grated lemon peel
2 teaspoons fresh squeezed lemon juice
⅛ teaspoon dried oregano leaves, crushed
Generous dash of onion salt
¼ cup salad or vegetable oil

1 loaf (about 12 inches long) Italian or French bread
4 ounces sliced salami, ham, or bologna
4 ounces sliced Swiss or Cheddar cheese
1 medium tomato, sliced
1 cup alfalfa sprouts

Makes 2 servings.

To make the dressing, thoroughly combine the mustard, lemon peel, lemon juice, oregano, and onion salt; gradually stir in the oil. Cut bread in half lengthwise; spread mustard dressing over bread halves. Layer with salami, cheese, tomato slices, and alfalfa sprouts. To serve, cut in half.

CRUNCHY CHICKEN SALAD SANDWICHES

Ordinary chicken salad? Not this flavorful sandwich mixture enhanced with almonds, orange pieces, and fresh grated peel.

1 package (3 ounces) cream cheese, softened
¼ cup chopped celery
¼ cup sliced almonds, toasted
2 tablespoons mayonnaise or salad dressing
1 teaspoon fresh grated orange peel
1 cup chopped cooked chicken
2 Sunkist oranges, peeled, cut into bite-size pieces, and drained
8 slices whole wheat bread
Lettuce

Makes 4 sandwiches.

In a bowl, combine the cream cheese, celery, almonds, mayonnaise, and orange peel; stir in chicken and orange pieces. Spread 4 slices of bread with the chicken mixture; top with lettuce and remaining bread.

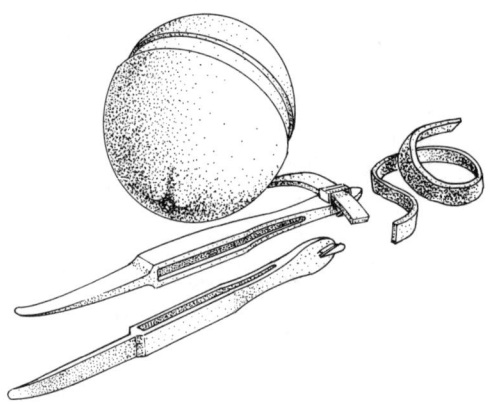

NEPTUNE POCKET SANDWICHES

This versatile sandwich filling can be made with oranges, tangerines, or pineapple and apple. Serve in store-bought or homemade pocket bread.

2 cans (about 7 ounces each) tuna, drained and flaked
Grated peel of 1 Sunkist orange
2 Sunkist oranges, peeled, cut into bite-size pieces, and drained
½ cup mayonnaise or salad dressing
¼ cup chopped green onions (scallions)
6 (6-inch) loaves pocket bread,* cut in half
Fresh spinach leaves, cut into thin strips.

Makes 6 sandwiches.

In a bowl, combine the tuna, orange peel, orange pieces, mayonnaise, and green onions. Spoon about ¼ cup of the tuna mixture in the pocket of each bread half; fill with spinach.

TANGERINE VARIATION: Substitute fresh grated peel of 1 tangerine and 3 medium tangerines, peeled, segmented, seeded, and cut in half for the orange peel and pieces.

DOUBLE APPLE VARIATION: Omit the orange peel and pieces. Substitute fresh grated peel and juice of ½ lemon, 1 can (8 ounces) crushed pineapple, drained, and 1 apple, chopped.

---

*For homemade bread, see Sesame Citrus Pocket Bread (page 194).

BAGELS AND ORANGE-CREAM CHEESE

Instead of sandwich-style, serve this as a spread on toasted bagel or English muffin halves.

2 packages (3 ounces each) cream cheese, softened	1 teaspoon fresh grated orange peel
½ cup shredded Cheddar cheese	⅛ teaspoon pumpkin pie spice
2 tablespoons chopped walnuts	4 bagels, sliced in half crosswise

Makes 4 sandwiches.

In a bowl, combine all the ingredients *except* the bagels. Spread the mixture on the sliced bagels and press halves together.

MONTEREY ENGLISH MUFFINS

A quick-to-make hot luncheon sandwich, or serve it as a sure-to-please "breakfast-on-the-run."

4 English muffins	4 slices (about 6 ounces) cooked ham
4 slices (about 4 ounces) Monterey Jack or other mild cheese	¼ cup orange marmalade
2 Sunkist oranges, peeled and cut into thick cartwheel slices	

Makes 4 sandwiches.

Split the muffins; place on a baking sheet. On 4 muffin halves, arrange cheese, orange cartwheel slices, and ham. Brush the top of the ham and the remaining 4 muffin halves with marmalade. Broil 6 inches from heat for 5 to 7 minutes, or until heated through. Press muffin halves together.

HUNGRYMAN'S GRILLED SANDWICHES

¼ cup butter or margarine, softened
Grated peel of ½ Sunkist orange
8 slices white, whole wheat, or rye bread
8 slices (about 8 ounces) Muenster or Monterey Jack cheese
2 Sunkist oranges, peeled, and cut into cartwheel slices
1 large avocado, sliced

Makes 4 sandwiches.

In a small bowl, combine the butter and orange peel. Lightly spread both sides of bread slices with butter mixture. Assemble 4 sandwiches with layers of cheese, orange cartwheel slices, and avocado slices. In a large skillet, grill sandwiches on both sides until they are lightly browned and cheese starts to melt.

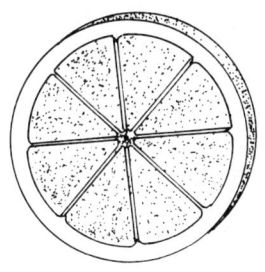

CALIFORNIA QUESADILLAS

These "glorified" grilled cheese sandwiches encase lots of good flavors in lightly grilled flour tortillas. They can also be made quickly in a microwave oven.

Butter or margarine
4 (8-inch) flour tortillas
2 cups shredded Monterey Jack or other mild cheese
1 can (4 ounces) whole chiles, drained and cut into strips
¼ cup chopped green onions (scallions)
1 cup alfalfa sprouts or shredded lettuce
1 to 2 Sunkist oranges, peeled and cut into thin cartwheel slices
Guacamole
Sour cream

Makes 4 quesadillas.

Prepare *each* quesadilla as follows: In a large buttered skillet or griddle, lightly brown the tortilla on one side. Turn; sprinkle with one quarter of the cheese, chiles, green onions, and alfalfa sprouts. Heat until cheese melts; top with one quarter of the orange cartwheel slices. Fold the tortilla in half. Keep warm while preparing remaining quesadillas. Cut into wedges, if desired. Serve with guacamole and sour cream.

Note: Fresh Anaheim chiles, peeled and cut into strips, can be substituted for canned chiles.

MICROWAVE—HIGH POWER SETTING

Prepare *each* quesadilla as follows: Arrange one quarter of the chiles on a tortilla; cook until heated through (approximately 30 seconds). Top with one quarter of the cheese, green onions, alfalfa sprouts, and orange cartwheel slices; cook until cheese melts (approximately 30 seconds). Fold the tortilla in half. Repeat for remaining quesadillas.

Preserves, Relishes, and Marmalades

"Something extra" is the best way to describe many of these nostalgic recipes. You may first remember seeing these condiments in pretty glass jars in your grandmother's kitchen. She always had just the right homemade relish or jewel-colored marmalade to complete any meal.

Today, orange relish is just as delicious as you remember it, complementing a succulent baked ham. Corn relish is the perfect addition to a sunny family picnic. Slow-cooked pear butter with oranges and spices tops any homebaked tea loaf with extra goodness.

Gently simmering lemon marmalade fills a kitchen with fragrance from the groves, and memories from the past. Quick jam also yields delicious results—without cooking, and lemon jellies, flavored with port wine or apple juice, make delightful gifts. Anyone on a sodium-restricted diet will appreciate the herb seasoning mix—a flavorful complement to meat, poultry or fish.

PRESERVES, RELISHES, AND MARMALADES

LEMON AND TOMATO PRESERVES
SPICED ORANGE-PEAR BUTTER
LEMON-CORN RELISH
EASY FRESH ORANGE JAM
A GEM OF A JELLY
SHIMMERING LEMON MARMALADE
NUTTY ORANGE RELISH
LEMON-SEASONED PEPPER
HIGH-FLAVOR LOW-SODIUM HERB SEASONING

LEMON AND TOMATO PRESERVES

This may be a nostalgic preserve recipe, but for flavor and appearance it's a modern-day classic.

2½ pounds tomatoes, peeled and cut into 6 to 8 wedges
4 cups sugar
2 cinnamon sticks
1 teaspoon whole cloves
2 unpeeled Sunkist lemons, cut into thin cartwheel slices

Makes four ½-pint jars.

In a large bowl, combine the tomatoes and sugar; stir well. Cover and let stand for 8 hours or overnight, stirring occasionally to dissolve the sugar. Drain off and reserve the juice. In a saucepot, bring reserved juice and spices (tied in a square of cheesecloth) to a boil, stirring occasionally. Boil rapidly, stirring constantly, to thread stage (230 to 234° F.). Add drained tomatoes and lemon cartwheel slices. Return to a boil and cook until thick and clear, about 30 minutes, stirring occasionally. Pour into hot sterilized ½-pint jars, filling to within ½ inch of the top. Wipe jars clean and seal. Process in a boiling water bath for 10 minutes.

SPICED ORANGE-PEAR BUTTER

5 pounds (about 10 large) unpeeled pears, cored and cut into chunks
Juice of 1 Sunkist orange
2½ cups sugar
1 teaspoon ground cinnamon
¼ teaspoon ground nutmeg
Grated peel of 2 Sunkist oranges

Makes five ½-pint jars.

In a saucepot, combine the pears and orange juice. Cook, uncovered, over medium heat until pears are very tender, about 30 minutes, stirring occasionally. Press through a food mill or sieve to yield about 7 cups of pulp. In the same saucepot, combine pear pulp, sugar, cinnamon, and nutmeg. Cook over medium heat until thick, about 1 to 1¼ hours, stirring frequently. Add orange peel during the last 5 minutes of cooking. Pour into hot sterilized ½-pint jars, filling to within ¼ inch of the top. Wipe jars clean and seal. Process in a boiling water bath for 10 minutes.

LEMON-CORN RELISH

A barbecue go-along or a gift to give the year round to food-loving friends.

2 cans (17 ounces each) whole-kernel corn, undrained
1 cup chopped onion
1 cup chopped celery
1 cup chopped sweet green pepper
¼ cup sugar
2 teaspoons dry mustard
1 teaspoon celery seed
1 teaspoon ground turmeric
½ teaspoon salt
¼ teaspoon white pepper
½ cup cold water
3 tablespoons all-purpose flour
Grated peel of 2 Sunkist lemons
Juice of 1 Sunkist lemon

Makes six ½-pint jars.

In a large saucepan, combine the undrained corn, onion, celery, green pepper, sugar, mustard, celery seed, turmeric, salt, and white pepper; bring to a boil. Reduce heat; cover and simmer for 10 minutes. Gradually blend the water into the flour; add to the corn mixture. Stir in lemon peel and juice; simmer 2 to 3 minutes longer, stirring until mixture thickens slightly. Pour into hot sterilized ½-pint jars with lids, filling to within ⅛ inch of top; cover. The relish will keep, refrigerated, up to one week.

Note: For longer storage, jars can be sealed and processed in a boiling water bath for 15 minutes.

EASY FRESH ORANGE JAM

The flavor of fresh oranges comes through in this refrigerated jam. It can also be frozen for longer storage.

3 to 4 Sunkist oranges, peeled and cut into chunks
4 cups sugar

1 pouch (3 ounces) liquid fruit pectin
2 tablespoons water

Makes five ½-pint jars.

In a food processor or blender, finely chop the oranges to yield 2 cups. In a bowl, combine the chopped oranges and sugar; let stand for 10 minutes, stirring occasionally. Combine the pectin and water; add to orange mixture, and stir for 3 minutes. Pour into sterilized ½-pint jars with lids, filling to within ½ inch of the top; cover. Set at room temperature for 24 hours; then refrigerate. Will keep refrigerated up to three weeks—or freeze for longer storage.

A GEM OF A JELLY

It would be hard to find an easier-to-make jelly. Other *pluses: It's not too sweet, can be made any time of year, and is the perfect "little gift to give" . . . so keep a few jars on hand.*

3 cups sugar
1½ cups apple juice
½ cup fresh squeezed lemon juice

1 pouch (3 ounces) liquid fruit pectin

Makes four ½-pint jars.

In a large saucepan, combine the sugar, apple juice, and lemon juice. Bring to a full rolling boil over high heat, stirring occasionally. Add pectin. Bring back to a full rolling boil, and boil for 30 seconds, stirring constantly. Skim off the foam. Pour into hot sterilized ½-pint jars, filling to within ¾ inch of the top. Wipe jars clean; seal. Process in a boiling water bath for 10 minutes.

Note: A spiral of lemon peel and a stick of cinnamon can be added to each jar before sealing.

LEMON PORT JELLY: Substitute 1½ cups of ruby, white, *or* tawny port for the apple juice. A perfect complement to roasted meat and poultry . . . and equally good spread on biscuits or popovers.

SHIMMERING LEMON MARMALADE

Of course this has to be a Sunkist classic! The early morning partner to English muffins, croissants, or even "plain" toast.

6 unpeeled Sunkist lemons, cut into thin half-cartwheel slices* and seeded (about 4 cups)	14 cups cold water 5½ cups sugar

Makes seven ½-pint jars.

In a large bowl, combine the lemon half-cartwheel slices and 7 cups of the water. Cover and let stand for 24 hours; drain. In a large saucepan, combine the drained lemon slices and 7 cups of fresh water. Bring to a boil. Boil rapidly for 25 minutes, stirring occasionally. Add sugar. Return to a boil, stirring to dissolve sugar. Boil rapidly to the jelly stage (220° F.), about 30 minutes, stirring frequently. Skim off the foam. Pour into hot sterilized ½-pint jars, filling to within ½ inch of the top. Wipe jars clean; seal. Process in a boiling water bath for 10 minutes.

*To make half-cartwheel slices, cut the lemon in half lengthwise. Place cut-side-down and cut into thin slices.

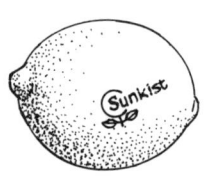

NUTTY ORANGE RELISH

2 cups golden raisins
Boiling water
3 Sunkist oranges, *peeled* and cut into chunks
3 tablespoons chopped crystallized ginger
1 Sunkist orange, *unpeeled* and cut into chunks
1 cup packed light brown sugar
1 cup coarsely chopped walnuts

Makes four ½-pint jars.

Cover the raisins with boiling water and let stand 10 minutes. Drain and reserve the raisins. In a food processor or blender, combine the peeled oranges and ginger; purée until almost smooth. Add unpeeled orange and blend until coarsely chopped. In a bowl, combine the orange mixture, drained raisins, brown sugar, and walnuts; stir to dissolve the sugar. Pour into sterilized ½-pint jars with lids, filling to within ½ inch of the top; cover. Will keep refrigerated up to two weeks. The relish thickens when chilled.

LEMON-SEASONED PEPPER

Give this as a gift in small decorated jars or serve it on baked potatoes, pasta, green salads, or barbecued or broiled beef, lamb, or pork.

6 tablespoons fresh grated lemon peel*
1 can (4 ounces) ground black pepper
½ cup toasted sesame seed
¼ cup celery seed
¼ cup onion salt
¼ cup salt
2 tablespoons monosodium glutamate (optional)
1 tablespoon garlic powder

Makes about 2 cups.

Spread the lemon peel on a baking sheet in a thin layer. Dry in the oven at 200° F. for 20 minutes. Cool and combine lemon peel with the remaining ingredients, mixing thoroughly. Store in jars with lids.

*Lightly packed, from about 6 Sunkist lemons.

HIGH-FLAVOR LOW-SODIUM HERB SEASONING

Grated peel of ½ Sunkist lemon
2 teaspoons dried parsley flakes
½ teaspoon garlic powder
½ teaspoon dried oregano *or* basil leaves, crushed
½ teaspoon dried marjoram leaves, crushed
¼ teaspoon ground allspice
¼ teaspoon pepper

Makes about 2 tablespoons.
About 2 calories and 1 mg. sodium per teaspoon.

Combine all the ingredients and refrigerate in a covered container. To use, sprinkle as desired over meat, poultry, or fish before broiling or baking.

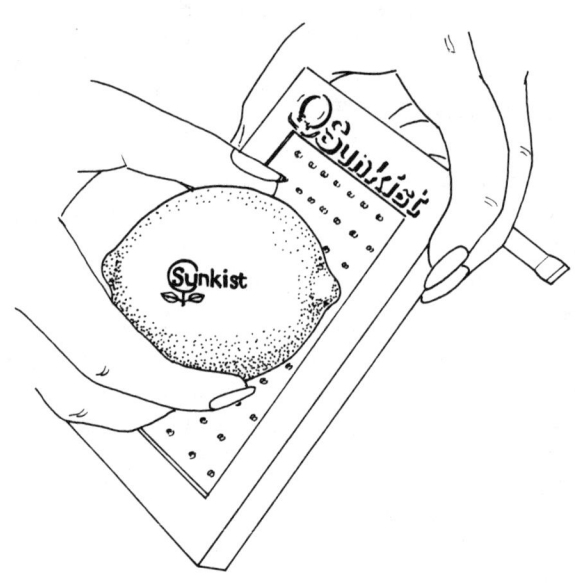

Quick and Yeast Breads

Nothing says joy in the kitchen like the smell of homemade bread in the oven. Every cook who invests a short time whipping up a quick bread batter, or more time letting yeast loaves rise, treasures the rewards. Add the tantalizing fragrance of citrus and the pleasure doubles.

Most of our recipes are for moist and flavorful quick breads. These easy-to-prepare loaves are as welcome with fruit or other toppings for dessert as they are with butter and jam for breakfast. Of course, any home-baked loaf makes a lovely and appreciated hostess or holiday gift.

There are familiar and family favorites here: lemony popovers, lemon corn bread, and cranberry-orange muffins. But do experiment with some new discoveries, like zesty pocket bread and orange English muffins. They're delicious variations on traditional recipes.

These breads and baked treats gain their unmistakable zest and rich citrus flavor from fresh grated peel. You'll find that using just a bit of peel for fresh flavor will become one of your treasured baking secrets.

QUICK AND YEAST BREADS

LEMONY GOOD POPOVERS
DOUBLE C RANCH CORN BREAD
ORANGE-HONEY MUFFINS
CRANBERRY-ORANGE MUFFINS
FRESH LEMON CAKE MUFFINS
BLENDER QUICK ORANGE BREAD
LEMON-GRANOLA QUICK BREAD
FRESH ORANGE–PUMPKIN BREAD (GROWER RECIPE)
WHOLE WHEAT ORANGE AND CARROT LOAF
HINT OF LEMON CRÊPES
HINT OF ORANGE CRÊPES
OLD-FASHIONED ENGLISH MUFFINS
ORANGE DROP BISCUITS
ORANGE DOUGHNUTS AND HOLES
LUSCIOUS LEMONY YEAST BRAID
SESAME-CITRUS POCKET BREAD

Salmon Pâté; Grapefruit and Shrimp with Zippy Cocktail Sauce; Citrus Ice Bowl; and Steamed Bucket of Clams

Mushroom-Almond Broiled Salmon Steaks and Scallop Sauté with Lemon

Lemon Chicken and Zucchini, and Green and Orange Salad with Blue Cheese Dressing

A Vegetable Medley: Fresh Broccoli and Pasta Combo; Cauliflower alla Parmesan; Stir-Fried Brussels Sprouts and Tangerines; Zucchini with Parsley-Dill Butter; Asparagus with Hollandaise Sauce

B. J.'s Omelette à l'Orange

California Quesadillas; Quick and Easy Lemon Fish Soup

From the Bakery: Fresh Lemon Cake Muffins; Luscious Lemony Yeast Braid; Fresh Orange-Pumpkin Bread; Double C Ranch Corn Bread; A Gem of a Jelly; and Shimmering Lemon Marmalade

Refreshing Desserts: Easy Fresh Ice Creams; Sim-Yet-Cee; Citrus Shells; and Lemon Boats

Tangerine-Almond Shortcake

Citrus Coolers: Tangy Orangeade; Real Old-fashioned Lemonade; Low-Cal Minty Lemonade

For the Cookie Jar: Orange Confetti Bars; Three-Way Orange Cookies; Fresh Orange Cookies; Candied Peel Citrus Drops

Fresh Lemon Meringue Pie

LEMONY GOOD POPOVERS

An often forgotten, yet versatile, quick bread. Serve it for breakfast with scrambled eggs, with a luncheon salad, or as a base for a saucy fish entrée such as Poached Fish and Wine Sauce (page 42).

1 egg, slightly beaten	1 teaspoon salad or vegetable oil
½ cup milk	⅛ teaspoon salt (optional)
Grated peel of 1 Sunkist lemon	½ cup all-purpose flour

Makes 4 large popovers. About 106 calories and 33 mg. sodium per popover without optional salt.

In a bowl, beat the egg, milk, lemon peel, oil and salt; add the flour, beating until smooth. Divide batter equally among 4 well-buttered 6-ounce custard cups set on a baking sheet. Bake at 450° F. for 15 minutes; reduce oven temperature to 350° F. and bake 20 minutes longer, or until popovers are firm and well browned. Remove from custard cups and serve warm.

DOUBLE C RANCH CORN BREAD

Cream-style corn and Cheddar cheese add flavor as well as moistness to this corn bread. Serve with Honey Lemon Butter and you're in for some good old-fashioned eating.

2 eggs, well beaten	1 cup yellow cornmeal
⅓ cup sour cream	2 tablespoons sugar
2 tablespoons salad or vegetable oil	Grated peel of 1 Sunkist lemon
2 cups (about 8 ounces) shredded Cheddar cheese	2 teaspoons baking powder
	½ teaspoon salt
1 can (about 8 ounces) cream-style corn	Honey Lemon Butter (page 184)

Makes 6 to 8 servings.

In a large bowl, combine the eggs, sour cream, and oil. Stir in 1½ cups of the cheese and the remaining ingredients; blend well. Pour into a greased 8- or 9-inch ovenproof skillet or baking pan. Bake at 400° F. for 25 minutes. Sprinkle with the remaining ½ cup of cheese. Bake 5 minutes longer, or until cheese melts. Cool 5 minutes; cut into serving pieces.

GREEN CHILE VARIATION: Add ¼ cup drained chopped canned green chiles to the batter.

HONEY LEMON BUTTER

½ cup butter or margarine, softened	1 teaspoon fresh grated lemon peel
2 tablespoons honey	1 tablespoon fresh squeezed lemon juice

Makes about ½ cup.

In a bowl, combine all the ingredients and beat with an electric mixer or wire whisk until light and fluffy.

ORANGE-HONEY MUFFINS

A "honey" of a muffin . . . good texture, easy to make, and excellent fresh orange flavor.

2 cups all-purpose flour	½ cup fresh squeezed orange juice
1 tablespoon baking powder	½ cup milk
½ teaspoon salt	¼ cup salad or vegetable oil
1 egg, slightly beaten	2 Sunkist oranges, peeled, sectioned, and drained
⅓ cup honey	1 tablespoon sugar
Grated peel of 1 Sunkist orange	

Makes 16 muffins.

In a large bowl, sift together the flour, baking powder, and salt. Combine the egg, honey, orange peel, orange juice, milk, and oil; add to dry ingredients all at once. Stir quickly until dry ingredients are *just* moistened but have a lumpy appearance. Spoon batter into 16 paper-lined 2½ × 1¼-inch muffin cups, filling about two-thirds full. Place one orange section on top of each muffin and sprinkle with sugar. Bake at 400° F. for 20 to 25 minutes.

CRANBERRY-ORANGE MUFFINS

1 cup all-purpose flour
1 cup whole wheat flour
⅓ cup *plus* 1 tablespoon sugar
1 tablespoon baking powder
¼ teaspoon salt
½ cup chopped fresh or frozen cranberries

Grated peel of ½ Sunkist orange
1 cup fresh squeezed orange juice
¼ cup salad or vegetable oil
1 egg, slightly beaten

Makes 12 muffins.

In a large bowl, combine the flours, ⅓ cup of the sugar, baking powder, and salt. Stir in the cranberries to lightly coat with the flour. Combine the orange peel, orange juice, oil, and egg; add to flour mixture all at once. Stir quickly until flour mixture is *just* moistened but has a lumpy appearance. Spoon batter into 12 paper-lined 2½ × 1¼-inch muffin cups, filling about three-quarters full. Sprinkle the tops with the remaining 1 tablespoon of sugar. Bake at 400° F. for 25 to 30 minutes.

FRESH LEMON CAKE MUFFINS

"Cake-like" in texture, these sweet-and-tart muffins also make a light dessert with tea or coffee.

1 cup all-purpose flour
1 teaspoon baking powder
¼ teaspoon salt
½ cup butter or margarine, softened

½ cup sugar
2 eggs, separated
Grated peel of ½ Sunkist lemon
Juice of 1 Sunkist lemon
Cinnamon Sugar (page 186)

Makes 8 to 9 muffins.

Sift together the flour, baking powder, and salt. In a large bowl, cream the butter; gradually add ¼ cup of the sugar, beating until light and fluffy. In a bowl, with an electric mixer, beat the egg yolks until thick and light in color; stir into the creamed butter. Add dry ingredients alternately with lemon juice. With clean beaters, beat the egg whites until foamy; gradually add the remaining ¼ cup sugar, beating until soft peaks form. Gently fold the egg whites and lemon peel into batter. Spoon batter into 8 to 9 paper-lined 2½ × 1¼-inch muffin cups, filling about three-quarters full. Sprinkle with Cinnamon Sugar. Bake at 375° F. for 18 to 20 minutes, or until lightly browned.

CINNAMON SUGAR
Combine 1 tablespoon sugar and ¼ teaspoon ground cinnamon.

BLENDER QUICK ORANGE BREAD

1 unpeeled Sunkist orange
½ cup fresh squeezed orange juice
2½ cups all-purpose flour
2 teaspoons baking powder
1 teaspoon baking soda
1 teaspoon pumpkin pie spice
½ teaspoon salt
1¼ cups sugar
2 eggs
¼ cup butter or margarine, melted
½ cup chopped walnuts or pecans

Makes 1 loaf.

Cut the orange into large chunks. In a blender, combine the orange chunks and juice; blend until almost smooth. Sift together the flour, baking powder, baking soda, pumpkin pie spice, and salt. In a large bowl, combine the sugar, eggs, and butter; beat until smooth. Add orange mixture and dry ingredients, stirring *just* until blended. Stir in the walnuts. Pour into a greased 9 × 5 × 3-inch loaf pan. Bake at 350° F. for 45 to 50 minutes, or until a toothpick inserted in the center comes out clean. Cool for 10 minutes; remove from pan. Cool on a wire rack.

LEMON-GRANOLA QUICK BREAD

The aroma of this lemon bread baking is so tempting you will surely have to serve it warm from the oven!

Granola Streusel Topping (below)
1 cup sugar
¾ cup all-purpose flour
¾ cup whole wheat flour
1 tablespoon baking powder
½ teaspoon salt
½ cup butter or margarine, melted
2 eggs, slightly beaten
½ cup water
Grated peel and juice of 1 Sunkist lemon (3 tablespoons juice)
1 cup granola

Makes 1 loaf.

Prepare Granola Streusel Topping and set aside. In a large bowl, combine the sugar, flours, baking powder, and salt. Combine the butter, eggs, water, lemon peel and juice; add to dry ingredients all at once. Stir quickly *just* until dry ingredients are moistened. Stir in the granola. Pour into a well-greased 9 × 5 × 3-inch loaf pan. Sprinkle with Granola Streusel Topping. Bake at 350° F. for 45 minutes, or until a toothpick inserted in the center comes out clean. Cool for 10 minutes; remove from pan. Cool on a wire rack.

GRANOLA STREUSEL TOPPING

1 tablespoon all-purpose flour
1 tablespoon sugar
1½ teaspoons butter or margarine, softened
2 tablespoons granola
Grated peel of ½ Sunkist lemon

In a small bowl, with a fork, blend together the flour, sugar, and butter. Stir in the granola and lemon peel.

FRESH ORANGE–PUMPKIN BREAD
Janis Karesh, Porterville, California
(Grower recipe contest winner)

Janis adapted a pumpkin-date bread recipe to use some of the fresh oranges her family grows. She really enjoys making this rich, moist bread when most of the ingredients, including the pumpkin, eggs, walnuts, and even sun-dried raisins, come from her own ranch. The bread keeps well, wrapped in aluminum foil in the refrigerator and, like fruitcake, improves as the flavors have more time to blend.

2 large unpeeled Sunkist oranges
4 cups all-purpose flour
2¾ cups sugar
2½ teaspoons baking soda
¾ teaspoon baking powder
1¼ teaspoons ground cloves
1¼ teaspoons ground cinnamon
1¼ teaspoons ground nutmeg
1¼ teaspoons pumpkin pie spice
½ teaspoon salt
5 eggs
2 cups mashed *cooked* pumpkin, *or* 1 can (16 ounces) solid-pack pumpkin
1 cup salad or vegetable oil
1¼ cups chopped walnuts
1¼ cups chopped dates
1¼ cups raisins

Makes 2 loaves.

Trim a thin slice from each end of the oranges; cut the fruit in half lengthwise. With a shallow "V" shape cut, remove the white center core. Cut the halves into small chunks. In a food processor or blender, purée the orange chunks to yield about 2 cups. Sift together the dry ingredients. In a large bowl, beat the eggs slightly; stir in the pumpkin, oil, and orange purée. Add dry ingredients and beat well. Stir in the walnuts, dates, and raisins. Pour into 2 greased and floured 9 × 5 × 3-inch loaf pans. Bake at 325° F. for 1 hour and 10 minutes, or until a toothpick inserted in the center comes out clean. Cool 10 minutes; remove from pans. Cool on wire racks.

THREE LOAF VARIATION: To make 3 loaves, pour batter into 3 greased and floured 9 × 5 × 3-inch loaf pans. Bake at 325° F. for

55 to 60 minutes, or until a toothpick inserted in the center comes out clean.

WHOLE WHEAT ORANGE AND CARROT LOAF

1¼ cups whole wheat flour
1 teaspoon ground cinnamon
½ teaspoon baking powder
½ teaspoon baking soda
¼ teaspoon salt
2 eggs, slightly beaten
Grated peel and juice of
   1 Sunkist orange
   (⅓ cup juice)

⅓ cup honey
¼ cup salad or vegetable oil
1 cup shredded carrots
½ cup chopped walnuts
½ cup raisins

Makes 1 loaf.

In a large bowl, combine the flour, cinnamon, baking powder, baking soda, and salt. Combine the eggs, orange peel and juice, honey, and oil; add to dry ingredients all at once. Stir quickly *just* until dry ingredients are moistened. Stir in carrots, walnuts, and raisins. Pour into a well-greased 9 × 5 × 3-inch loaf pan. Bake at 350° F. for 1 hour, or until a toothpick inserted in the center comes out clean. Cool 10 minutes; remove from pan. Cool on a wire rack.

HINT OF LEMON CRÊPES

Stack the crêpes on top of each other as they are cooked. No need to place wax paper between them, they won't stick together! Use them for the Tuna and Asparagus Crêpe Roll-ups (page 57) or Crêpes Huevos Rancheros (page 149), or any savory filling.

2 eggs
1 cup milk
⅔ cup all-purpose flour
Grated peel and juice of
   ½ Sunkist lemon

1 tablespoon salad or
   vegetable oil
½ teaspoon salt

Makes 12 crêpes.

In a blender or food processor, combine all the ingredients; blend until smooth. In a hot, lightly oiled 6-inch skillet, pour about 2 tablespoons of the batter, tilting the pan slightly to quickly spread the batter thinly and evenly. Lightly brown the first side; turn and cook on the second side for a few seconds.

HINT OF ORANGE CRÊPES

Use them in Chocolate and Orange Crêpe Sundaes (page 202) and many other elegant desserts.

2 eggs
1 cup milk
⅔ cup all-purpose flour
Grated peel of 1 Sunkist orange
1 tablespoon fresh squeezed orange juice
1 tablespoon sugar
1 tablespoon salad or vegetable oil
½ teaspoon salt

Makes 12 crêpes.

In a blender or food processor, combine all the ingredients; blend until smooth. In a hot, lightly oiled 6-inch skillet, pour about 2 tablespoons of the batter, tilting pan slightly to quickly spread batter thinly and evenly. Lightly brown the first side; turn and cook the second side for a few seconds.

OLD-FASHIONED ENGLISH MUFFINS

Half the fun of English muffins is in the making and, of course, the other half is in the eating!

¾ cup milk
3 tablespoons sugar
2 tablespoons butter or margarine
½ teaspoon salt
1 package active dry yeast
¾ cup warm water (105 to 115° F.)
Grated peel of 1 Sunkist lemon *or* orange
3¼ to 3½ cups all-purpose flour
½ cup uncooked quick oats
½ cup raisins
Cornmeal

Makes 1 dozen muffins.

In a small saucepan, heat the milk, sugar, butter, and salt, stirring to dissolve the sugar; cool to lukewarm. In a large bowl, sprinkle the yeast over the warm water, stirring to dissolve the yeast. Add milk mixture and grated peel. Stir in 1½ cups of the flour; beat until smooth. Stir in oats, raisins, and enough of the remaining flour to make a soft dough. Place dough on a lightly floured board; knead until smooth and elastic, about 5 minutes. Place in a greased bowl, turning dough to coat all sides. Cover; let rise in a warm place (80 to 85° F.) until doubled, about 45 minutes. Punch down dough. Place on a lightly floured board. Pat dough to ½-inch thickness. Cut into 3-inch rounds. Coat both sides of the rounds lightly with cornmeal; place on a baking sheet. Cover; let rise until doubled, about 30 minutes. Place 3 or 4 at a time in a lightly greased, preheated skillet or griddle. Cook over medium-low heat for 10 to 12 minutes on each side (check that the muffins brown slowly). Cool on wire racks. To serve, split and toast.

ORANGE DROP BISCUITS

Fresh grated citrus peel can enliven a variety of "convenience" baking mixes. Try adding fresh grated orange, lemon, or tangerine peel to your favorite cake, cookie, pancake, or yeast bread mix.

2 cups buttermilk biscuit mix
⅔ cup milk
Grated peel of 1 Sunkist orange

1 to 2 tablespoons butter or margarine, melted
2 tablespoons sugar

Makes about 18 small biscuits.

In a bowl, combine the biscuit mix, milk, and half the orange peel; beat well. Drop by tablespoons onto a greased baking sheet; brush biscuits with butter. Combine the remaining orange peel and sugar; sprinkle on top of biscuits. Bake at 450° F. for 8 to 10 minutes.

ORANGE DOUGHNUTS AND HOLES

Remember mama's homemade doughnuts? Even if your mom didn't make them, cook up some memories today.

2 eggs, slightly beaten
1 cup sugar
½ cup milk
¼ cup salad or vegetable oil
Grated peel of 1 Sunkist orange
½ cup fresh squeezed orange juice

4½ to 4¾ cups all-purpose flour
4 teaspoons baking powder
2 teaspoons baking soda
½ teaspoon salt
¼ teaspoon ground cinnamon
Salad or vegetable oil

Makes 20 to 24 doughnuts and 20 to 24 doughnut holes.

In a large bowl, combine the eggs and sugar, beating well. Stir in the milk, ¼ cup of the oil, orange peel, and orange juice. Sift together 4½ cups of the flour, baking powder, baking soda, salt, and cinnamon. Stir dry ingredients into egg mixture, mixing well. Add the remaining ¼ cup of flour, if necessary, to make a stiff dough. Chill the dough for 1 hour or longer. On a well-floured board, pat dough to a ½-inch thickness. Cut with a lightly floured doughnut cutter. Let stand for 10 minutes. In an electric skillet or a large saucepot, heat 1½ to 2 inches of oil to 375° F. Fry doughnuts 3 or 4 at a time, about 1 minute per side. Drain on paper toweling.

FROZEN O.J. VARIATION: Omit fresh squeezed orange juice. Substitute half a 3-ounce can Sunkist frozen concentrated orange juice, thawed, and add just enough milk to equal 1 cup liquid.

TOPPING IDEAS: Sprinkle with confectioners' sugar or spread with Orange Glaze, if desired. To make Orange Glaze, combine 1 cup confectioners' sugar, fresh grated peel of ½ orange, and 1 to 2 tablespoons fresh squeezed orange juice. Makes about ½ cup.

LUSCIOUS LEMONY YEAST BRAID

¾ cup milk
½ cup sugar
⅓ cup butter or margarine
1 teaspoon salt
2 packages active dry yeast
½ cup warm water (105 to 115° F.)
2 eggs, slightly beaten
Grated peel of 2 Sunkist lemons
5½ to 6 cups all-purpose flour
½ cup golden raisins
½ cup chopped walnuts
1 cup confectioners' sugar
Juice of ½ Sunkist lemon
Maraschino cherries, cut in half
Walnut halves

Makes 2 loaves.

In a small saucepan, heat the milk, sugar, butter, and salt, stirring to dissolve the sugar; cool to lukewarm. In a large bowl, sprinkle the yeast over the warm water, stirring to dissolve the yeast. Add milk mixture, eggs, and lemon peel. Stir in 2 cups of the flour; beat until smooth. Stir in enough of the remaining flour to make a stiff dough. Place dough on a lightly floured board; knead until smooth and elastic, about 5 to 10 minutes. Place in a greased bowl, turning dough to coat all sides. Cover; let rise in a warm place (80 to 85° F.) until doubled, about 1 hour and 15 minutes. Punch down dough. Place on a lightly floured board. Knead in raisins and chopped walnuts, about 5 minutes. Divide dough in half. Roll each half into a rectangle about 12 × 4 inches. Cut each lengthwise into 3 pieces. Roll to shape each piece into a "rope." To form one loaf, loosely braid 3 ropes together. Pinch and tuck ends under to seal. Place on a greased baking sheet. Repeat with remaining 3 ropes to form a second loaf. Cover; let rise until doubled, about 1 hour. Bake at 375° F. for 20 to 25 minutes. Remove to wire racks. To make the glaze, combine the confectioners' sugar and lemon juice; drizzle over warm bread. Garnish with maraschino cherries and walnut halves.

"RING" VARIATION: The dough can be formed into ring shapes. Divide the dough in half. Roll each half into a rectangle about 12 × 4 inches. Place each in a well-greased 2-quart ring mold or

10-inch tube pan. Overlap and pinch ends together well. Cover; let rise until doubled, about 1 hour. Bake at 375° F. for 25 to 30 minutes. Glaze as above. Makes 2 ring loaves.

SESAME-CITRUS POCKET BREAD

The secret to pocket bread is the perfect "puff" while baking. The Sunkist Kitchens have perfected the method to encourage the "puff" . . . thus the pocket. Use it for Neptune Pocket Sandwiches (page 165), or cut it into wedges and serve warm, with Hummus Bi Tahina (page 25).

3½ to 3¾ cups all-purpose flour
1 package active dry yeast
Grated peel of 1 Sunkist orange, tangerine, *or* lemon
½ teaspoon salt
½ teaspoon sugar
1⅓ cups very warm water (120 to 130° F.)
1 tablespoon salad or vegetable oil
Sesame seed

Makes 8 loaves.

In a large bowl, combine 1½ cups of the flour, yeast, peel, salt, and sugar. With an electric mixer on low speed, gradually add the warm water and oil. Increase the speed to medium, and beat for 3 minutes. With a wooden spoon, gradually stir in enough of the remaining flour (about 2 cups) to make a soft dough. Place the dough on a lightly floured board; knead until smooth and elastic, about 5 minutes, adding more flour as needed. Place in a greased bowl, turning dough to coat all sides. Cover; let rise in a warm place (80 to 85° F.) until doubled, about 1 hour. Punch down dough. Place on a lightly floured board; cut into 8 pieces. Shape into balls. Cover; let rest 10 minutes. Lightly sprinkle 4 sheets of wax paper, each about 18 inches long, with sesame seed. On a lightly floured board, roll each ball of dough into a 7-inch circle. Place 2 circles on each sheet of wax paper. Sprinkle tops with additional sesame seed; press into dough. Cover; let rise until doubled, about 45 minutes. Place an oven rack in the lowest position, but not on the oven floor, and preheat the oven to 475° F. To obtain optimum "puff" to each batch of pocket bread, preheat an ungreased large cookie sheet for 5 minutes. Carefully remove hot cookie sheet from the oven and arrange 2 or 3 circles of dough on sheet. Bake each batch at 475° F. for 7 minutes, or until puffed and just *lightly* browned. Cool on wire racks for 5 minutes. Cut each "loaf" of bread in half to form two "pockets." Place in plastic bags to keep pliable. Fill as desired.

To reheat: Wrap pocket bread in aluminum foil. Bake at 350° F. for 5 to 10 minutes, or until heated through.

Desserts and Ice Creams

Lighter fruit desserts are the perfect way to end a heavier meal, or to satisfy a dieter's craving for "just a little something sweet." Oranges combine with grapes, bananas, or kiwifruit, while grapefruit blend with cherries. Yogurt dips and toppings add flavor and richness without excessive calories. Traditional lemon curd is a favorite sauce for fruit, cake, or gingerbread.

Homemade lemon and orange ice creams are surprisingly easy to make, and are welcome for dessert on warm summer evenings. On frosty winter nights, consider serving lemony bread pudding or baked rice custard, still warm from the oven. For that special occasion, try a hot lemon soufflé with warm lemon sauce.

Let your meal dictate the dessert—whether you're looking for a light treat, a hearty, satisfying sweet, or just something new.

DESSERTS AND ICE CREAMS

HOT LEMON SOUFFLÉ
BEST-EVER BAKED RICE PUDDING
HINT OF LEMON BREAD PUDDING
WARM LEMON SAUCE
SLOW COOKING RICE CUSTARD
CHOCOLATE AND ORANGE CRÊPE SUNDAES
ORANGE BANANA FLAMBÉ
FOUR-STAR CITRUS AMBROSIA
ORANGE AMBROSIA À LA LAGOMARSINO (GROWER RECIPE)
GRAPEFRUIT AND CHERRY AMBROSIA
ORANGE-KIWIFRUIT AMBROSIA
CITRUS-YOGURT SUNDAES
MINTY ORANGE-GRAPE COMBO
SPICED POACHED PEARS
ORANGE-YOGURT DIP FOR FRESH FRUIT
FRESH LEMON GELATIN
LEMON TOFU DELIGHT
EASY FRESH LEMON ICE CREAM
EASY ORANGE ICE CREAM
FRESH BANANAS AND ORANGE ICE CREAM
SIM-YET-CEE (SIMPLE YET FANCY ICE) (GROWER RECIPE)
GRAPEFRUIT SNOW
"JUST FOR KIDS" FRUIT POPS
CLASSIC LEMON CURD

HOT LEMON SOUFFLÉ

A positively elegant dessert . . . light, airy, and so-o-o lemony!

3 tablespoons butter or margarine
3 tablespoons all-purpose flour
1 cup milk
Grated peel of ½ Sunkist lemon
Juice of 1 Sunkist lemon (3 tablespoons)
4 egg yolks
6 egg whites
½ teaspoon cream of tartar
½ cup sugar
Warm Lemon Sauce (page 201) (optional)

Makes 6 servings.

In a saucepan, melt the butter. Remove from the heat and stir in the flour. Cook for a few minutes, stirring constantly. Gradually blend in the milk. Cook over medium heat, stirring, until thickened. Add lemon peel and lemon juice. Remove from heat. In a bowl, with an electric mixer, beat the egg yolks until thick and light in color. Gradually stir a small amount of hot lemon mixture into beaten egg yolks; stir back into remaining lemon mixture in the pan, blending well. With clean beaters, beat the egg whites with the cream of tartar until foamy. Gradually add the sugar, beating until soft peaks form. Gently stir about one fourth of the egg whites into the lemon-yolk mixture. Fold in the remaining egg whites. Pour into a buttered and sugared 1½-quart soufflé dish. Bake at 350° F. for 30 to 35 minutes, or until set. Serve with Warm Lemon Sauce.

BEST-EVER BAKED RICE PUDDING

3 eggs
⅓ cup sugar
¼ teaspoon salt
2 cups milk
2 cups *cooked* rice
½ cup golden raisins
Grated peel of 1 Sunkist lemon
Warm Lemon Sauce (page 201)

Makes 6 servings (about 3½ cups).

In a bowl, beat the eggs slightly with the sugar and salt. Stir in the milk, cooked rice, raisins, and lemon peel. Pour into a well-buttered 1-quart casserole. Bake, uncovered, at 325° F. for 50 to 60 minutes, or until set. Serve with Warm Lemon Sauce.

HINT OF LEMON BREAD PUDDING

Fresh grated lemon peel makes this extra-good bread pudding even better. For an added touch of sweetness serve with Warm Lemon Sauce (page 201).

4 cups day-old bread cubes (about 6 slices)	2 tablespoons butter or margarine, melted
3 eggs, slightly beaten	Grated peel of 1 Sunkist lemon
3 cups milk	¼ teaspoon salt
½ cup sugar	Ground nutmeg
½ cup raisins	

Makes 6 servings (about 4½ cups).

In a large shallow baking pan, arrange the bread cubes in a single layer; bake at 350° F. for 10 minutes to lightly dry the bread. Meanwhile, combine all the remaining ingredients *except* the nutmeg; stir to dissolve the sugar. In a large bowl, pour the milk mixture over the dried bread cubes and stir well. Let soak for 10 minutes. Pour into a well-buttered 1½-quart casserole. Sprinkle with nutmeg. Set the casserole in a shallow baking pan filled with 1 inch hot water. Bake, uncovered, at 350° F. for 1 hour, or until a knife inserted in the center comes out clean. Remove from water bath and cool for 10 minutes. Serve warm.

WARM LEMON SAUCE

Serve with Hot Lemon Soufflé (page 199), Best-Ever Baked Rice Pudding (page 199), or Hint of Lemon Bread Pudding (page 200).

⅓ cup sugar
2 tablespoons cornstarch
⅛ teaspoon salt
Dash of nutmeg (optional)
¾ cup water
Grated peel of ½ Sunkist lemon

Juice of 1 Sunkist lemon
1 tablespoon butter or margarine
Few drops yellow food coloring (optional)

Makes about 1 cup.

In a small saucepan, combine the sugar, cornstarch, salt, and nutmeg. Gradually blend in the water, lemon peel and juice. Add the butter. Cook over medium heat, stirring, until thickened. Stir in the food coloring. Serve warm.

SLOW COOKING RICE CUSTARD

On a cool or rainy afternoon, warm up the kitchen with this slow cooking old-fashioned rice dessert.

1 quart milk
½ cup sugar
¼ cup raw regular rice
Grated peel of 1 Sunkist lemon

¼ teaspoon salt
2 eggs, well beaten
½ cup golden raisins
Ground cinnamon

Makes 6 servings (about 4 cups).

In a large bowl, combine the milk, sugar, rice, lemon peel, and salt; stir to dissolve the sugar. Pour into a well-buttered 2-quart casserole. Set the casserole in a shallow baking pan filled with 1 inch hot water. Bake, uncovered, at 325° F. for 1 hour. Remove from oven and stir well. Continue baking 45 minutes longer. Remove from oven. Gradually stir a small amount of hot milk mixture into beaten eggs; stir back into remaining milk mixture in the casserole, blending well. Stir in raisins. Return to oven and bake 30 minutes longer, or until the custard is set and rice is cooked. Remove from water bath. Sprinkle with cinnamon and serve warm.

CHOCOLATE AND ORANGE CRÊPE SUNDAES

Multiply this recipe several times and you have a great make-ahead dessert for large gatherings. The ice cream—filled crêpes can be made and frozen days in advance. Serve them with hot chocolate sauce, orange cartwheel slices, and almonds.

1 quart vanilla ice cream, softened
8 Hint of Orange Crêpes (page 190)
1 package (6 ounces) semi-sweet chocolate pieces
½ cup marshmallow creme

¼ cup almond-flavored liqueur or orange juice
Grated peel of ½ Sunkist orange
2 Sunkist oranges, peeled and cut into half-cartwheel slices
Sliced almonds

Makes 8 servings.

Spread the ice cream on the crêpes and roll up. Arrange on a serving platter or individual dessert plates and place in the freezer while preparing the sauce. To make the sauce, in a saucepan, over very low heat, melt the chocolate pieces. Stir in the marshmallow creme, liqueur, orange peel and heat. To serve, spoon the sauce over the crêpes and arrange orange half-cartwheel slices and almonds on top.

ORANGE BANANA FLAMBÉ

Serve the flambé over vanilla ice cream or slices of angel food cake.

3 Sunkist oranges, peeled and sectioned
3 bananas, cut lengthwise and crosswise
Juice of 1 Sunkist lemon
½ cup seedless raspberry jam *or* strawberry jelly or jam
¼ cup fresh squeezed orange juice
2 tablespoons sugar
Grated peel of ½ Sunkist orange
3 tablespoons Curaçao or other orange-flavored liqueur

Makes 6 servings.

In a bowl, combine the cut fruit with the lemon juice. In a chafing dish or large skillet, blend together the raspberry jam and orange juice; bring to a boil. Add fruit mixture and stir gently. Reduce heat and simmer for 1 to 2 minutes. Sprinkle with sugar and orange peel. In a metal ladle or butter warmer, heat the Curaçao and ignite it. Slowly pour it over fruit mixture.

FOUR-STAR CITRUS AMBROSIA

Combining the best of Sunkist . . . oranges, grapefruit, tangerines, and lemons. Serve it in shallow champagne glasses for that extra special touch.

2 eggs
½ cup sugar
Grated peel of ½ Sunkist lemon
¼ cup fresh squeezed lemon juice
¼ cup butter or margarine, melted
2 Sunkist oranges, peeled and cut into half-cartwheel slices
1 Sunkist grapefruit, peeled and sectioned
2 Sunkist tangerines, peeled, segmented, and seeded
Toasted shredded or flaked coconut
Fresh mint leaves (optional)

Makes 4 servings.

To make the sauce, in a saucepan, beat the eggs well. Stir in the sugar, lemon peel, lemon juice, and butter. Cook over low heat, stirring constantly, until thickened, about 10 minutes. Cover and chill. Meanwhile, divide fruit into 4 individual dessert dishes and chill. Spoon the sauce over the fruit, sprinkle with coconut, and garnish with fresh mint.

ORANGE AMBROSIA À LA LAGOMARSINO
U.S. Congressman & Mrs. Robert J. Lagomarsino,
19th District, California & Sunkist Grower

6 Sunkist oranges, peeled and cut into cartwheel slices
1 can (3½ ounces) flaked coconut (about 1 cup)
4 to 6 tablespoons confectioners' sugar
3 tablespoons fresh squeezed orange juice

Makes 6 to 8 servings (about 6 cups).

In a 1½-quart serving bowl, arrange layers of orange cartwheel slices, coconut, confectioners' sugar, and orange juice. Chill for 1 hour or longer.

GRAPEFRUIT AND CHERRY AMBROSIA

⅓ cup sugar
Grated peel of ½ Sunkist orange
Juice of 1 small Sunkist orange
2 tablespoons brandy
3 Sunkist grapefruit, peeled, sectioned, and drained
1 can (about 16 ounces) pitted dark sweet cherries, *well drained*
⅓ cup shredded or flaked coconut

Makes 4 to 6 servings (about 3½ cups).

In a small saucepan, combine the sugar, orange peel and juice; bring to a boil, stirring to dissolve the sugar. Cool slightly;

stir in the brandy. In a bowl, pour orange mixture over grapefruit sections and cherries; cover and chill. To serve, sprinkle with coconut.

ORANGE-KIWIFRUIT AMBROSIA

Colorful, refreshing, and so easy to prepare.

4 Sunkist oranges, peeled and cut into cartwheel slices
1 kiwifruit, peeled and thinly sliced
Grated peel of ½ Sunkist orange

Juice of 1 Sunkist orange
¼ cup almond- or orange-flavored liqueur
¼ cup whole natural almonds
2 tablespoons shredded or flaked coconut, toasted

Makes 4 servings (about 3½ cups).
About 203 calories and 4 mg. sodium per serving.

In a bowl, arrange the orange and kiwifruit slices. Combine the orange peel, orange juice, and liqueur. Pour over fruit mixture; cover and chill. To serve, spoon into individual dessert dishes and sprinkle with the almonds and coconut.

CITRUS-YOGURT SUNDAES

A fresh fruit dessert is most welcome after a filling meal. These "fruit sundaes" also make any brunch special.

1 carton (8 ounces) lowfat vanilla yogurt
1 teaspoon fresh grated orange peel
1 teaspoon fresh grated grapefruit peel
2 Sunkist grapefruit, peeled and sectioned

2 Sunkist oranges, peeled and cut into half-cartwheel slices
2 bananas, sliced
1 cup blueberries, strawberries, raspberries, *or* seedless grapes
1 tablespoon sugar
¼ teaspoon ground cinnamon

Makes 6 servings (about 4½ cups).
About 161 calories and 28 mg. sodium per serving.

Combine the yogurt, orange and grapefruit peels; cover and chill. In a large bowl, combine all the remaining ingredients; cover and chill. To serve, spoon fruit mixture into individual dessert dishes and top with the yogurt.

MINTY ORANGE-GRAPE COMBO

⅓ cup honey
Juice of 1 Sunkist lemon
1 to 2 tablespoons chopped
    fresh mint

2 Sunkist oranges, peeled and
    cut into quarter-
    cartwheel slices
2 cups seedless green grapes

Makes 6 servings (about 3 cups).
About 98 calories and 2 mg. sodium per serving.

In a bowl, combine the honey, lemon juice, and mint. Add the orange quarter-cartwheel slices and grapes; stir well. Chill for 2 hours or longer, stirring occasionally. Garnish with fresh mint leaves, if desired.

SPICED POACHED PEARS

1 cup sugar
1 cup water
⅓ cup fresh squeezed lemon
    juice
1 cinnamon stick
6 pears
24 whole cloves

1 unpeeled Sunkist lemon,
    cut into half-cartwheel
    slices
1 Sunkist orange, peeled and
    cut into half-cartwheel
    slices
1 cup seedless grapes

Makes 6 servings.

In a large saucepot, combine the sugar, water, lemon juice, and cinnamon. Cook over medium heat, stirring to dissolve the sugar. With a vegetable parer, peel the pears, leaving stem attached.

Cut a thin slice off blossom end of each pear and stud cut end with 4 whole cloves. Simmer the pears, uncovered, in the syrup for 20 minutes, turning occasionally; remove pears to a large serving dish. Bring the syrup to a boil and add the lemon half-cartwheel slices. Reduce heat and simmer for 2 minutes. Stir in orange half-cartwheel slices and grapes; heat. Remove the cinnamon stick and spoon the syrup and fruit over the pears. Serve warm or chilled.

ORANGE-YOGURT DIP FOR FRESH FRUIT

1 carton (8 ounces) lowfat plain yogurt
2 tablespoons honey
Grated peel of ½ Sunkist orange or tangerine

1 Sunkist orange and/or 2 large tangerines, peeled, segmented, and seeded
Apple slices
Banana slices

Makes about 1 cup dip.
About 17 calories and 10 mg. sodium per tablespoon dip.

In a small bowl, combine the yogurt, honey, and orange peel. Serve as a dip with orange and/or tangerine segments, apple and banana slices.

FRESH LEMON GELATIN

A "from-scratch" recipe with real, natural flavor.

1 cup sugar
2 envelopes unflavored gelatine
1⅔ cups cold water

⅔ cup strained, fresh squeezed lemon juice
Few drops yellow food coloring (optional)

Makes 4 to 5 servings (about 2½ cups).

In a saucepan, combine the sugar and gelatine; add water and heat, stirring to dissolve the sugar and gelatine. Remove from heat and stir in the lemon juice. Pour into a 2½- to 3-cup mold or bowl and chill until set, about 4 hours.

Desserts and Ice Creams

LEMON TOFU DELIGHT

1 package (3 ounces) lemon-flavored gelatin
2 tablespoons sugar
1 cup boiling water
½ cup cold water
1 package (about 14 ounces) tofu (kinugoshi or soft), drained, coarsely crumbled
2 egg whites
Grated peel and juice of 1 Sunkist lemon (3 tablespoons juice)

Makes 8 servings (about 4 cups).
About 92 calories and 50 mg. sodium per serving.

Dissolve the gelatin and sugar in the boiling water. Pour into a food processor or blender; add cold water, tofu, egg whites, lemon peel and juice. Blend until smooth. Pour into individual dessert dishes and chill until set.

EASY FRESH LEMON ICE CREAM

You've got to try it to believe it! No ice cream maker needed. Yet this easy lemon ice cream is as smooth as can be. It's rich, so small servings are in order.

2 cups heavy cream or whipping cream *or* half-and-half
1 cup sugar
Grated peel of 1 Sunkist lemon
⅓ cup fresh squeezed lemon juice
6 to 10 lemon shells or boats (page 290) (optional)

Makes 6 to 10 servings (about 3 cups).

In a large bowl, combine the cream and sugar; stir to dissolve the sugar. Blend in the lemon peel and juice. (The mixture will thicken slightly.) Pour into a shallow pan and freeze until firm, about 4 hours. Serve in lemon shells or boats, or in dessert dishes. Garnish with fresh mint leaves and strawberries, if desired.

LEMON AND FRUIT VARIATION: Stir ½ cup mashed strawberries, bananas, or kiwifruit into the slightly thickened lemon mixture before freezing. Makes about 3½ cups.

EASY ORANGE ICE CREAM

2 cups heavy cream or whipping cream
1 cup sugar
⅓ cup fresh squeezed lemon juice
Grated peel of 1 Sunkist orange
⅓ cup fresh squeezed orange juice

Makes 6 servings (about 3 cups).

In a large bowl, combine the cream and sugar; stir to dissolve the sugar. Blend in the lemon juice. (The mixture will thicken slightly.) Stir in the orange peel and juice. Pour into a shallow pan and freeze until firm, about 4 hours. Serve in dessert dishes or orange shells (page 290).

FRESH BANANAS AND ORANGE ICE CREAM

1 small banana, mashed
1 quart vanilla ice cream, softened
Grated peel of 1 Sunkist orange
½ cup coarsely chopped pecans
3 to 4 Sunkist oranges, peeled and cut into bite-size pieces

Makes 6 to 8 servings (about 4 cups ice cream).

In a bowl, combine all ingredients *except* the orange pieces. Freeze until firm, about 2 hours. To serve, scoop ice cream into dessert dishes and top with orange pieces. Garnish with fresh mint leaves, if desired.

SIM-YET-CEE (SIMPLE YET FANCY ICE)
George Roundtree, *Porterville, California*
(Grower recipe contest winner)

George and his wife Diane enjoy cooking together, and often serve guests a complete Japanese dinner. In experimenting with recipes for a light dessert, they discovered that less was really more. With only two ingredients, they perfected this flavorful ice. Decorated with kumquats or frozen grapes, it's a beautiful and refreshing finale to an Oriental meal.

5 cups fresh squeezed orange juice (about 15 Sunkist oranges)	2 medium bananas, cut into chunks

Makes about 6 cups.

In a blender or food processor, combine 1 cup of the orange juice and the bananas; blend until smooth. Combine with the remaining 4 cups of orange juice. Pour into the container of a 1½- to 2-quart ice-cream freezer and chill. Process according to the manufacturer's directions.

Note: The recipe can be doubled for a larger ice-cream freezer.

GRAPEFRUIT SNOW

1 envelope unflavored gelatine	2 egg whites
¾ cup water	1 Sunkist grapefruit, peeled, sectioned, and cut into bite-size pieces
1 cup sugar	
2½ cups fresh squeezed grapefruit juice	

Makes 6 to 8 servings (about 5 cups).

Soften the gelatine in ¼ cup of the water. In a small saucepan, combine ¾ cup of the sugar and the remaining ½ cup water. Bring to a boil, stirring to dissolve the sugar; cook for 2 minutes. Add the gelatine mixture, stirring to dissolve the gelatine. Add the grapefruit juice. Pour into a shallow pan and freeze *just* until slushy, about 1½ hours, stirring occasionally. In a bowl, with an electric mixer, beat the egg whites until foamy. Gradually add the remaining ¼ cup of sugar, beating until soft peaks form. In a chilled bowl, gradually fold beaten egg whites into grapefruit mixture. Fold in grapefruit pieces. Return to freezer for 2 hours, stirring occasionally. Continue freezing until firm.

TO SERVE IN GRAPEFRUIT SHELLS: After squeezing juice for above recipe, save 6 grapefruit halves; scrape the shells "clean" with a spoon. The edges may be notched with kitchen shears or a knife; or scalloped by using a coin to outline a pattern and then cutting around the pattern. Prepare recipe as above; return to freezer, *but* freeze until almost firm, about 2 hours. Spoon about ¾ cup of the mixture into each grapefruit shell. Return to freezer until firm, about 30 minutes or longer. Top with meringue (below) *or* garnish with additional grapefruit sections, maraschino cherries, fresh mint, or other fresh fruit, if desired. Makes 6 servings.

MERINGUE

3 egg whites
⅛ teaspoon cream of tartar
6 tablespoons sugar

In a bowl, with an electric mixer, beat the egg whites with cream of tartar until foamy. Gradually add the sugar, beating until stiff peaks form. Top each grapefruit half with about ⅓ cup of meringue, sealing well at the edges. Place on a baking sheet and bake at 450° F. for 3 to 4 minutes. Serve immediately.

212 *Desserts and Ice Creams*

"JUST FOR KIDS" FRUIT POPS

1½ cups fresh squeezed
    orange juice*
1 can (about 6 ounces) apple,
    grape, or pineapple juice
    or cranberry juice
    cocktail

6 (3-ounce) paper cups
6 small plastic spoons or
    wooden sticks

Makes 6 pops.
About 45 calories per pop.

Combine the juices and pour into the paper cups. Freeze until almost firm, about 30 to 45 minutes. For the handles, insert the plastic spoons or wooden sticks in an upright position. Freeze until firm. To serve, allow the "pops" to stand at room temperature for a few minutes and remove from the paper cups.

*Or use Sunkist chilled orange juice.

CLASSIC LEMON CURD

Hot or cold, this thick lemon sauce is excellent over fresh fruit, gingerbread, angel food, or pound cake.

1 egg
2 egg yolks
Grated peel of ½ Sunkist
    lemon
Juice of 2 Sunkist lemons (6
    tablespoons)

¾ cup sugar
¼ cup butter or margarine
Dash of salt

Makes about 1¼ cups.

In a saucepan, lightly beat the egg and yolks; add the remaining ingredients. Cook over low heat, stir constantly, until the mixture thickens, about 5 to 8 minutes. Serve hot or cold.

Cookies and Confections

Cookies are fun to make and to eat. With quick and tempting recipes like these, it will be easy to keep the cookie jar full of delectable treats.

And citrus-flavored snacks are the answer for easing pre-dinner hunger pangs. Afterwards, serve fresh, homemade citrus fudge for a special treat.

Each of these recipes brings unexpected pleasure. Make one today—just as a surprise—and be rewarded by the smiles it brings.

COOKIES AND CONFECTIONS

CANDIED PEEL CITRUS DROPS
APPLE AND ORANGE OATMEAL COOKIES
FRESH ORANGE COOKIES
THREE-WAY ORANGE COOKIES
FROSTED ORANGE COOKIES (GROWER RECIPE)
FAVORITE LEMON COOKIES
ORANGE CONFETTI BARS
ORANGE POPCORN BALLS
LEMON BUTTERED POPCORN
SEASONED SNACK MIX
1000 PALMS STUFFED DATES
FABULOUS ORANGE FUDGE
WHITE CITRUS FUDGE
CANDIED CITRUS PEEL

CANDIED PEEL CITRUS DROPS

Candied citrus peel adds delightful flavor to these drop cookies. A citrus glaze heightens the effect.

¼ cup minced lemon peel (page 307)
¾ cup granulated sugar
¼ cup water
1¼ cups all-purpose flour
½ teaspoon baking soda
½ teaspoon salt

½ cup butter or margarine, softened
¼ cup packed light brown sugar
1 egg
½ cup chopped pecans or walnuts
Citrus Glaze (below)

Makes about 3 dozen.

In a small saucepan, combine the lemon peel, ¼ cup of the granulated sugar, and water; bring to a boil, stirring to dissolve the sugar. Reduce heat and simmer briskly for 10 minutes, or until liquid is syrupy; cool slightly. Meanwhile, sift together the flour, baking soda, and salt. In a large bowl, cream together the butter, remaining ½ cup of granulated sugar, and brown sugar. Beat in the egg. Stir in nuts and peel with syrup. Gradually blend in dry ingredients; cover and chill for 1 hour or longer. Drop dough by teaspoons onto lightly greased cookie sheets. Bake at 375° F. for 10 to 12 minutes. Remove and cool on wire racks. Spread cookies with Citrus Glaze.

CITRUS GLAZE

1 cup confectioners' sugar
1 teaspoon fresh grated lemon peel
1 tablespoon fresh squeezed lemon juice

1 tablespoon water
1 tablespoon butter or margarine, softened

Makes about ½ cup.

In a small bowl, combine all the ingredients.

ORANGE VARIATION: Substitute ¼ cup diced orange peel (peel of ½ orange) for the lemon peel. For the glaze, substitute 1 teaspoon fresh grated orange peel for the lemon peel, and 2 tablespoons fresh squeezed orange juice for the lemon juice and water.

APPLE AND ORANGE OATMEAL COOKIES

1½ cups all-purpose flour
1 teaspoon baking soda
½ teaspoon ground cinnamon
½ teaspoon ground nutmeg
¼ teaspoon salt
¾ cup butter or margarine, softened
1¼ cups sugar
1 egg
Grated peel of 1 Sunkist orange
1 Sunkist orange, peeled and cut into bite-size pieces
1 unpeeled apple, cored and chopped
2 cups uncooked quick oats
½ cup chopped walnuts or pecans

Makes about 5½ dozen.

Sift together the flour, baking soda, cinnamon, nutmeg, and salt. In a large bowl, cream together the butter and sugar. Add the egg and orange peel and beat well. Gradually blend in dry ingredients. Stir in orange pieces, apple, oats, and nuts. Drop dough by teaspoons onto lightly greased cookie sheets. Bake at 375° F. for 15 minutes, or until lightly browned. Remove and cool on wire racks.

Note: For crisp cookies, do not store in an airtight container.

FRESH ORANGE COOKIES

Finely chopped fresh orange pieces and walnuts make these a sure "cookie jar" favorite.

1½ cups all-purpose flour
½ teaspoon baking soda
¼ teaspoon salt
½ cup butter or margarine, softened
½ cup granulated sugar
½ cup packed light brown sugar
1 egg
1 unpeeled Sunkist orange, finely chopped*
½ cup chopped walnuts
Orange Glaze (below)

Makes about 4 dozen.

Sift together the flour, baking soda, and salt. In a large bowl, cream together the butter and sugars. Add the egg and chopped orange and beat well. Gradually blend in dry ingredients. Stir in the walnuts. Cover and chill for 1 hour or longer. Drop dough by teaspoons onto lightly greased cookie sheets. Bake at 375° F. for 10 to 12 minutes. Remove and cool on wire racks. Spread cookies with Orange Glaze.

ORANGE GLAZE
1 cup confectioners' sugar
1 to 2 tablespoons fresh squeezed orange juice
1 tablespoon butter or margarine, softened
1 teaspoon fresh grated orange peel

Makes about ½ cup.

In a small bowl, combine all the ingredients.

*Chop the orange in a blender or food processor, or by hand, to equal ¾ cup chopped fruit.

THREE-WAY ORANGE COOKIES

This easy to handle cookie dough is versatile: Roll it flat or shape it into balls or logs. And coat it with any number of toppings.

2 cups all-purpose flour	Grated peel of 2 Sunkist oranges
2 teaspoons baking powder	3 tablespoons fresh squeezed orange juice
¼ teaspoon salt	
⅔ cup butter or margarine, softened	Chopped nuts, shredded or flaked coconut, colored sugar crystals, cinnamon sugar, etc., for topping
¾ cup sugar	
1 egg	

Makes about 3 dozen.

Sift together the flour, baking powder, and salt. In a large bowl, cream together the butter and sugar. Add the egg, orange peel and juice; beat well. Gradually blend in the dry ingredients. Cover and chill for 1 hour or longer. Shape dough into 1-inch balls, or 3 × ½-inch logs *or* roll to a ⅛-inch thickness and cut with lightly floured cookie cutters. Roll or sprinkle cookies with chopped nuts, coconut, etc. Place on ungreased cookie sheets. Bake at 350° F. for 12 to 15 minutes. Remove and cool on wire racks.

FROSTED ORANGE COOKIES
Eloise Pacey, *Valley Center, California*
(Grower recipe contest winner)

Eloise adapted the recipe for these tea cake cookies from an old one given her by a relative in Oregon. The soft, cake-like cookies are just as delicious today, and certainly worth a little extra time to prepare.

½ cup butter or margarine, softened	2 cups all-purpose flour
¾ cup sugar	½ teaspoon baking powder
1 egg	½ teaspoon baking soda
Grated peel and juice of 1 Sunkist orange (⅓ cup juice)	2 teaspoons fresh squeezed lemon juice and milk to equal ½ cup liquid
	¼ cup chopped walnuts
	Orange Frosting (page 221)

Makes 4 dozen.

In a large bowl, cream together the butter and sugar. Add the egg, orange peel and juice; beat well. Sift together the flour, baking powder, and baking soda. Add to the creamed mixture alternately with the lemon-milk. Stir in the walnuts. Drop dough by rounded teaspoons onto *ungreased* cookie sheets. Bake at 350° F. for 8 minutes (the cookies should not brown). Quickly remove from the cookie sheets and cool on wire racks. Spread the cookies with Orange Frosting.

ORANGE FROSTING

¼ cup butter or margarine, softened
1½ cups confectioners' sugar
Grated peel of ½ Sunkist orange
1½ tablespoons fresh squeezed orange juice

Makes about ¾ cup.

In a small bowl, cream together the butter and ½ cup of the confectioners' sugar. Add the orange peel, orange juice, and remaining 1 cup of sugar; beat well.

FAVORITE LEMON COOKIES

A basic lemon cookie for year round holiday baking. Cut them into Valentine hearts, Easter rabbits, or Halloween pumpkins. For Christmas ornaments, poke a small hole in each one before baking and hang them with yarn or ribbon on the Christmas tree.

2 cups all-purpose flour
½ teaspoon baking soda
¼ teaspoon salt
⅓ cup butter or margarine, softened
1 cup sugar
1 egg
Grated peel and juice of 1 Sunkist lemon
Lemon Frosting (page 222) *or* decorating icing*

*Decorating icing comes in tubes in assorted colors.

Makes about 4 to 5 dozen.

Sift together the flour, baking soda, and salt. In a large bowl, cream together the butter and sugar. Add the egg, lemon peel and juice; beat well. Gradually blend in the dry ingredients. Divide the dough in four parts; cover and chill for 1 hour or longer. On a lightly floured board, roll one fourth at a time to a ⅛-inch thickness. Cut with lightly floured cookie cutters and place on well-greased cookie sheets. Bake at 375° F. for 10 minutes, or until lightly browned. Remove and cool on wire racks. Spread cookies with Lemon Frosting or decorating icing.

LEMON FROSTING

¼ cup butter or margarine, softened
3 cups confectioners' sugar
1 egg yolk

Grated peel of ½ Sunkist lemon
1 to 2 tablespoons fresh squeezed lemon juice

Makes about 1¼ cups.

In a bowl, cream together the butter and 1 cup confectioners' sugar. Add the egg yolk and beat well. Add the remaining 2 cups of sugar, lemon peel and juice; mix until smooth. To prevent the frosting from drying out too quickly, cover with a damp cloth while frosting the cookies.

ORANGE CONFETTI BARS

12 Sunkist Fruit Gems (pectin candies in assorted flavors)
1½ cups all-purpose flour
1 teaspoon baking powder
1 teaspoon ground cinnamon
¼ teaspoon salt
½ cup butter or margarine, softened

1 cup packed light brown sugar
1 egg
Grated peel of 1 Sunkist orange
¼ cup fresh squeezed orange juice
½ cup coarsely chopped walnuts
Confectioners' sugar (optional)

Makes 18 bar cookies.

Cut the pectin candies into small pieces with kitchen shears.* Sift together the flour, baking powder, cinnamon, and salt. In a large bowl, cream together the butter and brown sugar. Add the egg, beating well. Add the orange peel and juice. Gradually blend in dry ingredients, pectin candies, and walnuts. Spread the mixture in a lightly greased 9-inch-square baking pan. Bake at 350° F. for 30 to 35 minutes. Cool on a wire rack and cut into bars. Sprinkle with confectioners' sugar.

*Dip shears in warm water to prevent sticking.

ORANGE POPCORN BALLS

Do have some extra hands available to shape these extra special popcorn balls quickly.

4 quarts popped popcorn (about ½ cup *plus* 2 tablespoons kernels)	½ cup fresh squeezed orange juice
1 cup coarsely chopped walnuts	½ cup half-and-half
2 cups sugar	1 tablespoon butter or margarine
	Grated peel of 1 Sunkist orange

Makes 18 to 20 popcorn balls, 2 inches in diameter.

In a large saucepot, combine the popcorn and walnuts; set aside. In a saucepan, combine the sugar, orange juice, and half-and-half; cook over low heat, stirring constantly, to dissolve the sugar. Cover and boil for 1 minute to dissolve the sugar from the sides of the pan. Increase the heat slightly and cook, uncovered, to hard ball stage (260° F.), stirring occasionally. Remove from heat and stir in the butter and orange peel. Slowly pour the hot syrup over the popcorn and nuts, tossing until evenly coated. Grease hands with additional butter or margarine and shape popcorn mixture into balls. The mixture is hot and sets quickly—so work fast.* Allow popcorn balls to cool on wax paper. When cool, wrap in plastic wrap or wax paper.

*This recipe works best with two people—one to pour, the other to stir, and both to quickly form balls.

LEMON BUTTERED POPCORN

2 tablespoons butter or margarine
Grated peel of ½ Sunkist lemon
1 tablespoon fresh squeezed lemon juice
12 cups popped popcorn (about ½ cup kernels)
Salt to taste (optional)

Makes about 12 cups.

In a small saucepan (*or* in a 1-cup glass measure in a microwave oven), heat the butter, lemon peel and juice; pour over the popcorn. Sprinkle with salt to taste.

SEASONED SNACK MIX

A munchie to serve anytime but *especially good served with tall glasses of Real Old-Fashioned Lemonade (page 265).*

1 cup natural whole almonds
1 tablespoon instant minced onion
2 to 3 tablespoons butter or margarine
Grated peel of 1 Sunkist lemon
1 tablespoon dried parsley leaves, crushed
½ teaspoon seasoned salt
½ teaspoon garlic salt
4 cups combination of assorted bite-size cereals (shredded wheat, corn, etc.), small Cheddar cheese crackers, *or* pretzel sticks

Makes about 5 cups.

In a large skillet, sauté the almonds and onion in the butter until lightly toasted. Add the lemon peel, parsley, seasoned and

Cookies and Confections 225

garlic salt and mix well. Add the cereal mixture; heat, stirring until well coated with the butter mixture. Cool.

1000 PALMS STUFFED DATES

A confection that's easy to make and fun to serve or give as gifts.

4 dozen dates
2½ cups confectioners' sugar
½ cup sweetened condensed milk
Grated peel of 1 Sunkist lemon

½ cup finely chopped walnuts or pecans
¼ cup finely chopped dried apricots
Walnut or pecan quarters or halves (optional)

Makes 4 dozen.

To prepare the dates for stuffing, cut each along one side and remove the pits. In a bowl, combine the confectioners' sugar, condensed milk, and lemon peel (mixture will be stiff). Stir in chopped nuts and apricots. Dust hands with additional confectioners' sugar and shape mixture into small balls (about ¾ inch); stuff into prepared dates. Top each with a nut quarter or half.

FABULOUS ORANGE FUDGE

A winner every time. Chocolate and orange team up in this easy-to-make sweet treat.

2 cups sugar
1 can (5⅓ ounces) evaporated milk
10 large marshmallows (or 100 miniature)
1 package (6 ounces) semisweet chocolate pieces

1 cup chopped walnuts
½ cup butter or margarine, cut into small pieces
Grated peel of 2 Sunkist oranges

Makes about 2 pounds or 25 pieces.

In a saucepan, combine the sugar, evaporated milk, and marshmallows. Bring to a boil over medium heat, stirring to dissolve the sugar. Boil for 6 minutes, stirring constantly. Remove from heat and add remaining ingredients. Beat well until fudge thickens, about 5 minutes. Pour into a buttered 8-inch-square baking pan. Chill until firm and cut into squares.

WHITE CITRUS FUDGE

The old-fashioned kind of fudge. Do not make it on rainy or very humid days.

2 tablespoons butter or margarine
2 cups sugar
¾ cup milk

Grated peel of 1 Sunkist lemon or orange
½ cup chopped walnuts

Makes about 1 pound.

In a saucepan, melt the butter over medium-low heat. Add the sugar and milk, stirring to dissolve the sugar. Cover and boil for 1 minute to dissolve the sugar from the sides of the pan. Cook, uncovered, without stirring, to the soft ball stage (239° F.). Cool to lukewarm, about 45 minutes, without stirring. Add lemon peel. Beat vigorously until the mixture loses its glossiness and is ready to set. Stir in walnuts and pour immediately onto wax paper. Cool and cut into squares.

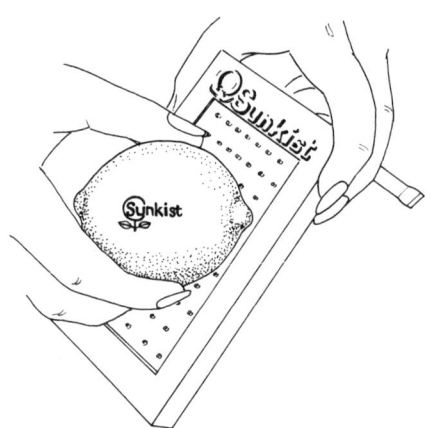

CANDIED CITRUS PEEL

Another Sunkist classic!

4 to 5 Sunkist oranges *or*	2 cups sugar
6 Sunkist lemons *or*	½ cup honey
2 Sunkist grapefruit	1¾ cups boiling water
12 cups cold water	

Makes 1 pound.

Score the citrus in quarters and remove sections of the peel. Cut into uniform strips about ⅜ inch wide to yield 3 cups peel. (Save the peeled fruit for other uses.) In a large saucepan, bring 6 cups of cold water and the peel to a boil; boil for 10 minutes. Drain and rinse. Repeat process with 6 cups fresh water. In the same saucepan, bring to a boil 1½ cups of the sugar, honey, and boiling water, stirring to dissolve the sugar; boil for 1 minute. Add drained peel and simmer briskly for 40 to 45 minutes, stirring frequently to avoid sticking. Drain well. In a large bowl, toss drained peel with the remaining ½ cup sugar to coat well. Spread on wax paper to dry. Store in a tightly covered container.

CHOCOLATE DIPPED CANDIED CITRUS PEEL

6 ounces sweet chocolate or white sweet chocolate   1 pound Candied Citrus Peel

In the top of a double boiler, over hot, not boiling, water, melt the chocolate; stir occasionally. Dip each piece of Candied Citrus Peel in the chocolate (covering one half to two thirds of each piece only); gently shake off any excess chocolate. Cool on wax paper until chocolate is set.

VARIATION: Substitute semi-sweet chocolate pieces and 2 teaspoons vegetable shortening for the sweet chocolate, melting the chocolate pieces with the shortening.

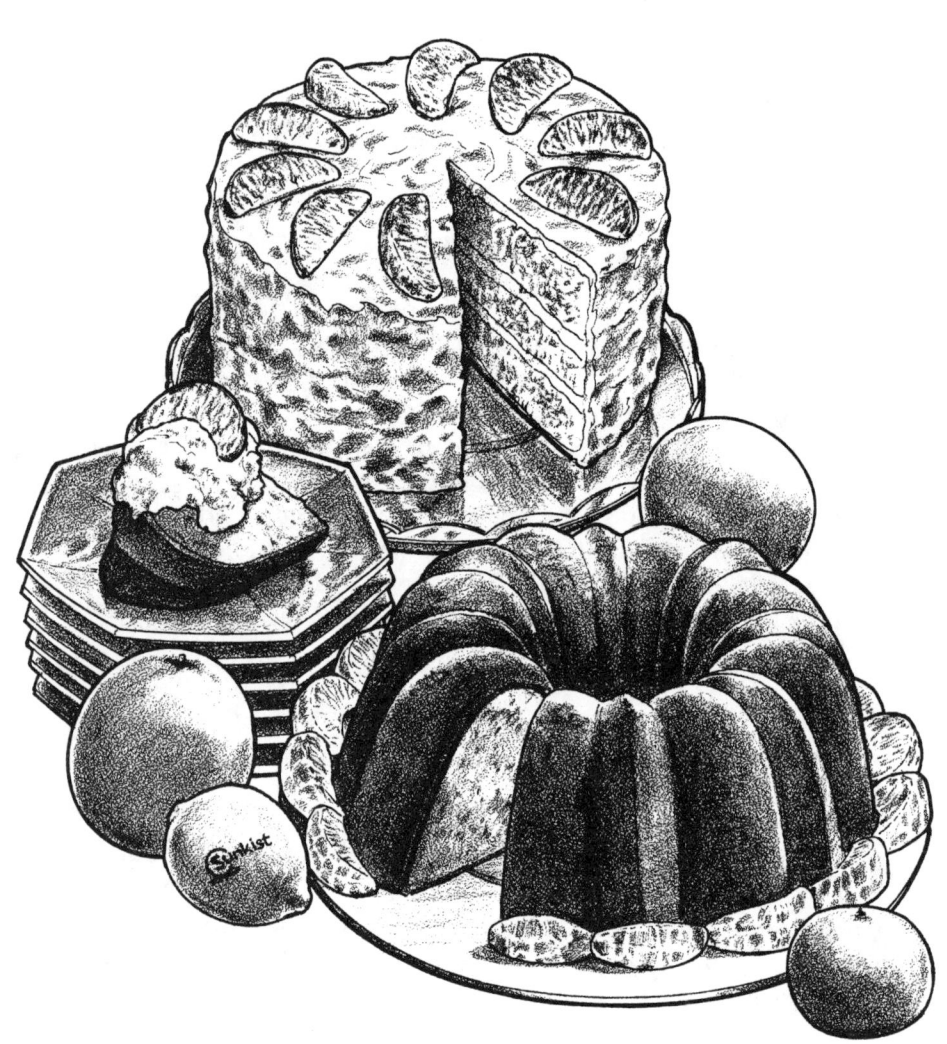

Cakes and Frostings

Homemade cakes are always special. The best cakes seem to come from a treasured family recipe, made with special ingredients and a little extra attention. We're sharing some of our own family favorites here.

For entertaining, orange and chocolate flavors blend in a rich and dramatic cake filled with an orange icing and topped with a satin chocolate glaze.

For traveling to potlucks or a neighborhood get-together, take an orange-flavored carrot cake, rich with spices and a cream cheese icing or filling.

Plan ahead for the holidays with a dark molasses fruitcake, or a light golden fruitcake with orange glaze.

And for special family occasions, bake a special lemon layer cake, moist with sour cream.

CAKES AND FROSTINGS

FRESH ORANGE AND CARROT CAKE
ORANGE AMBROSIA CAKE ROLL
TANGERINE-ALMOND SHORTCAKE
KAREN ANN'S LEMON CAKE
FRESH ORANGE-COCOA CAKE
DARK ORANGE LOAF CAKE (GROWER RECIPE)
FLOWERPOT CAKE
SPICED GRAPEFRUIT UPSIDE-DOWN CAKE
GRANDMA'S FAVORITE MOLASSES FRUITCAKE
WESTERN GOLDEN FRUITCAKE
SWEET AND TART LEMON CAKE
ZESTY CITRUS FROSTING

FRESH ORANGE AND CARROT CAKE

Whether served from the pan, or shaped jellyroll fashion, this moist orange carrot cake is a flavor favorite!

1 unpeeled Sunkist orange	2 teaspoons ground nutmeg
1½ cups sugar	¼ teaspoon salt
1 cup salad or vegetable oil	2 cups shredded carrots
4 eggs	½ cup chopped walnuts
2 cups all-purpose flour	½ cup raisins
2 teaspoons baking powder	Fresh Orange Cream Cheese Spread (page 232) or Fresh Orange Ice Cream (page 232)
2 teaspoons baking soda	
2 teaspoons ground cinnamon	

Makes 12 servings.

Trim a thin slice from each end of the orange; cut the fruit in half lengthwise. With a shallow "V" shape cut remove the white center core. Cut the halves into small chunks. In a blender or food processor, purée the orange chunks to yield ⅔ cup. In a large bowl, combine the sugar and oil. Beat in the eggs one at a time. Sift together the dry ingredients and gradually add them to the egg mixture. Stir in orange purée, carrots, walnuts, and raisins. Pour the batter into a greased 13 × 9 × 2-inch baking pan. Bake at 350° F. for 45 to 50 minutes, or until a toothpick inserted in the center comes out clean. Cool on a wire rack. Frost with Fresh Orange Cream Cheese Spread or serve with Fresh Orange Ice Cream.

ORANGE CARROT CAKE ROLLS: Prepare the batter as above. Line two 15½ × 10½ × 1-inch jellyroll pans with greased aluminum foil. Divide the batter equally (about 3 cups each) between the prepared pans. Bake, one at a time, at 350° F. for 25 minutes. Cool for 5 minutes. Invert each cake onto a large, wax paper–lined cookie Invert sheet; carefully remove the foil. Roll up each cake *with* wax paper from the narrow end; cool completely on wire racks. Unroll *one* cake and spread with Fresh Orange Cream Cheese Spread. Reroll without the wax paper and refrigerate. Unroll *second* cake and spread with *softened* Fresh Orange Ice Cream. Reroll without wax paper and freeze. To serve, sprinkle cakes with confectioners' sugar and garnish with orange half-cartwheel slices, if desired. Each cake makes 8 to 12 servings.

HALF-AND-HALF VARIATION: Bake half the cake batter in a jellyroll pan as above. Bake the remaining batter in a greased 8- or 9-inch-square baking pan at 350° F. for 40 minutes, or until a toothpick inserted in the center comes out clean.

FRESH ORANGE CREAM CHEESE SPREAD

1 package (8 ounces) cream cheese, softened
1 cup confectioners' sugar
Grated peel of 1 Sunkist orange
1 cup heavy cream or whipping cream, whipped

Makes about 3 cups.

In a bowl, combine the cream cheese, sugar, and orange peel. Fold in the whipped cream and chill.

FRESH ORANGE ICE CREAM

1 quart vanilla ice cream, softened
Grated peel of 1 Sunkist orange

Makes about 4 cups.

In a bowl, combine the ice cream and orange peel. Return to the freezer.

ORANGE AMBROSIA CAKE ROLL

When making any jellyroll-type cake, it is important to cool the rolled up cake thoroughly. But don't leave it rolled up too long after it's cooled, or it will crack as it is unrolled.

CAKE
1 cup cake flour
1 teaspoon baking powder
¼ teaspoon salt
3 eggs
1 cup sugar
Grated peel of ½ Sunkist orange
⅓ cup fresh squeezed orange juice

ORANGE FILLING AND GLAZE
¾ cup sugar
1 tablespoon cornstarch
1 cup fresh squeezed orange juice
4 egg yolks, beaten
1 cup heavy cream or whipping cream, whipped
Grated peel of 1 Sunkist orange
¼ cup shredded or flaked coconut

Makes 8 to 12 servings.

To make the cake, line a 15½ × 10½ × 1-inch jellyroll pan with greased aluminum foil. Sift together the cake flour, baking powder, and salt. In a large bowl, with an electric mixer, beat the eggs well. Gradually add the sugar and orange juice, beating until well blended. Gradually add the dry ingredients, beating just until smooth. Stir in the orange peel. Pour the batter into the prepared pan. Bake at 375° F. for 13 to 15 minutes. Cool for 5 minutes. Invert the cake onto a large, wax paper–lined cookie sheet; carefully remove the foil. Roll up the cake *with* the wax paper from the narrow end; cool completely on a wire rack. Meanwhile prepare the Orange Filling and Glaze.

To make the Orange Filling and Glaze, in a saucepan, combine the sugar and cornstarch. Gradually blend in the orange juice and beaten egg yolks. Bring to a boil over medium heat, stirring until thickened. Cool thoroughly. Reserve ½ cup of the cooled filling for the glaze. Gently fold the whipped cream and orange peel into the remaining 1 cup of filling.

To assemble the cake roll, unroll the cake and spread it with the filling. Reroll without the wax paper and place on a serving platter. Spread the top with the reserved glaze and sprinkle with the coconut. Chill for at least 1 hour before serving. Garnish with orange half-cartwheel slices and well-drained maraschino cherries with stems, if desired.

TANGERINE-ALMOND SHORTCAKE

Almonds and tangerines seem to have a natural affinity. This attractive shortcake can also be made with fresh oranges for year round enjoyment.

1½ cups all-purpose flour
2 teaspoons baking powder
¼ teaspoon salt
⅓ cup butter or margarine, softened
⅓ cup sugar
1 egg
⅔ cup milk
¼ cup finely chopped almonds

2 teaspoons fresh grated tangerine peel
3 medium Sunkist tangerines, peeled, segmented, and seeded
¼ cup almond- or orange-flavored liqueur
2 cups prepared whipped topping or sweetened whipped cream
Whole natural almonds (optional)

Makes 6 to 8 servings.

To make the shortcake, sift together the flour, baking powder, and salt. In a large bowl, cream together the butter and sugar. Add the egg and beat well. Stir in the milk, chopped almonds, and tangerine peel. Add the dry ingredients, stirring just until blended. Spread batter into an aluminum foil–lined and lightly greased 8-inch-round cake pan. Bake at 375° F. for 30 minutes, or until a toothpick inserted in the center comes out clean. Cool slightly. Remove from pan and carefully remove foil. Cool on a wire rack. Cut horizontally into 2 layers. Meanwhile, combine the tangerine segments and liqueur; chill. To assemble, spoon tangerines and whipped topping between the cake layers and over the top. Garnish with whole almonds.

NON-ALCOHOLIC VARIATION: Substitute ¼ cup fresh squeezed tangerine juice and ⅛ teaspoon almond extract for the liqueur.

ORANGE VARIATION: Substitute 3 small oranges, peeled and segmented, for the tangerines. Substitute fresh grated peel of ½ fresh orange for the tangerine peel.

KAREN ANN'S LEMON CAKE

CAKE
- 2 cups all-purpose flour
- 1½ teaspoons baking powder
- ½ teaspoon baking soda
- ¼ teaspoon salt
- ⅔ cup butter or margarine, softened
- 1¼ cups sugar
- 3 eggs, separated
- ¾ cup sour cream
- Grated peel of 1 Sunkist lemon

LEMONY FROSTING
- ½ cup butter or margarine, softened
- 3 cups confectioners' sugar
- 1 egg yolk
- Grated peel of ½ Sunkist lemon
- 2 tablespoons fresh squeezed lemon juice

Makes 12 servings (about 1¾ cups frosting).

To make the cake, sift together the flour, baking powder, baking soda, and salt. In a large bowl, with an electric mixer, cream together the butter and sugar. Beat in the egg yolks one at a time; continue beating until light in color. Add dry ingredients to creamed mixture alternately with sour cream, beating *just* until smooth. With clean beaters, beat the egg whites until soft peaks form. Gently fold beaten egg whites and lemon peel into batter. Pour the batter into two 8-inch-round cake pans (bottoms lined with wax paper). Bake at 350° F. for 30 to 35 minutes, until a toothpick inserted in the center comes out clean. Cool for 10 minutes. Remove from pans and peel off wax paper. Cool on wire racks. Fill and frost with Lemony Frosting.

To make the Lemony Frosting, in a bowl, cream together the butter and 1 cup confectioners' sugar. Add the egg yolk and beat well. Add lemon peel, lemon juice, and remaining 2 cups sugar; beat until smooth.

FRESH ORANGE-COCOA CAKE

Very light in texture, with a subtle chocolate flavor and just a hint of orange in the cake and icing.

1 unpeeled Sunkist orange
2 cups *sifted* cake flour
1¾ cups sugar
½ cup cocoa
1½ teaspoons baking powder
¾ teaspoon baking soda
¼ teaspoon salt

⅔ cup fresh squeezed orange juice
¾ cup vegetable shortening
1 teaspoon vanilla extract
4 eggs
¾ cup finely chopped walnuts
Fresh Orange Icing (page 237)
Satin Chocolate Glaze (page 237)

Makes 12 servings.

Trim a thin slice from each end of the orange; cut the fruit in half lengthwise. With a shallow "V" shape cut, remove the white center core. Cut the halves into small chunks. In a blender or food processor, purée the orange chunks to yield ⅔ cup. In a large bowl, sift together the dry ingredients; add the orange purée, orange juice, shortening, and vanilla. With an electric mixer, beat at medium speed for 2 minutes. Add the eggs and beat 2 minutes longer. Stir in the walnuts. Pour the batter into two 9-inch-round cake pans (bottoms lined with oiled wax paper). Bake at 375° F. for 30 to 35 minutes, or until a toothpick inserted in the center comes out clean. Cool for 10 minutes. Carefully remove from pans and peel off wax paper. Cool on wire racks. Spread 1 cup Fresh Orange Icing between cake layers; frost sides of cake with remaining icing. Frost top of cake with Satin Chocolate Glaze, allowing some glaze to drizzle over the sides.

FRESH ORANGE ICING

⅓ cup instant nonfat dry milk (powder)
2 tablespoons fresh squeezed orange juice
2 teaspoons fresh squeezed lemon juice
3 cups *sifted* confectioners' sugar
1 egg white
½ cup vegetable shortening
¼ cup butter or margarine, softened
Grated peel of 1 Sunkist orange

Makes about 2⅔ cups.

In a bowl, dissolve the dry milk in the orange and lemon juices. Add the confectioners' sugar and egg white. With an electric mixer, beat at high speed for 5 minutes, or until thick. Add the shortening and butter; beat 5 minutes longer, or until fluffy. Stir in the orange peel.

SATIN CHOCOLATE GLAZE

1 cup *sifted* confectioners' sugar
¼ cup cocoa
2 tablespoons butter or margarine, softened
1½ to 2½ tablespoons boiling water
½ teaspoon vanilla extract

Makes about ½ cup.

In a small bowl, combine all the ingredients and beat until smooth. (For a thinner glaze use the maximum amount of water.)

DARK ORANGE LOAF CAKE
Ruth Brady, *Fillmore, California*
(Grower recipe contest winner)

Fortunately, Ruth Brady loves to cook. Packing lunches every day for seven children was a challenge to her creativity instead of an endurance trial. When she and her mother began developing this recipe, they wanted a moist, flavorful dessert like a fruitcake. The winning results have been welcome in lunch boxes for years. The cake also freezes well, so Ruth always has a sweet treat on hand for family and friends.

1 Sunkist orange
1 cup raisins
2 cups all-purpose flour
1 teaspoon baking powder
¼ teaspoon baking soda
¼ teaspoon salt
1 cup chopped walnuts

½ cup butter or margarine, softened
1½ cups sugar
2 eggs
1 cup buttermilk
1 teaspoon vanilla extract

Makes 1 loaf cake.

Cut the orange in half, ream out the juice and reserve it. Cut off and discard the ends of the orange shells and cut the peel into 1-inch pieces. In a food processor or blender, finely chop the orange peel with the raisins. Sift together the flour, baking powder, baking soda, and salt; stir in the walnuts to coat with the flour. In the large bowl of an electric mixer, cream together the butter and 1 cup of the sugar. Beat in the eggs, buttermilk, and vanilla. By hand, stir in the orange-raisin mixture. Add dry ingredients, stirring until well blended. Pour into a well-greased 9 × 5 × 3-inch loaf pan. Bake at 350° F. for 55 to 60 minutes, or until a toothpick inserted in the center comes out clean. Meanwhile, in a small saucepan, combine the reserved orange juice and remaining ½ cup of sugar. Bring to a boil, stirring constantly. Slowly pour over the hot cake in the pan. Cool cake on a wire rack for 1 hour. (The cake will absorb all the syrup mixture.) Remove from the pan.

FLOWERPOT CAKE

Fun for kids to decorate, but equally "adult" as the centerpiece for a bridal or baby shower.

CAKE
- 1 (6-inch diameter) new clay flowerpot
- 1 package (about 16 ounces) pound cake mix
- 2 eggs
- Milk *or* water
- Grated peel of 1 Sunkist lemon

FROSTING
- 1 egg white
- ⅛ teaspoon cream of tartar
- ¾ cup confectioners' sugar
- Grated peel of ½ Sunkist lemon

CANDY FLOWERS
- Vanilla wafers
- Sunkist Fruit Gems (pectin candies in assorted colors)
- Decorating icing*
- Plastic straws
- Peppermint stick candy
- Candy canes

Makes 8 to 10 servings.

To make the cake, use crumpled foil to plug the hole in the bottom of the flowerpot. Cut a 16-inch-long piece of wax paper in four 3-inch-wide strips. Line the sides and bottom of the flowerpot with overlapping strips of wax paper. In a large bowl, prepare the pound cake mix with the eggs and milk *or* water following the package directions; stir in the lemon peel. Carefully pour the batter into the prepared flowerpot. Place in a shallow baking pan for ease in handling. Bake at 325° F. for 1¼ hours, or until a long skewer inserted in the center comes out clean. Cool 10 minutes; then turn out of the pot onto a wire rack; peel off the wax paper and cool completely. Turn the wide end up to frost.

---

*Decorating icing comes in tubes in assorted colors.

To make the frosting, in a bowl, with an electric mixer, beat the egg white with the cream of tartar until foamy. Gradually add the sugar, beating until stiff peaks form. Stir in the lemon peel. Frost the top of the flowerpot cake, allowing some of the frosting to drizzle over the sides. (Reserve a small amount of frosting to "glue" the flower parts together.)

To assemble the flowers: (Let assembled flowers dry before "planting.")

Use vanilla wafers as backs of flowers.

Use pectin candies whole as flowers or cut into strips for petals.

Use green candy or decorating icing for leaves.

Use white decorating icing to outline leaves, for flower centers, or as additional "glue."

Use plastic straws or peppermint sticks as flower "stems." Push straws or peppermint sticks into pectin candy. "Plant" along with candy canes in frosted flowerpot cake.

SPICED GRAPEFRUIT UPSIDE-DOWN CAKE

CAKE

⅓ cup butter or margarine
½ cup packed light brown sugar
1 Sunkist grapefruit, peeled, cut into 6 cartwheel slices, and *well drained*
Walnut halves (about 18)

1 package (about 16 ounces) pound cake mix
2 eggs
Milk *or* water
1 teaspoon ground cinnamon
⅛ teaspoon ground cloves
Grated peel of 1 Sunkist grapefruit

WHIPPED TOPPING

1 cup heavy cream or whipping cream*
2 tablespoons confectioners' sugar

Grated peel of ½ Sunkist grapefruit

Makes 8 to 9 servings (about 2 cups topping).

*Or substitute 1 envelope (1½ ounces) whipped topping mix for 1 cup whipping cream *and* sugar. Prepare the whipped topping mix with ½ cup cold milk following the package directions. Stir in the grapefruit peel.

To make the cake, melt the butter in a 9-inch-square baking pan while the oven is preheating to 325° F. Carefully remove the hot baking pan from oven; sprinkle the brown sugar evenly over the melted butter. Arrange the grapefruit cartwheel slices and walnut halves over the brown sugar. In a large bowl, prepare the pound cake mix with the eggs and milk *or* water following the package directions, adding the cinnamon and cloves. Stir in the grapefruit peel. Pour the batter over the grapefruit. Bake for 50 to 55 minutes, or until a toothpick inserted in the center comes out clean. Run a knife around the sides of the pan; remove the cake by inverting it onto a serving plate. Serve warm or cool with Whipped Topping.

To make the Whipped Topping, in a bowl, whip the cream with the confectioners' sugar. Stir in the grapefruit peel; chill for 10 to 15 minutes.

GRANDMA'S FAVORITE MOLASSES FRUITCAKE

This holiday cake can be baked in three different sizes, and that's especially nice for entertaining or gift-giving.

2 unpeeled Sunkist oranges	6 eggs
1 cup light molasses	3 cups all-purpose flour
1 package (about 16 ounces) raisins	1 teaspoon baking soda
	1½ teaspoons ground cinnamon
1 package (8 ounces) pitted dates, chopped	1 teaspoon ground nutmeg
2 containers (16 ounces each) glacé fruit mix	½ teaspoon ground allspice
	½ teaspoon ground cloves
1 cup butter or margarine, softened	1 cup fresh squeezed orange juice
1¼ cups sugar	2 cups walnut or pecan halves

Makes 12 to 16 servings.

Cut the oranges into large chunks. In a food processor or blender, finely chop the oranges to yield 1⅓ cups. In a large saucepot, combine the chopped oranges, molasses, raisins, and dates; bring to a boil. Reduce heat and simmer for 5 to 10 minutes.

Remove from heat and stir in the fruit mix. In a large bowl, with an electric mixer, cream together the butter and sugar. Beat in the eggs one at a time. Sift together the flour, baking soda, and spices. Add to the creamed mixture alternately with the orange juice. Stir the batter into the fruit mixture. Add the nuts. Spoon 8 cups of the batter into a *well-greased* 10-inch Bundt or tube pan. With the remaining 6 cups batter make 2 dozen cupcakes *or* 8 dozen mini fruitcakes (see below). Bake the large fruitcake at 300° F. for 2 hours, or until a toothpick inserted in the center comes out clean. Cool for 10 minutes. Remove from the pan and cool on a wire rack. To serve, sprinkle with confectioners' sugar and garnish with unpeeled orange cartwheel slices, quartered, and candied cherries, if desired.

"CUPCAKE" FRUITCAKES: Spoon about ¼ cup batter into each of 24 paper-lined 2½ × 1¼-inch muffin cups. Press a candied cherry or nut half into the top of each, if desired. Bake at 300° F. for 40 to 45 minutes. Makes 2 dozen cupcake-size fruitcakes.

"MINI" FRUITCAKES: Spoon about 1 tablespoon batter into each of 96 paper-lined 1¾ × 1-inch "miniature" muffin cups. Press a candied cherry or nut half into the top of each, if desired. Bake at 300° F. for 30 to 35 minutes. Makes 8 dozen miniature fruitcakes.

WESTERN GOLDEN FRUITCAKE

1 cup butter or margarine, softened
2 cups sugar
4 eggs
4 cups all-purpose flour
1½ teaspoons baking soda
1 cup buttermilk
½ cup fresh squeezed orange juice
2 cups pecan or walnut halves
1 package (8 ounces) pitted dates, chopped
8 ounces candied cherries, halved
8 ounces candied pineapple chunks
Grated peel of 2 Sunkist oranges
Fresh Orange or Lemon Glaze (page 243)

Large cake makes 12 to 16 servings and small loaf 4 to 6 servings.

Cakes and Frostings

In a large bowl, with an electric mixer, cream together the butter and sugar. Beat in the eggs one at a time. Sift together the flour and baking soda. Add to the creamed mixture alternately with the buttermilk and orange juice, beating until smooth. Stir in the nuts, dates, cherries, pineapple, and orange peel. Spoon 7½ cups of the batter into a *well-greased* 10-inch Bundt or tube pan and spoon the remaining 2½ cups of batter into a *well-greased* 7½ × 3½ × 2¼-inch loaf pan. Bake both cakes at 300° F. for 2 hours, or until a toothpick inserted in the center comes out clean. Cool for 10 minutes. Remove from the pans and cool on wire racks. To serve, drizzle the cakes with Fresh Orange or Lemon Glaze and garnish with nut halves, if desired.

FRESH ORANGE GLAZE

In a small bowl, combine 1 cup confectioners' sugar, 1 teaspoon fresh grated orange peel, and 1½ to 2 tablespoons fresh squeezed orange juice.

FRESH LEMON GLAZE

In a small bowl, combine 1 cup confectioners' sugar and fresh grated peel and juice of ½ lemon.

SWEET AND TART LEMON CAKE

Convenient to make and full of fresh tangy lemon flavor. It's the perfect take-along cake for any occasion.

CAKE
1 package (about 18 ounces) lemon cake mix with pudding
4 eggs
1 cup water
⅓ cup salad or vegetable oil
Grated peel of ½ Sunkist lemon
Juice of 1 Sunkist lemon (3 tablespoons)

TART LEMON GLAZE
1½ cups confectioners' sugar
Grated peel of ½ Sunkist lemon
Juice of 1 Sunkist lemon (3 tablespoons)

Makes 12 servings.

To make the cake, in a large bowl, combine all the ingredients. With an electric mixer, beat at medium speed for 2 minutes (by hand, 300 strokes). Pour the batter into a *well-greased* 10-inch Bundt pan. Bake at 350° F. for 45 to 50 minutes, or until a toothpick inserted in the center comes out clean. Cool for 10 minutes. Combine all the glaze ingredients and beat until smooth. Invert the cake onto a serving plate. Prick the cake well with a toothpick and drizzle with half the glaze. Cool the cake completely; then drizzle with the remaining glaze.

ZESTY CITRUS FROSTING

Spread this frosting on doughnuts, cupcakes, or between cookies to form "sandwiches."

1 package (3 ounces) cream cheese, softened
2 cups confectioners' sugar
1 tablespoon fresh squeezed lemon or orange juice
1 tablespoon apricot, peach, or pineapple preserves
Grated peel of ½ Sunkist lemon or orange

Makes about 1 cup frosting.

In a bowl, with an electric mixer, beat the cream cheese until smooth. Add the confectioners' sugar, juice, and preserves; beat well. Stir in the peel.

Note: To fill and frost an 8- or 9-inch two-layer cake, double the frosting ingredients.

Pies and Pastries

Every citrus variety makes deliciously flavored pies.

End a meal with a perfect lemon pie, and your guests will remember that high, golden meringue and tart-sweet filling. After years of preparations and variations, we think we've perfected the classic.

But there's more to lemon pies than meringue. A double-crust lemon pie is a nice surprise, and a frosty polar pie with lemon flavored crust, vanilla ice cream, and thick lemon filling is wonderful on a hot summer night.

Showcase the sweetness of oranges in an easy-to-make cream cheese pie, or the tang of grapefruit in a fluffy chiffon pie. Two other favorites—fresh peach pie with peach nectar, and the light but rich lemon charlotte russe.

PIES AND PASTRIES

FRESH LEMON MERINGUE PIE
EASY LEMON MERINGUE PIE
ORANGE MERINGUE PIE
GRAPEFRUIT MERINGUE PIE
FROZEN LEMON ICE CREAM PIE
DOUBLE-CRUST LEMON PIE
GRAPEFRUIT CHIFFON PIE
MARGARITA COCKTAIL PIE
ORANGE-CREAM CHEESE PIE
GLAZED FRESH PEACH PIE
ORANGE-COCONUT FLAN
CREAM PUFFS WITH A'PEEL
TINT OF MINT GRAPEFRUIT CHARLOTTE RUSSE
THE CLASSIC LEMON CHARLOTTE RUSSE
ALL-PURPOSE PIE CRUST

FRESH LEMON MERINGUE PIE

When you're in the mood for lemon meringue pie, try this Sunkist classic... it's the real thing!

1½ cups sugar
¼ cup *plus* 2 tablespoons cornstarch
¼ teaspoon salt
½ cup cold water
½ cup fresh squeezed lemon juice
3 egg yolks, well beaten
2 tablespoons butter or margarine
1½ cups boiling water
Grated peel of ½ Sunkist lemon
2 to 3 drops yellow food coloring (optional)
1 (9-inch) baked pie crust (page 260)
Three-Egg Meringue (below)

Makes 6 servings.

In a saucepan, thoroughly combine the sugar, cornstarch, and salt. Gradually blend in the cold water and lemon juice. Stir in the egg yolks. Add the butter and boiling water. Bring to a boil over medium-high heat, stirring constantly. Reduce heat to medium and boil for *1 minute*. Remove from heat and stir in the lemon peel and food coloring. Pour into baked pie crust. Top with Three-Egg Meringue, sealing well at edges. Bake at 350° F. for 12 to 15 minutes. Cool for 2 hours before serving.

THREE-EGG MERINGUE

3 egg whites
¼ teaspoon cream of tartar
6 tablespoons sugar

In a bowl, with an electric mixer, beat the egg whites with the cream of tartar until foamy. Gradually add the sugar and beat until stiff peaks form.

VARIATION: For a higher meringue use Four-Egg Meringue (page 253).

EASY LEMON MERINGUE PIE

Quick to make, fresh lemon juice and grated peel add the zest. And if you don't tell, no one will know you started with a mix.

1 package (about 3 ounces) lemon pudding and pie filling
½ cup sugar
2 cups water
Juice of 1 Sunkist lemon (3 tablespoons)
3 egg yolks, well beaten
Grated peel of ½ Sunkist lemon
1 (9-inch) frozen deep-dish pie shell, thawed and baked
Three-Egg Meringue (page 249)

Makes 6 servings.

In a saucepan, thoroughly combine the pudding mix and sugar. Gradually blend in the water and lemon juice. Stir in the egg yolks. Bring to a full boil over medium heat, stirring constantly, until thickened. Stir in lemon peel. Pour into baked pie crust. Top with Three-Egg Meringue, sealing well at the edges. Bake at 350° F. for 12 to 15 minutes. Cool for 2 hours before serving.

ORANGE MERINGUE PIE

A delicious change-of-pace meringue pie.

1 cup sugar
¼ cup cornstarch
⅛ teaspoon salt
2 cups fresh squeezed orange juice
¼ cup fresh squeezed lemon juice
3 egg yolks, well beaten
2 tablespoons butter or margarine
Grated peel of ½ Sunkist orange
1 (9-inch) baked pie crust (page 260)
Three-Egg Meringue (page 249)

Makes 6 servings.

In a saucepan, thoroughly combine the sugar, cornstarch, and salt. Gradually blend in the orange and lemon juices. Stir in the egg yolks. Add the butter and bring to a boil over medium-high heat, stirring constantly. Reduce heat to medium and boil for *1 minute*. Remove from heat and stir in orange peel. Pour into baked pie crust. Top with Three-Egg Meringue, sealing well at the edges. Bake at 350° F. for 12 to 15 minutes. Cool for 2 hours before serving.

VARIATION: For a higher meringue use Four-Egg Meringue (page 253).

GRAPEFRUIT MERINGUE PIE

1 Sunkist grapefruit, peeled and sectioned
1 tablespoon *plus* 1½ cups sugar
¼ cup *plus* 2 tablespoons cornstarch
¼ teaspoon salt
1¾ cups fresh squeezed grapefruit juice
¾ cup cold water
3 egg yolks, well beaten
2 tablespoons butter or margarine
1 (10-inch) baked pie crust (page 260)
Five-Egg Meringue (below)

Makes 6 to 8 servings.

Sprinkle the grapefruit sections with 1 tablespoon of the sugar; set aside. In a saucepan, thoroughly combine 1½ cups of the sugar, cornstarch, and salt. Gradually blend in the grapefruit juice and water. Stir in the egg yolks. Add the butter and bring to a boil over medium-high heat, stirring constantly. Reduce heat to medium and boil for 3 to 4 minutes. Pour into baked pie crust. Top with Five-Egg Meringue, sealing well at the edges. Bake at 350° F. for 12 to 15 minutes. Cool for 2 hours before serving. Garnish each serving with 1 or 2 grapefruit sections.

FIVE-EGG MERINGUE
5 egg whites
¼ teaspoon cream of tartar
10 tablespoons sugar

In a bowl, with an electric mixer, beat the egg whites with the cream of tartar until foamy. Gradually add the sugar and beat until stiff peaks form.

FROZEN LEMON ICE CREAM PIE

This spectacular dessert sits waiting in the freezer... for the ohs and ahs that are sure to come when it is served.

Hint of Lemon Pie Crust (below) *or* other 10-inch baked pie crust (page 260)
Lemon Filling (page 253)
2 pints vanilla ice cream, softened
Four-Egg Meringue (page 253)

Makes 8 to 10 servings.

Prepare and bake the pie crust. Cool and then chill. Prepare the Lemon Filling; then chill, stirring occasionally. *To assemble the pie*: Spread 1 pint of softened ice cream into the chilled baked pie crust; freeze until firm. Top with half the lemon filling; freeze until firm. Repeat the layers with the remaining ice cream and lemon filling, freezing after each addition. Make Four-Egg Meringue. Top the frozen pie with meringue, sealing well at edges. Bake at 500° F. for 3 minutes, or until lightly browned. Serve immediately and refreeze any unused pie. *Or* freeze *unbaked* meringue-topped pie and bake as above before serving.

HINT OF LEMON PIE CRUST

1½ cups all-purpose flour
2 tablespoons sugar
½ teaspoon salt
Grated peel of ½ Sunkist lemon
½ cup vegetable shortening
4 to 5 tablespoons cold water

In a large bowl, sift together the flour, sugar, and salt. Stir in the lemon peel. With a pastry blender or two knives, cut in the shortening until the pieces are the size of small peas. Gradually add the water, tossing mixture with a fork to incorporate *just* enough moisture so that mixture can be formed into a ball. Flatten onto a lightly floured board. Roll out to a 12-inch circle. Line a 10-inch pie plate with the pastry and flute edges as desired. Prick the bottom and sides well with a fork; chill for 30 minutes or longer, then bake at 450° F. for 10 to 12 minutes; cool.

LEMON FILLING

6 tablespoons butter or margarine
1½ cups sugar
½ cup fresh squeezed lemon juice
4 egg yolks (reserve whites for the meringue)
2 whole eggs
¼ teaspoon salt
Grated peel of 1 Sunkist lemon

In a saucepan, melt the butter. Remove from the heat and blend in the sugar and lemon juice. Add the egg yolks, whole eggs, and salt; beat well with an electric mixer. Cook over medium-low heat, stirring constantly, until thickened, about 8 to 10 minutes. Stir in lemon peel. Chill, stirring occasionally.

FOUR-EGG MERINGUE

4 egg whites
¼ teaspoon cream of tartar
½ cup sugar

In a bowl, with an electric mixer, beat the egg whites with the cream of tartar until foamy. Gradually add the sugar and beat until stiff peaks form.

DOUBLE-CRUST LEMON PIE

No meringue—but all the flavor of fresh lemon.

1¼ cups sugar
¼ cup cornstarch
¼ cup cold water
1¼ cups boiling water
2 tablespoons butter or margarine, softened
Grated peel of 1 Sunkist lemon
⅓ cup fresh squeezed lemon juice
2 eggs, slightly beaten
2 drops yellow food coloring (optional)
Pastry for a 2-crust pie (page 260)
1 egg white, slightly beaten
Sugar

Makes 6 servings.

In a saucepan, thoroughly combine 1¼ cups of the sugar and the cornstarch. Gradually blend in the cold water. Add the boiling water and cook over medium heat, stirring constantly, until the mixture boils. Boil for 2 minutes; then remove from heat. Stir in the butter until melted. Add the lemon peel, lemon juice, 2 eggs, and food coloring; blend until smooth. Cool, stirring occasionally. Line a 9-inch pie plate with half the pastry. Pour in the cooled filling. Top with the remaining pastry. Trim and flute the edges as desired. With a knife, make 6 leaf-shaped cutouts from the pastry trimmings. Brush the top of the pie with egg white. Arrange the leaves, spoke-wheel-fashion, on the pie. Cut slits in the top crust to allow steam to escape. Sprinkle lightly with sugar. Bake at 425° F. for 20 to 25 minutes; cool.

GRAPEFRUIT CHIFFON PIE

Airy goodness and fresh grapefruit flavor served in a toasted coconut crust. The filling is so versatile, it doubles as a chilled soufflé.

1 envelope unflavored gelatine
1 cup fresh squeezed
   grapefruit juice
4 eggs, separated
½ cup sugar
¼ teaspoon salt

1 tablespoon fresh grated
   grapefruit peel
1 cup heavy cream or
   whipping cream,
   whipped
Toasted Coconut Pie Crust
   (page 255)

Makes 8 servings.

Soften the gelatine in the grapefruit juice. In the top of a double boiler, with an electric mixer, beat the egg yolks well with ¼ cup of the sugar, and salt. Gradually beat in the gelatine mixture. Cook over boiling water, stirring constantly, until the mixture *starts* to thicken, about 10 minutes. Pour into a large bowl and add the grapefruit peel. Chill until mixture begins to thicken, about 1 hour, stirring occasionally. With clean beaters, beat the egg whites until foamy. Gradually add the remaining ¼ cup of sugar, beating until soft peaks form. Fold the beaten egg whites and whipped cream into grapefruit-gelatine mixture. Spoon into Toasted Coconut Pie Crust. Chill for 2 hours or longer. Garnish with grapefruit sections, if desired.

TOASTED COCONUT PIE CRUST

3 cups shredded or flaked coconut, toasted
¼ cup packed light brown sugar
6 tablespoons butter or margarine, melted
1 tablespoon fresh grated grapefruit peel

Thoroughly combine all the ingredients. Press firmly onto the bottom and sides of a 10-inch pie plate; chill.

CHILLED GRAPEFRUIT SOUFFLÉ: Omit the Toasted Coconut Pie Crust. Attach an aluminum foil or wax paper collar to a 1-quart soufflé dish. Lightly oil the inside of the foil collar. Spoon the mixture into the prepared dish. Chill for 3 hours, or until firm. Remove collar before serving. Garnish with grapefruit sections and fresh mint.

MARGARITA COCKTAIL PIE

A surprise dessert for Margarita fans.

1 envelope unflavored gelatine
½ cup fresh squeezed lemon juice
5 eggs, separated
1 cup sugar
¼ teaspoon salt
3 to 4 tablespoons tequila
¼ cup triple sec or other orange-flavored liqueur
Grated peel of 1 Sunkist lemon
Pretzel Crumb Crust (page 256)

Makes 8 servings.

Soften the gelatine in the lemon juice. In the top of a double boiler, with an electric mixer, beat the egg yolks well with ½ cup of the sugar, and salt. Stir in the gelatine mixture. Cook over boiling water, stirring constantly, until the mixture *starts* to thicken, about 5 minutes. Pour into a large bowl and add the liquors and lemon peel. Chill until mixture begins to thicken, about 45 minutes, stirring occasionally. With clean beaters, beat the egg whites until foamy. Gradually add the remaining ½ cup of sugar, beating until soft peaks form. Fold beaten egg whites into lemon-gelatine mixture. Spoon into chilled Pretzel Crumb Crust and chill for 2 hours or longer. Garnish with lemon cartwheel twists and fresh mint leaves, if desired.

PRETZEL CRUMB CRUST

1½ cups finely crushed salted pretzels
¼ cup packed light brown sugar
½ cup butter or margarine, melted

Thoroughly combine all ingredients. Press firmly onto the bottom and sides of a 10-inch pie plate. Bake at 400° F. for 5 minutes. Cool and then chill.

ORANGE-CREAM CHEESE PIE

3 Sunkist oranges
1 (9-inch) unbaked pie shell (page 260)
1 egg white, slightly beaten
½ cup finely chopped walnuts
2 packages (3 ounces each) cream cheese, softened
1 cup confectioners' sugar
1 cup heavy cream or whipping cream, whipped
2 teaspoons cornstarch
¼ cup granulated sugar
½ cup fresh squeezed orange juice
Juice of ½ Sunkist lemon

Makes 6 to 8 servings.

Grate the peel from 1 orange and reserve it. Peel and cut all three oranges into half-cartwheel slices and *drain well*. Brush the pie shell with the egg white; press the walnuts into the bottom and sides of the shell. Bake at 450° F. for 10 to 12 minutes; cool. In a bowl, blend the cream cheese, confectioners' sugar, and reserved orange peel until smooth; fold in the whipped cream. Carefully spread the cream cheese mixture over the nuts. Arrange the orange half-cartwheel slices, overlapping, on the cream cheese mixture. To make the glaze, in a small saucepan, combine the cornstarch and granulated sugar; gradually blend in the orange and lemon juices. Cook over medium heat, stirring, until thickened; spoon the glaze over orange slices. Chill for 4 hours or longer.

GLAZED FRESH PEACH PIE

This, unfortunately, is a seasonal recipe. But when fresh, ripe peaches are available, this pie can't be beat.

¾ cup sugar	3 pounds fresh, ripe but firm peaches, peeled, thickly sliced, and chilled
3 tablespoons cornstarch	
1 can (12 ounces) peach nectar	
	Hint of Lemon Pie Crust (page 252), *or* other 10-inch baked pie crust (page 260), chilled
Grated peel of ½ Sunkist lemon	
Juice of 1 Sunkist lemon	

Makes 8 servings.

To make the glaze, in a saucepan, thoroughly combine the sugar and cornstarch; gradually blend in the peach nectar, lemon peel and juice. Cook over medium heat, stirring, until thickened. Chill, stirring occasionally. Arrange half the peaches in the pie crust; pour half the chilled glaze over the peaches. Repeat the layers, ending with the glaze. Chill. Best served 3 hours or so after making.

ORANGE-COCONUT FLAN

Fresh grated orange peel, coconut, and half-and-half enrich the flavor of a packaged pudding mix. This simple filling is then turned into an eye-catching, orange-encircled flan.

1⅔ cups fine vanilla wafer crumbs (30 to 42 wafers)	1 package (about 3½ ounces) instant vanilla pudding and pie filling
⅓ cup butter or margarine, melted	2 cups half-and-half
Grated peel of 1½ Sunkist oranges	¼ cup shredded or flaked coconut, toasted
¼ teaspoon ground cinnamon	2 to 3 Sunkist oranges, peeled and cut into half-cartwheel slices

Makes 6 to 8 servings.

In a bowl, combine the vanilla wafer crumbs, butter, peel of 1 orange, and cinnamon. Press firmly onto the bottom and sides of a 9½- or 10-inch flan, quiche, tart, or pie pan. Bake at 350° F. for 10 minutes. Cool. Meanwhile, in a bowl, prepare the pudding with half-and-half following the package directions; let stand for 5 minutes. Stir in the toasted coconut and remaining orange peel. Spoon into the prepared crust. Arrange orange half-cartwheel slices on the pudding mixture, overlapping slices around outer edges of the flan only, leaving center open. Sprinkle with additional toasted coconut, if desired.

CREAM PUFFS WITH A'PEEL

1 cup water
½ cup butter or margarine
Grated peel of 1 Sunkist orange or lemon
¼ teaspoon salt
1 cup all-purpose flour
4 eggs

Makes 8 cream puffs.

In a saucepan, combine the water, butter, peel, and salt; bring to a boil. Reduce heat to low. With a wooden spoon, quickly stir in the flour until the mixture forms a ball and leaves the sides of the pan; remove from heat. Beat the eggs into the mixture, one at a time, until thoroughly blended. On a greased baking sheet, spoon dough (or squeeze through a pastry tube) into eight mounds, about 3 inches apart. Bake at 375° F. for 45 minutes. Remove from oven and cut a slit in the side of each puff. Bake 10 minutes longer. Cool on wire racks. Cut each puff in half horizontally; remove any damp center.

FILLING SUGGESTION: Fill the cream puff shells with your favorite vanilla or chocolate ice cream *or* with Fresh Bananas and Orange Ice Cream (page 209) and orange sections or pieces. Replace the tops and sprinkle with confectioners' sugar.

FILLING SUGGESTION: Fill the cream puff shells with *cooled* Easy Lemon Meringue Pie *filling* (page 250). Replace the tops and sprinkle with confectioners' sugar.

TINT OF MINT GRAPEFRUIT CHARLOTTE RUSSE

1 envelope unflavored gelatine
1 cup fresh squeezed grapefruit juice
4 eggs, separated
½ cup sugar
¼ teaspoon salt
¼ cup mint-flavored apple jelly
2 to 3 drops green food coloring (optional)
1 tablespoon fresh grated grapefruit peel
16 to 20 ladyfingers, split
1 cup heavy cream or whipping cream, whipped

Makes 12 servings.

Soften the gelatine in the grapefruit juice. In the top of a double boiler, with an electric mixer, beat the egg yolks well with ¼ cup of the sugar, and salt. Gradually beat in the gelatine mixture, mint jelly, and food coloring. Cook over boiling water, stirring constantly, until the mixture *starts* to thicken, about 10 minutes. Pour into a large bowl; add the grapefruit peel. Chill until mixture begins to thicken, about 1 hour, stirring occasionally. Meanwhile, line the bottom and sides of an 8- or 9 × 3-inch springform pan with ladyfingers. With clean beaters, beat the egg whites until foamy. Gradually add the remaining ¼ cup of sugar, beating until soft peaks form. Fold the beaten egg whites and whipped cream into the grapefruit-gelatine mixture. Spoon into ladyfinger-lined pan. Chill for 4 hours or overnight. Carefully remove the sides of the springform pan. Garnish with grapefruit sections and fresh mint leaves, if desired.

THE CLASSIC LEMON CHARLOTTE RUSSE

This recipe, once tried, becomes like a friend . . . never forgotten and invited to many special occasions.

1 envelope unflavored gelatine
½ cup fresh squeezed lemon juice
4 eggs, separated
1 cup sugar
¼ teaspoon salt
Grated peel of 1 Sunkist lemon
16 to 20 ladyfingers, split
1 cup heavy cream or whipping cream, whipped

Makes 12 servings.

Soften the gelatine in the lemon juice. In the top of a double boiler, with an electric mixer, beat the egg yolks well with ½ cup of the sugar, and salt. Gradually beat in the gelatine mixture. Cook over boiling water, stirring constantly, until the mixture *starts* to thicken, about 10 minutes. Pour into a large bowl; add the lemon peel. Chill until the mixture begins to thicken, about 45 minutes, stirring occasionally. Meanwhile, line the bottom and sides of an 8- or 9 × 3-inch springform pan with ladyfingers. With clean beaters, beat the egg whites until foamy. Gradually add the remaining ½ cup of sugar, beating until soft peaks form. Fold the beaten egg whites and whipped cream into the lemon-gelatine mixture. Spoon into ladyfinger-lined pan. Chill for 4 hours or overnight. Carefully remove the sides of the springform pan. Garnish with lemon cartwheel slices and fresh mint leaves, if desired.

ALL-PURPOSE PIE CRUST

1½ cups all-purpose flour
½ teaspoon salt
½ cup vegetable shortening
4 to 5 tablespoons cold water

In a large bowl, sift together the flour and salt. With a pastry blender or two knives, cut in shortening until pieces are the size of small peas. Gradually add the water, tossing mixture with a fork to incorporate *just* enough moisture so that mixture can be formed into a ball. Flatten onto a lightly floured board. Roll out to an 11- to 12-inch circle. Line a 9- or 10-inch pie plate with the pastry and flute the edges as desired. Prick bottom and sides well with a fork; chill for 30 minutes or longer, then bake at 450° F. for 10 to 12 minutes; cool. Makes a 9- or 10-inch pie crust.

UNBAKED PIESHELL: Do not prick bottom and sides; chill for 30 minutes or longer. Use for Orange-Cream Cheese Pie (page 256). Prick bottom and sides. Use for Springtime Asparagus Quiche (page 153).

PASTRY FOR 2-CRUST PIE: Double ingredients and *mix* as above. Divide dough and roll out each half. Use for Double-Crust Lemon Pie (page 253).

Beverages

In 1916, Sunkist introduced America to a whole new idea: "Drink an Orange." The Sunkist-designed glass citrus reamer helped fresh-squeezed orange juice become a morning ritual.

Later, Sunkist suggested a wedge of fresh lemon in iced tea, another innovation that became standard practice. And, of course, old-fashioned homemade fresh lemonade has long been a favorite refresher.

Today's light meals and active lifestyles have encouraged more trendsetter ideas from our kitchens: mock-cocktails. Instead of serving plain soft drinks or mineral waters, offer your guests a selection of delicious non-alcoholic beverages. With one of our easy and dramatic citrus garnishes, these richly colored and flavored drinks are beautiful and satisfying.

Build a handsome buffet table around a refreshing bowl of citrus punch, complete with a showy Citrus Ice Ring (page 279). Or serve an ice cream-based orange dessert drink as the perfect finale to a delicious dinner.

From the neighborhood lemonade stand to elegant entertaining, count on citrus beverages to quench your thirst and brighten any gathering.

BEVERAGES

REAL OLD-FASHIONED LEMONADE
LEMONADE SYRUP BASE
LOW-CAL MINTY LEMONADE
HOT BUTTERED LEMONADE
TANGY ORANGEADE
LEMON APPLEADE
LEMON AND MINT ICED TEA
SPICED CITRUS ICED TEA
HOT RUSSIAN TEA
MINTED CITRUS COOLER (GROWER RECIPE)
FRESH GRAPEFRUIT AND ORANGE COOLER
TWOSOME ORANGE-CRAN NOG
LOW CALORIE FRUIT NOG
BANANA FLIP
STRAWBERRY ORANGE FROSTEE
GRAPEFRUIT AND BERRY FROTH
ORANGE "EGGNOG" SHAKE
3 ORANGE "SODA"
OLD-FASHIONED RAMOS FIZZ
SANGRIA ROSÉ
SANGRIA BLANCA
CITRUS GOLD RIESLING PUNCH
HOT CRAN-LEMON WINE PUNCH
DOUBLE ORANGE CHAMPAGNE PUNCH
LEMON PINK CHAMPAGNE PUNCH
SPARKLING FRUIT PUNCH
CROWD-PLEASING SPICED PUNCH
ORANGE GRAND FINALE
CAFÉ BRÛLOT
ORANGE OR LEMON BRANDY
LIVELY LEMON LIQUEUR
"MADE-AT-HOME" ORANGE FLAVORED COFFEE MIX

REAL OLD-FASHIONED LEMONADE

A Sunkist classic . . . zesty, thirst-quenching, and not too sweet.

Juice of 6 Sunkist lemons (1 cup)
¾ cup sugar, or to taste
4 cups cold water

1 Sunkist lemon, cut into cartwheel slices
Ice cubes

Makes about 6 cups (six 8-ounce servings).

In a large pitcher, combine the lemon juice and sugar; stir to dissolve the sugar. Add the remaining ingredients and blend well.

"PINK LEMONADE" VARIATION: Add a few drops of red food coloring or grenadine syrup.

HONEYED LEMONADE VARIATION: Substitute honey to taste for the sugar.

LEMONADE SYRUP BASE

This lemonade base is one to keep on hand. Serve it hot or serve it cold, serve it by the pitcherful!

BASE MIXTURE
1½ cups sugar
½ cup boiling water
Grated peel of 1 Sunkist lemon

1½ cups fresh squeezed lemon juice

Makes about 2⅔ cups base.

Combine the sugar and boiling water; stir to dissolve the sugar. Add the lemon peel and lemon juice. Store in a covered container in the refrigerator.

LEMONADE BY THE GLASS

¼ to ⅓ cup Lemonade Syrup Base
¾ cup cold water
Ice cubes

Makes one 8-ounce serving.

In a large glass, combine all the ingredients and stir well.

LEMONADE BY THE PITCHER

2⅔ cups Lemonade Syrup Base
5 cups cold water
Ice cubes

Makes about 8 cups (eight 8-ounce servings).

In a large pitcher, combine all the ingredients and stir well.

HOT LEMONADE BY THE MUG

¼ cup Lemonade Syrup Base
¾ cup boiling water

Makes one 8-ounce serving.

Preheat a mug with hot tap water. Pour the base and boiling water into the mug and stir.

LOW-CAL MINTY LEMONADE

2 cups cold water
Juice of 3 Sunkist lemons (½ cup)
Low calorie sugar substitute to equal ¼ cup sugar*
⅛ teaspoon mint extract
4 drops green food coloring (optional)
1 can (12 ounces) low calorie lemon-lime flavored soda, chilled
Ice cubes
½ Sunkist lemon, cut into cartwheel slices

Makes about 4 cups (four 8-ounce servings).
About 15 calories and 18 mg. sodium per serving.

*For a few more calories use ¼ cup sugar in place of sugar substitute.

In a large pitcher, combine the water, lemon juice, sugar substitute, mint extract, and food coloring. To serve, add soda, ice, and lemon cartwheel slices. Garnish with fresh mint, if desired.

HOT BUTTERED LEMONADE

A warmer-upper in wintertime or on a chilly spring or fall evening. The optional rum makes it an adult pleaser.

Grated peel of ½ Sunkist lemon
Juice of 3 Sunkist lemons (½ cup)
3 cups water
½ cup sugar
¼ cup light rum (optional)
1 tablespoon butter or margarine

Makes about 4 cups (five 6-ounce servings).

In a saucepan, combine all the ingredients and heat.

TANGY ORANGEADE

Here's an old-time classic updated with the convenience of ready-to-drink chilled orange juice available in supermarket dairy departments. If you're a traditionalist, make this easy, tangy cooler with fresh squeezed O.J.

Juice of 6 Sunkist lemons (1 cup)
¾ to 1 cup sugar
1 quart Sunkist chilled orange juice
Ice cubes

Makes about 5½ cups (six 7-ounce servings).

In a large pitcher, combine the lemon juice and sugar; stir to dissolve the sugar. Add the orange juice. Serve over ice. Garnish with orange and lemon cartwheel slices, if desired.

FRESH O.J. VARIATION: Substitute 3 to 4 cups fresh squeezed orange juice for the chilled orange juice.

LEMON APPLEADE

BASE MIXTURE

½ cup sugar
¾ cup boiling water
Grated peel of ½ Sunkist lemon

Juice of 6 Sunkist lemons (1 cup)
2 cups apple juice, chilled

Makes about 4 cups base.

Dissolve the sugar in the boiling water. Add the lemon peel and fruit juices. Store in a covered container in the refrigerator.

LEMON APPLEADE BY THE GLASS

½ cup Lemon Appleade base
⅓ to ½ cup water or club soda

Ice cubes

Makes one 8-ounce serving.

In a large glass, combine all the ingredients and stir well.

LEMON APPLEADE BY THE PITCHER

4 cups Lemon Appleade base
1 bottle (1 Liter) club soda, chilled, *or* 4 cups water

Ice cubes

Makes about 8 cups (eight 8-ounce servings).

In a large pitcher, combine all the ingredients and stir well.

LEMON AND MINT ICED TEA

Mint adds an extra liveliness to this refreshing lemony iced tea.

3 cups boiling water
6 tea bags*
1 teaspoon chopped fresh mint, *or* ¼ teaspoon dried mint flakes
¾ cup sugar
3 cups cold water
Juice of 3 Sunkist lemons (½ cup)
Ice cubes
Lemon cartwheel slices

Makes about 7 cups (seven 8-ounce servings).

Pour the boiling water over the tea bags and mint. Cover and steep for 5 minutes; strain. In a large pitcher, combine the tea and sugar; stir to dissolve the sugar. Add the cold water and lemon juice; cool. Serve over ice in tall glasses. Garnish with lemon cartwheel slices.

*Or use 2 family size tea bags or 2 tablespoons of loose tea.

SPICED CITRUS ICED TEA

For a real citrus flavor, the outer colored peel of oranges or lemons, rich in natural oils, is chilled with the spiced tea mixture. Sweeten, if desired, with a touch of sugar, honey, or orange-flavored liqueur.

2 Sunkist lemons *or* oranges
6 cups boiling water
5 tea bags
12 whole cloves
2 cinnamon sticks
Ice cubes
Sugar, honey, or orange-flavored liqueur, to taste (optional)

Makes about 6 cups (six 6-ounce servings).

With a vegetable parer, peel each lemon *or* orange in a continuous spiral, removing the outer colored layer of peel only. (Save the fruit for other uses.) Pour the boiling water over the tea bags, spices, and peel. Cover and steep for 5 minutes. Remove the tea bags and spices; chill the tea mixture with peel. To serve, remove the peel and serve the tea over ice. Sweeten with sugar, honey, or orange-flavored liqueur to taste and serve with cinnamon stick stirrers, if desired.

HOT RUSSIAN TEA

The Russians prefer their hot tea sweetened and with plenty of fresh lemon. Sometimes spices are added. Here's our version for you to enjoy.

3 cups boiling water	1 strip (about 3 inches) fresh orange peel
3 tea bags	⅓ cup sugar
20 whole cloves	Juice of 2 Sunkist oranges
1 cinnamon stick	Juice of 1 Sunkist lemon

Makes about 3½ cups (five 6-ounce servings).

Pour the boiling water over the tea bags, spices, and orange peel. Cover and steep for 5 minutes; strain. Stir in the sugar, orange and lemon juices; heat. Garnish with lemon cartwheel slices studded with whole cloves, if desired.

MINTED CITRUS COOLER
Nancy Graham, *Ventura, California*
(Grower recipe contest winner)

Nancy's mother first prepared this cooling citrus punch for her daughter's engagement party. Today, Nancy lives with her husband John and their three children in a wonderful family home that has housed four generations of Grahams. The surrounding 20-acre ranch produces the juicy lemons and oranges that flavor many of the foods and beverages from Nancy's kitchen.

3½ cups pineapple juice
3 cups fresh squeezed orange juice
1½ cups fresh squeezed lemon juice
⅓ cup fresh squeezed lime juice
2 cups sugar
15 to 20 fresh mint leaves
1 bottle (1 Liter) ginger ale, chilled
1 bottle (1 Liter) club soda, chilled
Ice cubes
1 Sunkist orange and 1 lemon, cut into cartwheel slices

Makes about 18 cups (eighteen 8-ounce servings).

In a large glass container, combine the fruit juices, sugar, and mint leaves; stir to dissolve the sugar. Cover and chill for 4 hours or overnight. Remove the fresh mint with a slotted spoon. To serve, in large punch bowl, combine the juice mixture with the remaining ingredients.

FRESH GRAPEFRUIT AND ORANGE COOLER

Juice of 2 Sunkist grapefruit
Juice of 2 Sunkist oranges
¼ cup sugar
1 bottle (1 Liter) lemon-lime flavored soda, chilled
Ice cubes
Orange half-cartwheel slices
Fresh mint leaves

Makes about 6 cups (six 8-ounce servings).

In a large pitcher, combine the fruit juices and sugar; stir to dissolve the sugar. Add soda and ice cubes. Garnish with orange half-cartwheel slices and fresh mint.

TWOSOME ORANGE-CRAN NOG

A quick "breakfast-on-the-run" for two, or a fruity refresher anytime. Milk can be substituted for the cream, if desired.

1 cup crushed ice	¼ cup light cream or half-and-half
½ cup fresh squeezed orange juice	2 eggs
½ cup cranberry juice cocktail	2 tablespoons sugar
	2 orange cartwheel slices

Makes two 8-ounce servings.

In a blender, combine all the ingredients *except* the orange cartwheel slices; blend until smooth. Pour into two 10-ounce glasses. Garnish each serving with an orange cartwheel slice.

LOW CALORIE FRUIT NOG

Light in calories, yet long in fruit flavor, this beverage satisfies any time of day.

Juice of 1 Sunkist orange	Low calorie sugar substitute to equal 2 teaspoons sugar
½ medium banana, cut into chunks	2 to 3 ice cubes
¼ cup nonfat milk	
1 egg white	

Makes two 6-ounce servings.
About 67 calories and 42 mg. sodium per serving.

In a blender, combine all the ingredients and blend until smooth.

STRAWBERRY VARIATION: Substitute ½ cup strawberries for the banana. About 52 calories and 42 mg. sodium per serving.

BANANA FLIP

1 cup crushed ice
Juice of 1 Sunkist orange
⅓ cup light cream or half-and-half

1 small banana, cut into chunks
1 tablespoon sugar

Makes two 6-ounce servings.

In a blender, combine all the ingredients and blend until smooth. Pour into two 8-ounce glasses. Garnish each serving with an orange cartwheel slice, banana chunk, and fresh mint, if desired.

MILK VARIATION: Substitute lowfat or whole milk for the cream.

STRAWBERRY ORANGE FROSTEE

Fresh fruit drinks are "blender easy." This strawberry and fresh orange cooler looks as good as it tastes.

½ cup crushed ice
Juice of 1 Sunkist orange
7 fresh or frozen strawberries

2 teaspoons sugar
1 orange cartwheel twist

Makes one 8-ounce serving.
About 100 calories and 3 mg. sodium per serving.

In a blender, combine the ice, orange juice, 6 strawberries, and sugar; blend until smooth. Pour into a large champagne glass. Garnish with an orange cartwheel twist and a strawberry.

GRAPEFRUIT AND BERRY FROTH

An unlikely combination... fresh grapefruit juice, berries, and pineapple sherbet? Not really. The result is a cool, colorful, not-too-sweet sippin' treat.

Juice of 2 Sunkist grapefruit (1½ cups)	1 pint pineapple sherbet, softened
1 cup fresh or frozen raspberries, strawberries, *or* boysenberries	

Makes about 3½ cups (four 7-ounce servings).

In a food processor or blender, combine all the ingredients and blend until smooth.

ORANGE "EGGNOG" SHAKE

½ can (3 ounces) Sunkist frozen concentrated orange juice, thawed	1 quart vanilla ice cream, softened
	¼ teaspoon ground nutmeg

Makes about 4 cups (four 8-ounce servings).

In a food processor or blender, combine the orange juice, half the ice cream, and nutmeg; blend *just* until smooth. Add the remaining ice cream and blend until smooth but still thick.

3 ORANGE "SODA"

The soda fountain in the old drugstore may never have served an orange soda like this, but when you feel like a kid, try this grown-up version. For the "real" kids, omit the orange liqueur.

1 can (12 ounces) Sunkist orange carbonated soft drink
2 small scoops orange sherbet
2 small scoops vanilla ice cream
2 to 4 tablespoons orange-flavored liqueur (optional)
Fresh mint leaves

Makes 2 servings.

In two 12-ounce soda glasses, divide the orange soft drink. Carefully top each serving with 1 scoop of sherbet and 1 scoop of vanilla ice cream. Pour the orange liqueur over each, as desired. Garnish with fresh mint.

OLD-FASHIONED RAMOS FIZZ

Many cities are known for a particular food or beverage: San Francisco for cioppino, Buffalo for chicken wings, Chicago for pizza. This airy, slightly tart drink, is but one of New Orleans' contributions. For brunch, it's a winner.

Juice of ½ Sunkist lemon
½ cup crushed ice
1 egg white
1½ ounces heavy cream or half-and-half
1 to 1½ ounces gin
1 tablespoon confectioners' sugar, or to taste
3 drops orange flower water

Makes one 7-ounce serving.

In a cocktail shaker, combine all the ingredients and shake well (about 1 minute). Strain into a chilled fizz or other 8-ounce glass.

SANGRIA ROSÉ

Juice of 2 Sunkist oranges
Juice of 1 Sunkist lemon
¼ cup sugar
1 bottle (750 mL) rosé wine, chilled
1 can (12 ounces) lemon-lime flavored soda, chilled
¼ cup brandy
Orange and lemon cartwheel slices
Ice cubes

Makes about 6 cups (six 8-ounce servings).

In a large pitcher, combine the orange juice, lemon juice, and sugar; stir to dissolve the sugar. Add the remaining ingredients and stir well.

RED WINE VARIATION: Substitute Burgundy or other red wine for rosé wine.

SANGRIA BLANCA

This white sangria has been a winner at many a Cinco de Mayo gathering. But you don't need a special occasion, just friends to enjoy it.

½ cup fresh squeezed orange juice
½ cup fresh squeezed lemon juice
½ cup sugar
1 bottle (750 mL) Chablis or other dry white wine, chilled
1 bottle (10 ounces) club soda, chilled
¼ cup Curaçao or other orange-flavored liqueur
1 Sunkist lemon, cut into cartwheel slices
Ice cubes

Makes about 6 cups (six 8-ounce servings).

In a large pitcher, combine the orange juice, lemon juice, and sugar; stir to dissolve the sugar. Add the remaining ingredients and stir well. Garnish each serving with an orange cartwheel twist, a strawberry, and fresh mint, if desired.

LOWER IN CALORIE VARIATION: Omit the sugar and club soda. Substitute 1 can (12 ounces) low calorie lemon-lime flavored soda.

CITRUS GOLD RIESLING PUNCH

For a bridal shower, retirement party, or class reunion, this smooth citrus punch is enlivened with white wine and vodka.

2 cups boiling water
2 tea bags
1½ cups sugar
1 can (6 ounces) Sunkist frozen concentrated orange juice, reconstituted
2 cups fresh squeezed lemon juice
1 bottle (750 mL) Riesling or other dry white wine
1 cup vodka
Ice cubes
1 Sunkist orange, cut into half-cartwheel slices

Makes about 12 cups (sixteen 6-ounce servings).

Pour the boiling water over the tea bags; cover and steep for 5 minutes. Remove the tea bags. Add the sugar, orange and lemon juices; stir to dissolve the sugar. Chill. To serve, combine the juice-tea mixture, wine, vodka, and ice in a large punch bowl. Float orange half-cartwheel slices in the punch.

FRESH O.J. VARIATION: Substitute 3 cups fresh squeezed orange juice for the frozen juice.

HOT CRAN-LEMON WINE PUNCH

3 cups water
¾ to 1 cup sugar
20 whole cloves
2 cinnamon sticks
1 bottle (32 ounces) cranberry juice cocktail
1 bottle (750 mL) rosé wine
Juice of 6 Sunkist lemons (1 cup)

Makes about 11 cups (seventeen 5-ounce servings).

In a saucepot, combine the water, sugar, and spices. Bring to a boil; stir to dissolve the sugar. Reduce heat and simmer for 5 minutes. Remove the spices. Add the remaining ingredients and heat. Float lemon cartwheel slices studded with whole cloves in the punch, if desired.

CHILLED PUNCH VARIATION: After simmering the water, sugar, and spices, chill spiced mixture. To serve, remove the cloves and cinnamon; in a large punch bowl, combine the spiced mixture and remaining ingredients. Add ½ cup brandy (optional). Add ice or float a Citrus Ice Ring (page 279).

DOUBLE ORANGE CHAMPAGNE PUNCH

For an added touch and a conversation piece as well, float a Citrus Ice Ring (page 279) in this double orange-flavored champagne punch. Omit the ice cubes and citrus cartwheel slices.

2 bottles (750 mL each) champagne, chilled
1 bottle (1 Liter) club soda, chilled
1 can (6 ounces) Sunkist frozen concentrated orange juice, thawed
½ cup Curaçao or other orange-flavored liqueur
½ cup brandy (optional)
Ice cubes
Orange and lemon cartwheel slices

Makes about 12 cups (sixteen 6-ounce servings).

In a large punch bowl, combine the champagne, club soda, concentrated orange juice, Curaçao, and brandy. Add ice. Float orange and lemon cartwheel slices in the punch.

LEMON PINK CHAMPAGNE PUNCH

Juice of 6 Sunkist lemons (1 cup)
1 cup sugar
1 bottle (750 mL) Chablis or other dry white wine, chilled
1 bottle (750 mL) pink champagne, chilled
1 bottle (1 Liter) club soda, chilled
½ cup brandy (optional)
½ cup Curaçao or other orange-flavored liqueur (optional)
Citrus Ice Ring (page 279)

Makes about 11 cups (seventeen 5-ounce servings).

In a large punch bowl, combine lemon juice and sugar; stir to dissolve the sugar. Add Chablis, champagne, soda, brandy, and Curaçao. Float Citrus Ice Ring in punch.

CITRUS ICE RING

1 Sunkist lemon, cut into cartwheel slices	1 Sunkist orange, cut into half-cartwheel slices
	Fresh mint leaves

Fill a 1½-quart metal ring mold half full with water. Freeze until firm. Arrange the citrus slices and fresh mint on top of the ice ring. Add water to cover the citrus to within ¼ inch of the rim of the mold; freeze. To unmold the ice ring, place the metal mold briefly in warm water; remove the Citrus Ice Ring and float in punch.

SPARKLING FRUIT PUNCH

This sparkling punch is an excellent blending of fruit flavors, not too sweet and not too tart.

Juice of 3 Sunkist oranges	1 can (12 ounces) lemon-lime flavored soda (regular or low calorie), chilled
Juice of 1 Sunkist lemon	
1 can (6 ounces) unsweetened pineapple juice, chilled	
	Ice cubes
1 can (6 ounces) apple juice, chilled	Orange cartwheel slices
	Lemon cartwheel slices

Makes about 4 cups (four 8-ounce servings).

In a large pitcher, combine the fruit juices and soda. Add the ice, orange and lemon cartwheel slices and stir well.

CROWD-PLEASING SPICED PUNCH

For non-alcoholic entertaining with the "taste-of-the-grape" this fruity punch is sure to be a crowd pleaser.

4 cups water	1 bottle (24 ounces) white grape juice, chilled
⅔ cup sugar	Juice of 6 Sunkist lemons (1 cup)
20 whole cloves	Ice cubes
2 cinnamon sticks	
1 bottle (32 ounces) apple cider, chilled	

Makes about 12 cups (sixteen 6-ounce servings).

In a saucepan, combine the water, sugar, and spices. Bring to a boil; stir to dissolve the sugar. Reduce heat and simmer for 5 minutes. Chill; remove the spices. To serve, combine all the ingredients in a punch bowl. Float lemon cartwheel slices in the punch, if desired.

ORANGE GRAND FINALE

A dessert and after-dinner drink all in one!

2 Sunkist oranges, peeled and cut into chunks	1 quart vanilla ice cream, softened
½ cup orange- or almond-flavored liqueur	Whipped cream
	Grated chocolate or chocolate curls
	Fresh grated orange peel

Makes about 4 cups (four 8-ounce servings).

In a food processor or blender, combine the orange chunks and liqueur; blend until smooth. Add half the ice cream and blend *just* until smooth. Repeat with remaining ice cream. To serve, pour into 4 brandy snifters or other stemmed glasses. Garnish with whipped cream, chocolate, and grated orange peel.

CAFÉ BRÛLOT

Café Brûlot is an elegant ending to a fine meal. Lightly sweetened coffee is infused with brandy, Curaçao, and the citrus oils of fresh orange and lemon.

12 sugar cubes	¾ cup brandy
1 Sunkist orange	¼ cup Curaçao or other
1 Sunkist lemon	orange-flavored liqueur
12 whole cloves	4 cups hot strong black coffee
2 cinnamon sticks	

Makes about 4½ cups (six 6-ounce servings).

To extract some of the citrus oils, rub 6 sugar cubes over the whole unpeeled orange and 6 over the lemon. With a vegetable parer, peel the orange and lemon in continuous spirals, removing the outer colored layer of peel only. (Save the fruit for other uses.) In a chafing dish or large skillet, place the sugar cubes, orange and lemon peels, cloves, and cinnamon. Add the brandy and liqueur. With the back of a wooden spoon, crush the sugar cubes and peel into the liquor. Quickly heat until the liquid begins to bubble. With a metal ladle, dip out a small amount of liquid; carefully ignite it. Pour over the remaining liquid in the chafing dish to ignite. Slowly pour in the hot coffee, stirring until the flames die. Ladle into cups. Garnish each with a cinnamon stick wrapped with additional peel and secured with a whole clove, if desired.

ORANGE OR LEMON BRANDY

1 Sunkist orange *or* lemon   1 cup sugar
3 cups brandy

Makes about 2½ cups.

With a vegetable parer, peel the orange *or* lemon in a continuous spiral, removing the outer colored layer of peel only. (Save the fruit for other uses.) Place the peel and brandy in a jar with a tight-fitting lid. Let stand one week; shake occasionally. Remove the peel. Add the sugar; shake until the sugar dissolves. Let stand seven days longer. Serve as a drink straight or over crushed ice. For dessert, pour over fresh fruits or vanilla ice cream.

LIVELY LEMON LIQUEUR

This is definitely a liqueur with a kick! But also a pleasant, surprise ending to a meal when served over vanilla ice cream.

2 Sunkist lemons   1 cup sugar
2 cups vodka

Makes about 2½ cups.

With a vegetable parer, peel the lemons in continuous spirals, removing the outer colored layer of peel only. (Save the fruit; squeeze the juice for other uses). Place the lemon peel and vodka in a jar with a tight-fitting lid. Let stand for one week; shake occasionally. Remove the lemon peel. Add the sugar and shake until the sugar dissolves. Let stand seven days longer. Serve as a drink straight or over crushed ice. For dessert, serve over fresh fruits or vanilla ice cream.

"MADE-AT-HOME" ORANGE FLAVORED COFFEE MIX

Many flavored instant coffee/chocolate mixes can be found on supermarket shelves. Here's a "made-at-home" version to keep on hand or give as gifts to coffee-loving friends.

2 Sunkist oranges
½ cup powdered instant coffee (not crystals)
¾ cup instant cocoa mix
¾ cup powdered instant non-dairy creamer

Makes about 2 cups mix or 16 servings.

With a vegetable parer, peel the oranges in continuous spirals, removing the outer colored layer of peel only. (Save the fruit for other uses.) Place the peel on a baking sheet and dry in the oven at 200° F. for 2 hours. Place the dried peel and remaining ingredients in a jar with a tight-fitting lid. Store the mix for 1 week or longer to blend flavors; shake occasionally. To serve, spoon 2 level tablespoons of the mix into each cup (leaving dried peel in jar). Add ¾ cup boiling water and stir well.

CINNAMON ORANGE COFFEE VARIATION: Add 2 teaspoons ground cinnamon to the dry mix.

CLOVE ORANGE COFFEE VARIATION: Add ¼ teaspoon ground cloves to the dry mix.

Fresh Citrus Garnishes

A simple, colorful garnish can be almost as important to a recipe as any key ingredient. It's been said that first you "eat with your eyes." The visual feast must precede and tantalize your senses, encouraging you to sample and enjoy the fare. Successful restaurateurs know this and use garnishes, from the simplest parsley sprig or lemon slice, to the most elaborate creations.

Often a simple citrus cartwheel or lemon wedge dipped in paprika is all that's needed to dress a plate to perfection. Most of the garnishes suggested here yield a great return for a very small investment of time. You'll probably find several that will become your own personal signature on frosty beverages, delicate fish dinners, and elegant desserts.

Most of the ingredients are probably staples in your kitchen. But if you're out of parsley, try paprika or substitute a pickle slice for an olive. Experiment with colors, shapes, and flavors. Just a touch of citrus brightens any meal, and adds color and freshness.

Fresh Citrus Garnishes

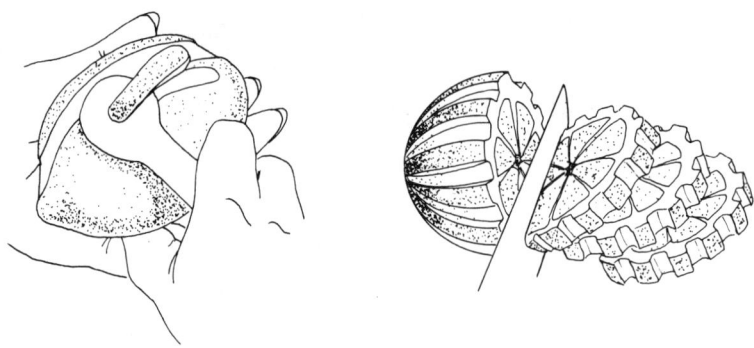

FLUTED CARTWHEEL SLICES: Use a citrus zester or SNACKER™ citrus peeler. Hold the stem and blossom ends of the unpeeled fruit between your thumb and middle finger. Pull the zester through the peel from end to end, leaving about ¼ to ½ inch between each cut. Cut cartwheel slices of desired thickness. If you don't have a citrus tool, use kitchen shears or a knife to cut notches around the peel of each cartwheel slice.

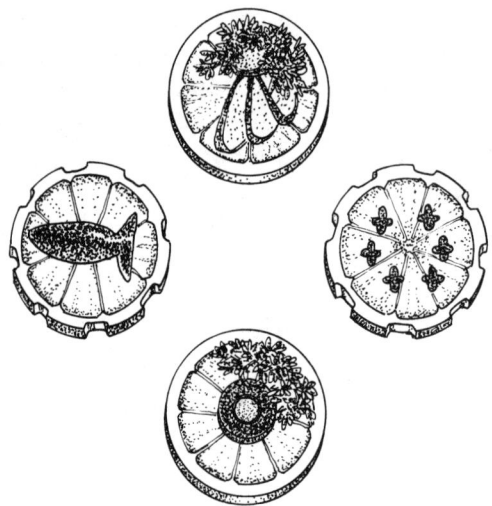

DECORATED CARTWHEEL SLICES: Use any one of the following to decorate cartwheel slices:

>   whole cloves
>   pimiento strips or cutouts
>   pickle fans

sprinkles of paprika, chopped parsley,
    ground cloves or cinnamon
berries
anchovy rolls
maraschino cherries
sculptured mushrooms
sprigs of mint or parsley
broccoli flowerets
sliced stuffed green or ripe (black) olives

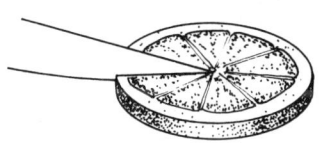 

CARTWHEEL TWISTS: Make one cut from the center of an unpeeled cartwheel slice through the outer peel. Twist the ends in opposite directions, standing the cartwheel gently. Use plain or decorate with parsley or watercress.

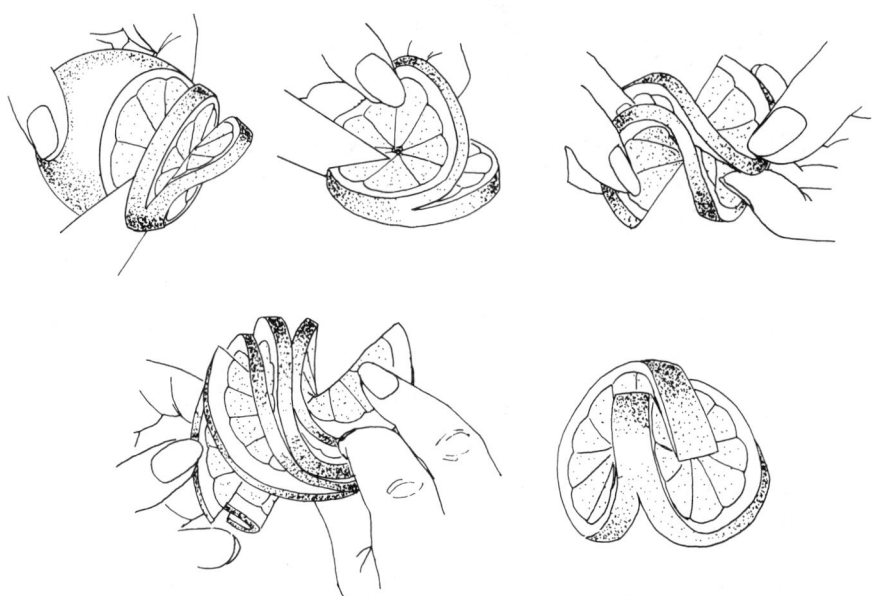

DOUBLE CARTWHEEL TWISTS, FLOWERS, AND BUTTERFLIES: 1. Cut a thin slice from each end of an unpeeled orange or lemon. Cut the fruit crosswise, but not quite through; make a second cut crosswise, cutting off the double cartwheel slice. 2. Make one cut from the center through the outer peel where the slices are attached. 3. Twist the cut ends in opposite directions for "double cartwheel twists." 4. Twist *two* double cartwheel slices together to form a "flower." 5. Bring the cut ends of a double cartwheel slice together and overlap; gently spread the slices to form a "butterfly" garnish.

FANS OR QUARTER CARTWHEEL SLICES: Cut the peeled or unpeeled cartwheels into quarters or sixths.

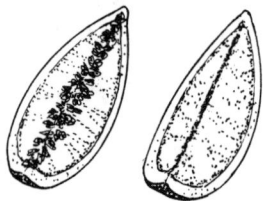

DECORATED WEDGES: The center edge of lemon or orange wedges can be dipped in paprika, chopped parsley or mint, ground cinnamon, cloves, or nutmeg.

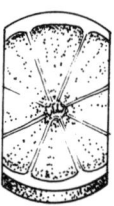

OBLONG SLICES: Cut a small slice off the opposite sides of an unpeeled cartwheel slice. Decorate as desired.

CURLS: Cut half the "meat" from a cartwheel slice, leaving the peel intact. Curl the peel from the cut side to the center of the fruit slice.

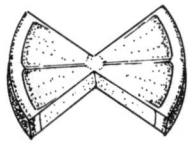

BOW TIES: Cut two pie-shaped wedges on the opposite sides of the unpeeled cartwheel slice, leaving the membrane in the center intact to hold the slice together.

LEMON BOATS: Prepare as for citrus shells (page 290), cutting the lemon in half lengthwise.

CITRUS SHELLS: Cut an orange, grapefruit, or large lemon in half crosswise. Carefully ream out the juice or cut out the "meat" with a curved grapefruit knife. Then scrape the shell "clean" with a spoon. The edges may be notched with kitchen shears or a paring knife; for scallops, use a coin to outline the pattern; then cut around the pattern. To prevent tipping, cut a thin slice from the bottom of the shell. If desired, place in a plastic bag, seal, and store in the refrigerator or freezer until ready to use.

Shells may be used in many ways: for individual servings of ice cream, puddings, fruit cups, or gelatin desserts; for holding cranberry and other sauces; or for nuts and candy.

Fresh Citrus Garnishes

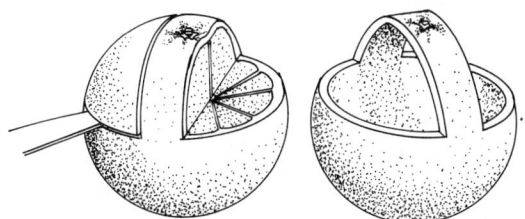

BASKETS: Using unpeeled fruit, make two cuts from the stem end, cutting straight down to the center of the fruit, and leaving about ¼ inch of peel on either side of the stem. Finish cutting two wedges from the fruit by making two horizontal cuts just meeting the vertical cuts. This leaves a handle; carefully cut away the "meat" from the handle, leaving it attached to the basket. Carefully cut out the "meat" from the basket or bottom half of the fruit; scrape "clean" with a spoon.

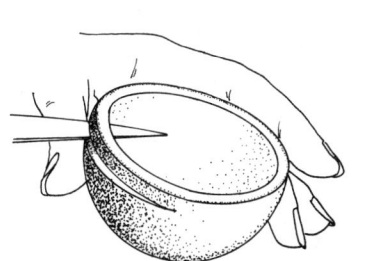 

For another type of basket, cut the fruit in half crosswise. Cut around the "meat" and carefully remove; reserve for use in salads, etc. Scrape the shells "clean" with a spoon. Cut a ¼-inch strip around the top of each shell, leaving about ½ inch intact on each side. Pull the strips together at the center and tie with ribbon or string.

Baskets are perfect for small flowers, votive candles, or to hold nuts and candy.

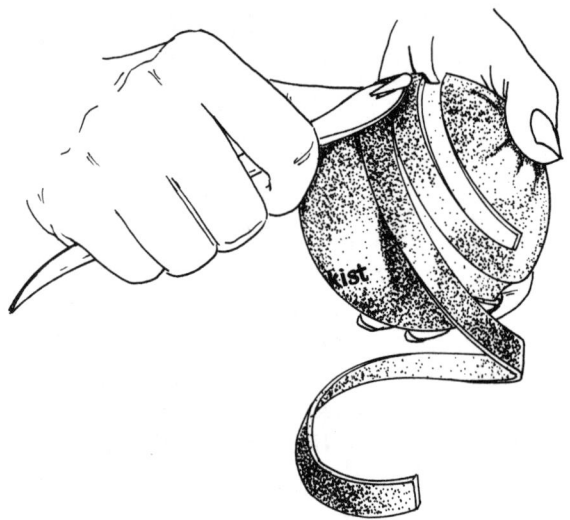

CITRUS PEEL STRIPS: With a sharp knife, zester, or SNACKER™ citrus peeler, cut a narrow strip of peel from the fruit in a circular fashion. Use to wrap around vegetable bunches or in special drinks.

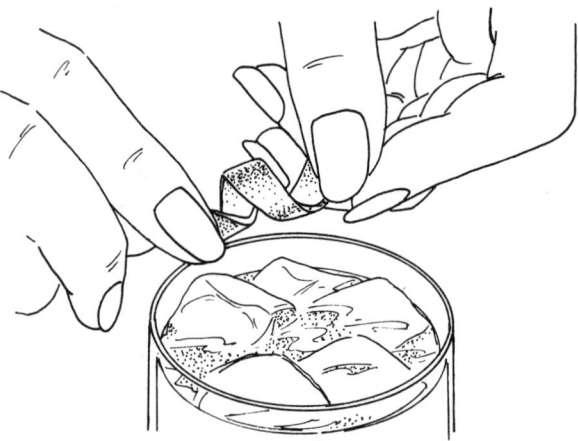

LEMON TWISTS: Give 2-inch strips of lemon peel a "twist" before dropping them into your favorite beverage. Twisting the peel releases the fragrant lemon oils.

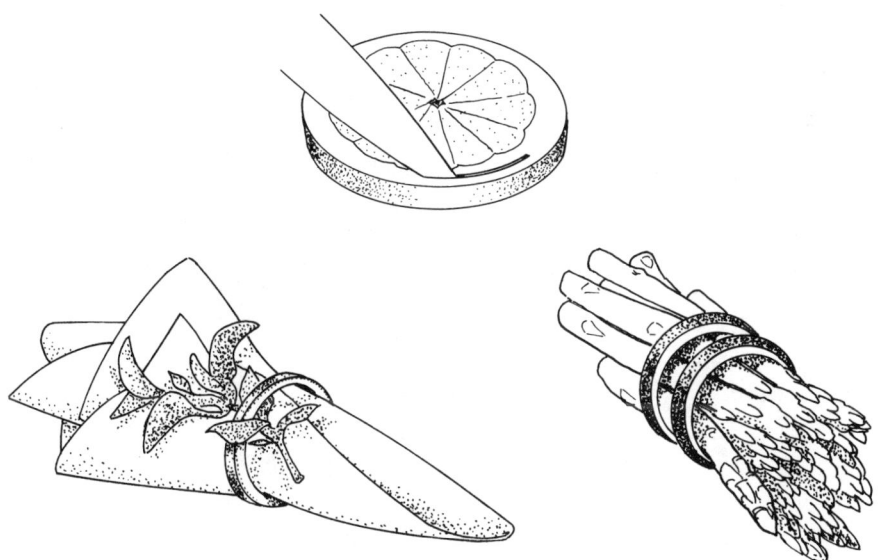

LEMON RINGS: Cut a lemon into cartwheel slices. With a knife or your fingers, carefully remove the "meat" from the lemon, leaving the peel intact. Use lemon rings as napkin rings or to encircle small bunches of cooked asparagus, broccoli spears, green beans, or carrot sticks. (Use the peeled lemon slices as desired for cooking or garnishing fish.)

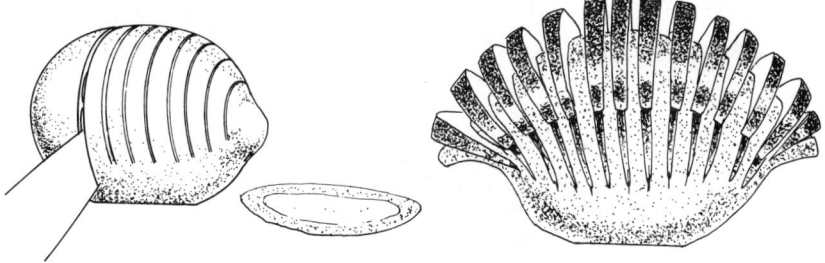

LEMON CUCUMBERS: To prevent tipping, cut a thin slice from one side of the lemon. Make 12 to 16 vertical cuts, three-quarters of the way through the lemon. Insert half-slices of unpeeled cucumber or zucchini into the cuts. This is an attractive garnish for large serving platters.

294 Fresh Citrus Garnishes

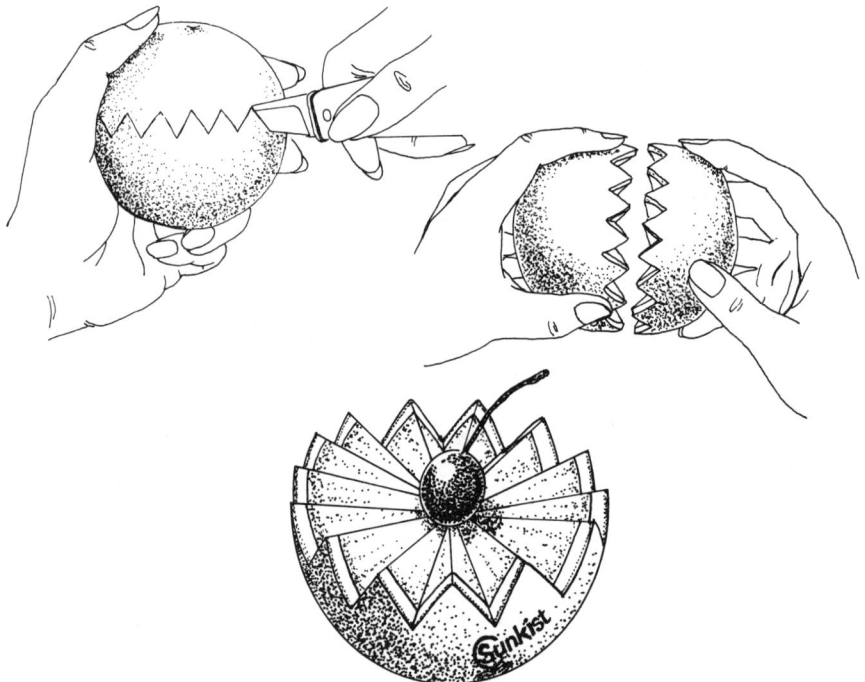

STAR GARNISHES: 1. Hold the stem and blossom ends of unpeeled fruit between your thumb and middle finger. With a knife, make sawtooth-cuts around the middle, cutting to the inside center only. Cut sharply through to allow clean separation. 2. Twist and gently pull the fruit apart to provide two star garnishes. 3. An attractive way to serve grapefruit halves, or to serve individual lemon stars with seafood entrées.

STAR CUPS: With a grapefruit knife, remove the "meat" from the star garnish, leaving enough "meat" next to the peel for color. You

can also juice or remove all the "meat" and then scrape the shells clean with a spoon. Fill with berries, sherbets, pudding, or relishes.

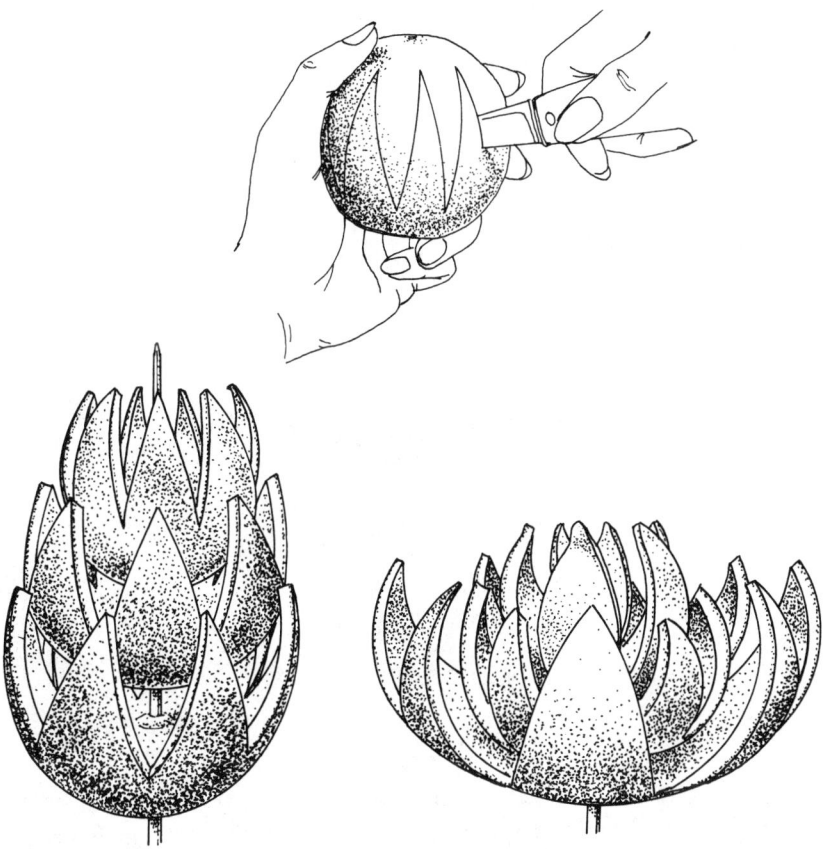

CHRYSANTHEMUM FLOWERS: 1. Make long sawtooth-cuts around unpeeled oranges, lemons, grapefruit or tangerines, cutting to within ¾ inch of each end of fruit. Separate the two halves of the fruit. Keeping the peel intact, remove the "meat" from the peel with a spoon or your fingers; save the "meat" for use in fruit cups. Scrape the peel "clean" with a spoon. Place the flowers on wooden skewers; cut the skewer "stem" to the desired length. Surround with watercress or other greens. 2. and 3. For a more spectacular flower, start with a grapefruit "mum," fill with an orange "mum" and then a lemon or tangerine "mum." If the flowers are not to be used for some time, place them in cold water or a plastic bag and refrigerate.

CHRYSANTHEMUM SALAD BOWLS: After cutting the grapefruit or large oranges for chrysanthemums and removing the "meat," scrape the peel "clean" with a spoon. Use the "bowls" for fresh fruit or tossed salad.

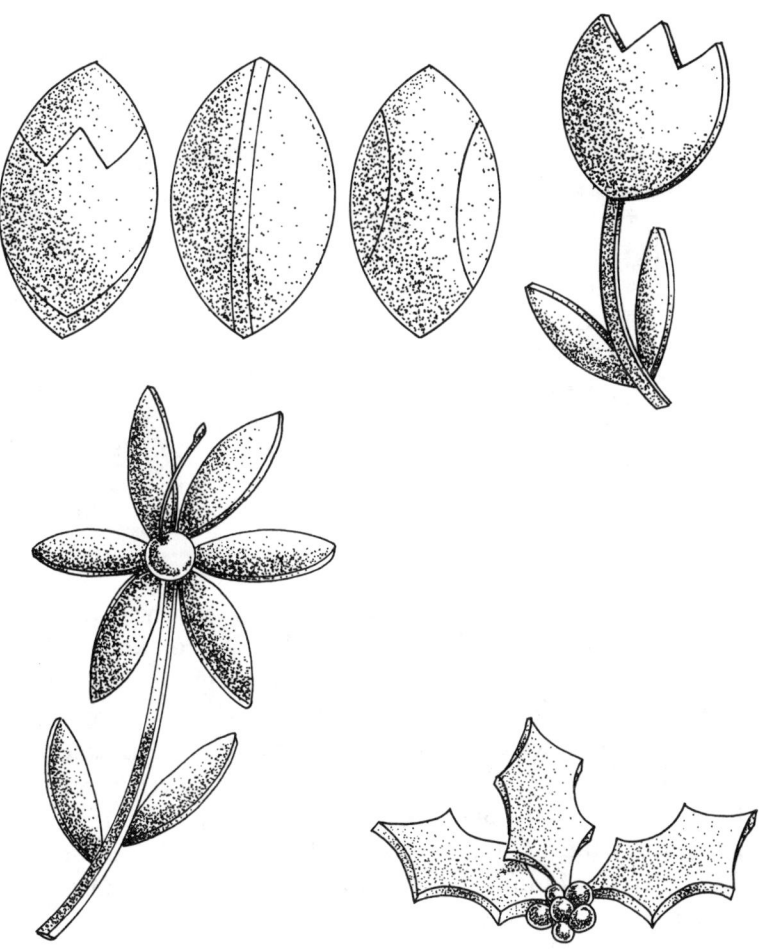

ORANGE PEEL FLOWERS: Score the peel of a large orange lengthwise into quarters; remove the peel with your fingers. With a paring knife or kitchen shears, cut the peel quarters into petal, stem, and leaf shapes of a tulip, poinsettia, or holly. Attach the flower to ham or other meat with toothpick halves just before the glaze is added. Remove the toothpicks before serving; the flower will cling to the meat. Or position flower on top of a cake or molded salad shortly before serving.

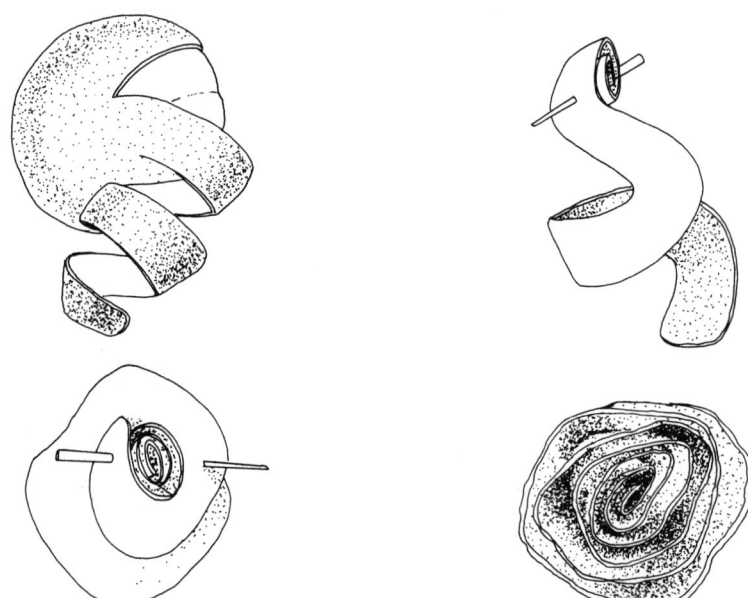

CITRUS ROSES: 1. Roses can be made from grapefruit, orange, lemon, and tangerine peel. With a vegetable parer or knife, cut a thin continuous spiral from the outer colored layer of the citrus peel, about 1 inch wide. If necessary, place the peel in near-boiling water for 1 or 2 minutes to make it more flexible; cool in cold water for easier handling. 2. To make a rose, wind the peel in reverse, with the colored side in. Starting with the center of the rose, form the peel into a tight "bud"; secure with a toothpick half at the base. 3. Continue winding the peel around the "bud" to form the rose. Secure with toothpick halves at the base, cutting off any excess toothpick. 4. Place the peel in cold water to set the flower. Roses will keep in cold water or a plastic bag in the refrigerator for several days.

BEVERAGE GARNISHES:

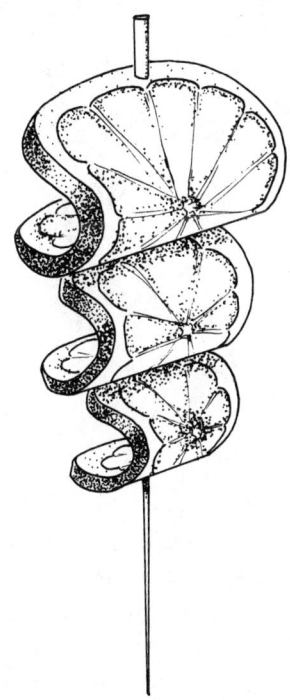

TIKI SAILS: Using unpeeled cartwheel slices of orange and lemon, double each over and thread them through the peel onto a long wooden skewer. Use graduated-size cartwheel slices, beginning with the largest.

Fresh Citrus Garnishes

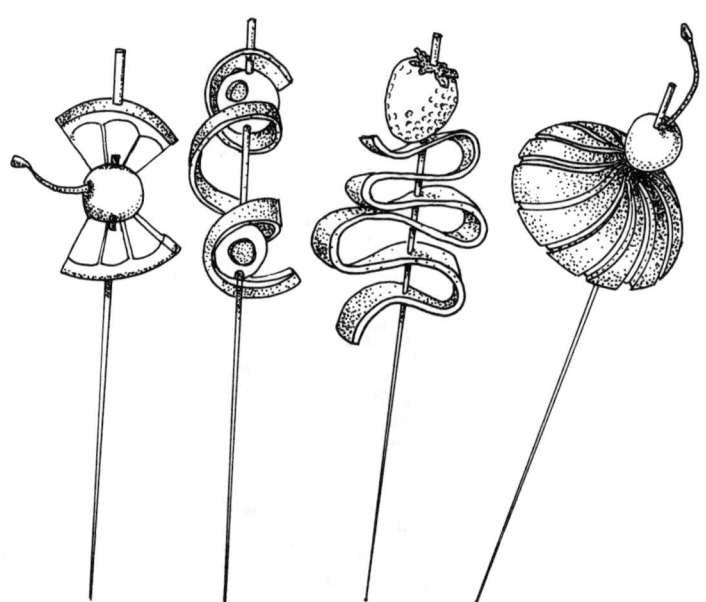

KABOBS: 1. Cut unpeeled cartwheel slices into quarters. Thread two quarters onto wooden skewers, placing a maraschino cherry between them. 2. and 3. Thread either a lemon or orange peel twist onto a wooden skewer, along with an olive, strawberry, cherry, or cocktail onion. 4. Cut off the end of an orange or lemon that has been zested diagonally, as in making fluted cartwheel slices. Place on the end of a wooden skewer, topped with a maraschino cherry.

CITRUS PEEL FLOWERS: These flowers can be made from the reamed-out shells of grapefruit, oranges, lemons, or tangerines. Cut the fruit in half crosswise; ream out the juice and reserve. Scrape the shells "clean" with a spoon. With a paring knife or kitchen shears, cut each citrus shell from the outer edge to within ½ inch of the center, making six petals. Petals can be left as cut, rounded, or pointed. Flowers can be made ahead and placed flat between damp paper toweling. To make the centers, attach maraschino cherries, cranberries, or olives with toothpicks. Use with seasonal greenery and candles for attractive decorations, or with parsley or watercress to garnish large trays or platters.

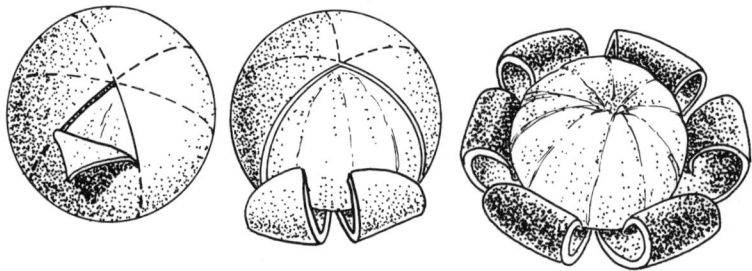

TANGERINE FLOWERS: Score the peel lengthwise into sixths, cutting to within 1 inch of the stem end. Gently pull back the peel; then curl each peel petal back toward the fruit. Gently separate the segments.

Citrus Preparation Techniques

To help you get the best from every piece of fresh citrus, here are some basic techniques to use when preparing citrus for serving or cooking. Just remember when you do prepare fresh citrus, it is easier and you'll get more attractive results by using a sharp knife.

Remember, too, that citrus juice, grated peel, and reamed-out shells can be frozen for future use. So when citrus is especially plentiful and economical, prepare a little extra and freeze it.

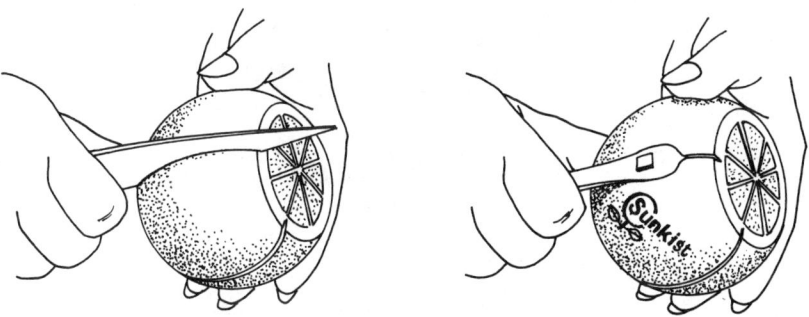

ORANGE OR GRAPEFRUIT PEELING METHOD 1: Basketball Method. Slice off the stem end of the fruit. Without cutting into the "meat" of the fruit, score the peel with a knife or the SNACKER™ citrus peeler into quarters like a basketball. Pull the peel away with your fingers.

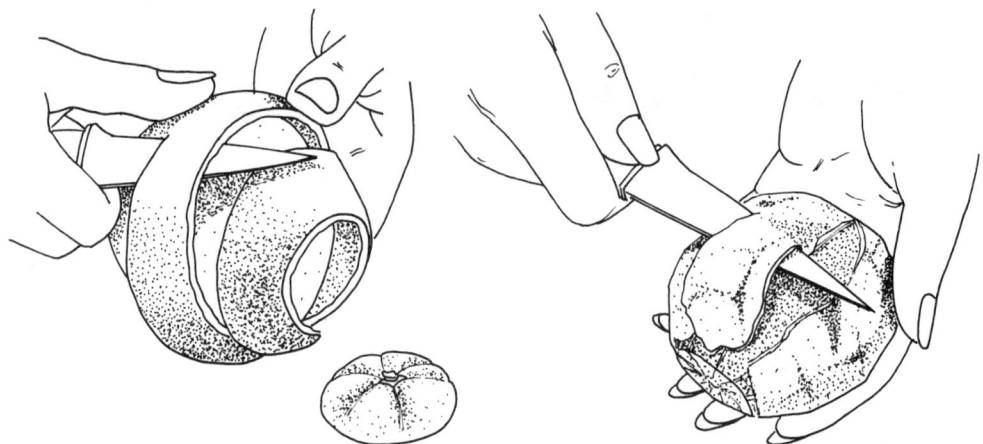

ORANGE OR GRAPEFRUIT PEELING METHOD 2: Round and Round Method. Using a slightly sawing motion, cut only the outer colored peel away in a continuous spiral, leaving the white membrane. Cutting lengthwise with curve of fruit, remove the white membrane.

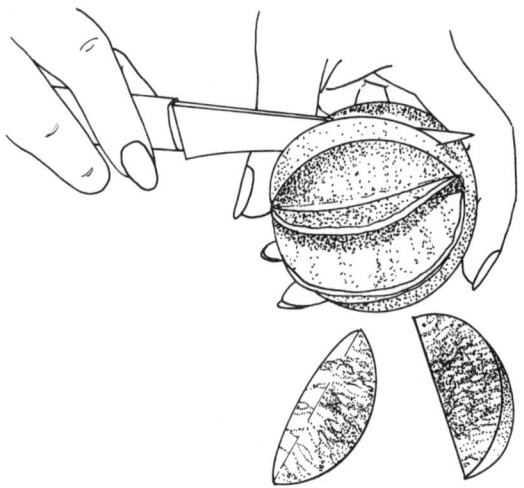

CITRUS SECTIONS: With knife, peel an orange or grapefruit. Working over a bowl to reserve the juice, cut along both sides of each dividing membrane and lift out sections from center.

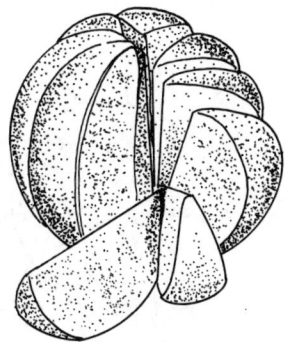

CITRUS SEGMENTS: Peel an orange, grapefruit, or tangerine by hand, or with the SNACKER™ citrus peeler. Gently separate the fruit along the natural divisions.

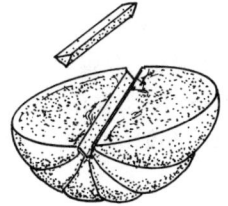 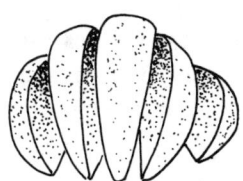 

BITE-SIZE PIECES: Cut a peeled orange or grapefruit in half lengthwise and, with a shallow "V" shape cut, remove the white center core. Place the halves cut-side-down; cut lengthwise and crosswise.

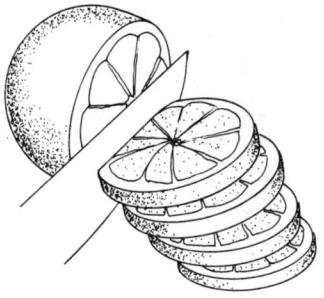 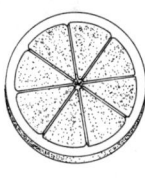 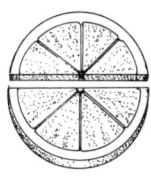

BASIC CARTWHEEL SLICES: Cut a thin slice from both ends of peeled or unpeeled fruit. Then slice the fruit crosswise into the desired thickness. Cut cartwheels in half for half-cartwheel slices.

Citrus Preparation Techniques

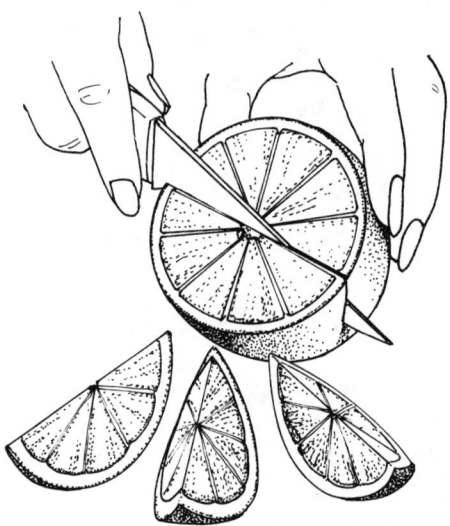

UNPEELED "SMILES" OR WEDGES: For "easy-to-eat" orange "smiles," cut the fruit in half crosswise; then cut 3 or 4 wedges from each half. For traditional wedges, cut the fruit in half lengthwise; then cut each half into wedges.

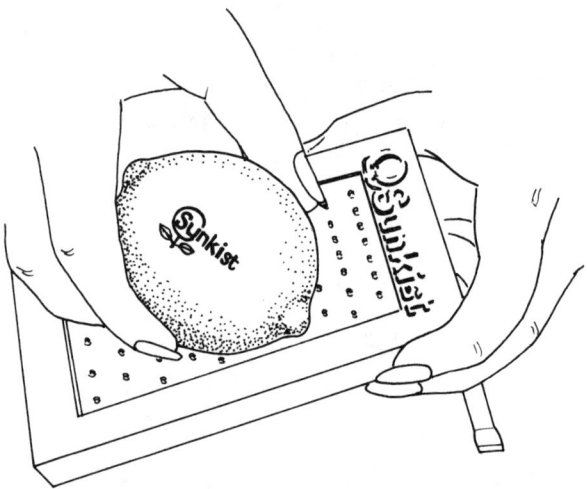

GRATED PEEL: Wash the fruit; then dry. Using a citrus peel grater, with quick downward strokes, remove the outer colored layer of peel only. Grate over wax paper. Measure *lightly* in a spoon; do not pack. To store fresh grated peel, seal in a plastic bag and freeze for later use.

Citrus Preparation Techniques 307

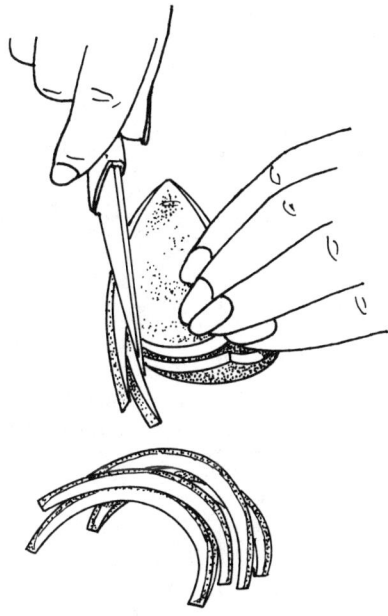

SLIVERED PEEL: Score the peel of the fruit into quarters; remove with your fingers. With the tip of a spoon scrape most of the white membrane from the peel. Stack 2 or 3 pieces at a time on a cutting board. Cut into the thinnest possible strips.

MINCED PEEL: Cut the slivered peel strips crosswise into very small pieces.

Citrus Preparation Techniques

FRESH CITRUS JUICE: Fruit at room temperature gives up more juice. Roll the fruit on the counter top with the palm of your hand, to break the juice sacs. Cut in half crosswise and ream out the juice on a hand or electric juicer. Save citrus shells for containers (page 290) by freezing in sealed plastic bags.

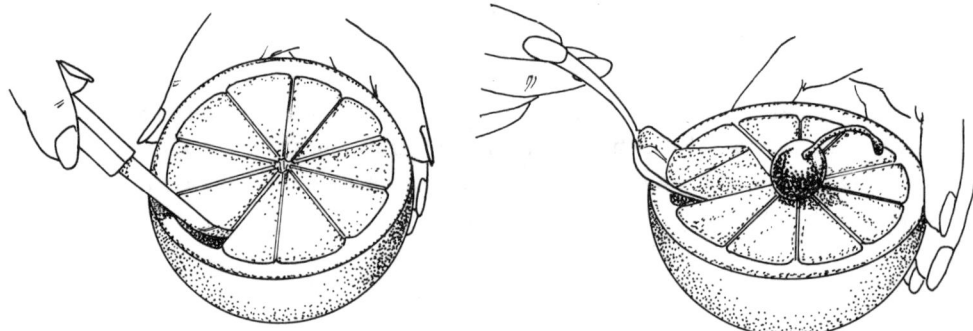

GRAPEFRUIT HALVES: Cut a grapefruit in half crosswise. Using a paring or curved grapefruit knife, cut around each fruit half, separating the "meat" from the peel. Cut along both sides of each dividing membrane so the sections can be removed easily with a spoon. Serve with a sprinkling of sugar or another topping, if desired. *Or* serve each grapefruit with a serrated grapefruit spoon, which eliminates preparation time.

Western Citrus Information

WESTERN CITRUS INFORMATION

Purchasing and Storage

Most varieties of citrus from California and Arizona are tree-ripened. You can be assured that any fruit shipped to market has reached full maturity and is ready to eat. The only exception is lemons, which actually ripen, or cure, better in storage at the packinghouse than on the tree.

Fresh citrus is packed by size, and occasionally advertised or displayed in stores by size designation. For example, oranges can be 72s or 113s, indicating the number of pieces of fruit packed in a standard size citrus carton. The higher the number, the smaller the fruit.

TRAITS	SEASONS	PURCHASING TIPS	STORAGE TIPS
Navel Oranges			
—seedless —finest for eating —navel formation opposite stem end —peel and segment easily	November to May; peak supplies January, February, and March.	Look for smooth skins, free of soft spots. Fruit should feel firm and heavy for its size.	At room temperature, 1 to 2 weeks. For longer storage, place in plastic bag in refrigerator.

TRAITS	SEASONS	PURCHASING TIPS	STORAGE TIPS
Valencia Oranges			
–thinner skins –only a few seeds –excellent for juice, as well as eating	February to October; peak supplies May, June, and July.	Look for smooth skins, free of soft spots. Fruit should feel firm and heavy for its size. Fruit is fully ripe, despite occasional greenish tinge, called regreening.	At room temperature, 1 to 2 weeks. For longer storage, place in plastic bag in refrigerator.
Lemons			
–low in sodium –low in calories	Available year round.	Look for smooth skins, firm and heavy fruit. Avoid bruised, bumpy, wrinkled fruit that may be old, or was improperly handled.	At room temperature, 7 to 10 days. In plastic bag in refrigerator, at least 1 month.
Grapefruit			
–white –ruby –available all year –tart-sweet flavor –few seeds –low in calories	Winter grapefruit comes from desert areas November to June or early July. Summer grapefruit from Central and Southern California is available June to October.	Look for almost flawless, firm, smooth skins and heavy fruit.	At room temperature, up to 2 weeks. For longer storage, place in plastic bag in refrigerator.

TRAITS	SEASONS	PURCHASING TIPS	STORAGE TIPS
Mandarins			
–*Kinnows* are most plentiful –*Satsumas* –light orange color –smooth skins –mild, sweet flavor –some seeds	January to May	Avoid bruised, blemished fruit that may be old, or was improperly handled.	At room temperature, up to a week. Best storage is in refrigerator in plastic bag.
Tangelos			
–*Orlandos* –*Minneolas* (knob-like at stem end) –cross between a tangerine and grapefruit –tart-sweet flavor	December to April	See above.	See above.
Tangerines			
–*Dancies* –pebbly-skinned	November to January	See above.	See above.
Royal Mandarins			
–cross between a tangerine and orange –red orange color –similar to orange in flavor	January to March	See above.	See above.

BASIC QUESTIONS ABOUT FRESH CITRUS

Q: *Why is wax added to the peel of citrus fruits?*

A: Practically all citrus fruits are washed and cleaned to remove the debris and field dust that accumulate during the growing period. In order to prevent abnormal shrinkage and shriveling, a small quantity of vegetable wax is used to replace the natural wax that is removed during the washing process. These waxes have been tested and approved for use on foods and meet the requirements of the U.S. Food and Drug Administration.

Q: *Are citrus fruits dyed to enhance their color?*

A: Citrus fruits grown in California and Arizona are not artificially colored with dyes. California–Arizona state laws prohibit the addition of color to the peel of citrus fruits.

Q: *Why does some western-grown fruit have thicker peel?*

A: The thickness of citrus peel is dependent upon annual variables, the most critical of which is weather. Extremely hot or cold temperatures and the degree of rainfall can all affect the thickness of peel. The occasions of thicker peel are actually nature's way of protecting the quality of the fruit's interior.

Q: *Can I freeze whole citrus fruits?*

A: The result of freezing whole citrus in a home freezer will be disappointing. As the fruit freezes, the juice sacs burst, and after the fruit thaws the pulp will be dry and the peel mushy.

Q: *Can valencia and navel oranges both be used in cooking?*

A: In most cases valencia and navel oranges can be interchanged in the recipes in this cookbook. Any exceptions are noted. It is not recommended that navel oranges be exposed to prolonged cooking times. So if using navel orange segments, bite-size pieces or cartwheel slices in poultry, pork, beef, or fish entrées, whether skillet-cooked or oven-baked, add the oranges during the last 5 minutes of cooking, giving them just enough time to heat through.

Q: *Can orange and lemon juice be frozen successfully at home?*

A: Fresh squeezed lemon, grapefruit, and valencia orange juice may be frozen for up to four months. Navel orange juice may become bitter. It's especially handy to freeze lemon juice in ice cube trays. Pre-measure the volume of each ice cube compartment so that you know exactly how much juice is in each cube. When a recipe calls for just a few tablespoons of fresh lemon juice, you'll be prepared. For convenient storage, remove the hardened juice cubes from trays and place in sealed plastic bags in the freezer. Freeze grapefruit and valencia orange juice in appropriately sized containers. Thaw in the refrigerator; the juice will separate, so shake or stir before using.

Q: *What is the difference between the outside colored peel and the white layer underneath the colored peel?*

A: Flavedo, the outer colored peel of citrus, has tiny oil sacs which provide the distinctive citrus flavors in so many of today's popular food items. The fresh grated citrus peel used in recipes throughout this cookbook provides a wonderful aroma and subtle citrus flavor.

Albedo, the white portion just beneath the colored peel, contains valuable nutrients. It contains fiber that aids the digestive process in the intestinal tract. Albedo also contains pectin, the substance that causes jellies and jams to jell. That's one reason fresh citrus peel is often called for in jelly and jam making.

Q: *If navel oranges don't have seeds, how can the trees be grown?*

A: Seedless navel oranges, as well as all other varieties of citrus fruits, are reproduced by "budding." The seeds of other citrus varieties are planted to grow citrus rootstock known to be disease resistant. When they are about two or three years old, the seedlings are budded with a slip from a mature navel orange tree producing the very best quality fruit. The bud is grafted into the bark of the seedling. The bud eventually takes hold and becomes a new tree, producing the variety of fruit that was budded into the rootstock. All citrus fruits are propagated in this manner.

Q: *Why do summer valencia oranges sometimes appear green and unripe?*

A: Valencias, because they are ripening in the warmer months, are subject to a phenomenon known as *regreening*. The oranges turn golden before they are fully ripe. As the weather gets warmer and they hang on the tree to ripen, they actually begin to turn green again, starting at the stem end. The warm temperatures apparently cause chlorophyll, the greening substance, to return to the peel. Oranges ripen only on the tree, and regardless of outside color, are never picked until fully ripe.

Q: *What are blood oranges and when are they in season?*

A: The blood orange is distinguished by its deep internal red color. The intensity of coloration seems to vary according to variety, as well as the conditions of temperature and light under which the fruit is grown. Most blood oranges display some red blush on the peel. Blood oranges have been very popular in Europe and are grown primarily in the Mediterranean regions. Very limited supplies of blood oranges are marketed from California and Arizona between mid-January and mid-May.

Q: *Are any limes grown in California and Arizona?*

A: Yes, a limited supply of fresh limes are available from western groves from August to February. They are seedless and lighter in color than those grown in Florida and Mexico, the two major producing areas for U.S. lime supplies.

NUTRITION

Citrus fruits contribute to a healthful, nutritious diet. Citrus is one of the best sources of vitamin C and is low in calories and sodium. It's a good source of potassium, fiber, and complex carbohydrates, and supplies some vitamin A and other nutrients, as well. Fresh citrus and citrus products are available year round, making them especially valuable as reliable sources of important nutrients.

The following is specific information on the nutrients found in different varieties of fresh western-grown citrus marketed by Sunkist.

FRESH CALIFORNIA–ARIZONA ORANGES*

	Size 88 Navel Oranges (2⅞" Diameter)	Size 113 Valencia Oranges (2⅝" Diameter)
Food Energy (calories)	65.0 calories	59.0 calories
Protein	1.4 grams	1.3 grams
Fat	0.1 grams	0.4 grams
Carbohydrates	16.3 grams	14.4 grams
Fiber	0.6 grams	0.6 grams
Calcium	56.0 mg.	48.0 mg.
Iron	0.2 mg.	0.1 mg.
Phosphorus	27.0 mg.	21.0 mg.
Potassium	250.0 mg.	217.0 mg.
Sodium	1.0 mg.	0.0 mg.
Ascorbic Acid (vitamin C)	80.3 mg.	58.7 mg.
Thiamin	0.1 mg.	0.1 mg.
Riboflavin	0.1 mg.	trace
Niacin	0.4 mg.	0.3 mg.
Folacin	47.2 mcg.	46.7 mcg.
Vitamin A	26.0 RE 256.0 IU	28.0 RE 278.0 IU

*Agriculture Handbook No. 8-9, Composition of Foods, United States Department of Agriculture, Human Nutrition Information Service, August 1982.

FRESH CALIFORNIA–ARIZONA LEMONS*

	Size 165 (Raw-With Peel) (2⅛" Diameter)	1 Tablespoon Fresh Lemon Juice
Food Energy (calories)	22.0 calories	4.0 calories
Protein	1.3 grams	0.1 grams
Fat	0.3 grams	0.0 grams
Carbohydrates	11.6 grams	1.3 grams
Fiber	**	**
Calcium	66.0 mg.	1.0 mg.
Iron	0.8 mg.	0.0 mg.
Phosphorus	16.0 mg.	1.0 mg.
Potassium	157.0 mg.	19.0 mg.
Sodium	3.0 mg.	0.0 mg.
Ascorbic Acid (vitamin C)	83.2 mg.	7.0 mg.
Thiamin	0.1 mg.	trace
Riboflavin	trace	trace
Niacin	0.2 mg.	trace
Folacin	**	2.0 mcg.
Vitamin A	3.0 RE / 32.0 IU	0.0 RE / 3.0 IU

*Agriculture Handbook No. 8-9, Composition of Foods, United States Department of Agriculture, Human Nutrition Information Service, August 1982.

**Data not available.

FRESH CALIFORNIA–ARIZONA GRAPEFRUIT*

	½ Size 40 (3¾" Diameter) White Grapefruit	½ Size 40 (3¾" Diameter) Ruby Grapefruit
Food Energy (calories)	43.0 calories	46.0 calories
Protein	1.0 grams	0.6 grams
Fat	0.1 grams	0.1 grams
Carbohydrates	10.7 grams	11.9 grams
Fiber	0.2 grams	0.3 grams
Calcium	14.0 mg.	13.0 mg.
Iron	0.1 mg.	0.1 mg.
Phosphorus	14.0 mg.	14.0 mg.
Potassium	169.0 mg.	181.0 mg.
Sodium	0.0 mg.	1.0 mg.
Ascorbic Acid (vitamin C)	39.3 mg.	46.8 mg.
Thiamin	trace	trace
Riboflavin	trace	trace
Niacin	0.3 mg.	0.2 mg.
Folacin	13.9 mcg.	15.0 mcg.
Vitamin A	1.0 RE / 12.0 IU	32.0 RE / 318.0 IU

*Agriculture Handbook No. 8-9, Composition of Foods, United States Department of Agriculture, Human Nutrition Information Service, August 1982.

FRESH TANGERINES*
1 Medium
(2⅜" Diameter)

Food Energy (calories)	37.0	calories
Protein	0.5	grams
Fat	0.2	grams
Carbohydrates	9.4	grams
Fiber	0.3	grams
Calcium	12.0	mg.
Iron	0.1	mg.
Phosphorus	8.0	mg.
Potassium	132.0	mg.
Sodium	1.0	mg.
Ascorbic Acid (vitamin C)	25.9	mg.
Thiamin	0.1	mg.
Riboflavin		trace
Niacin	0.1	mg.
Folacin	17.1	mcg
Vitamin A	77.0	RE
	773.0	IU

*Agriculture Handbook No. 8-9, Composition of Foods, United States Department of Agriculture, Human Nutrition Information Service, August 1982.

For nutritional information on processed citrus products marketed by Sunkist, or by other manufacturers under license agreement from Sunkist Growers, Inc., please write to:

Consumer Services Department
Sunkist Growers, Inc.
Box 7888
Van Nuys, CA 91409

Equivalent Measures

The following information indicates equivalents for the juice, fruit, and peel from Western citrus. These are approximate measures, and may vary from season to season, but they will help you plan for recipes and servings.

FRESH ORANGES:
- Oranges, medium 2 to 4 = 1 cup juice
- Oranges, medium 2 = 1 cup bite-size pieces
- Orange, medium 1 = 10 to 12 sections
- Orange, medium 1 = 4 teaspoons grated peel

FRESH LEMONS:
- Lemons, medium 6 = 1 cup juice
- Lemon, medium 1 = 3 tablespoons juice
- Lemon, medium 1 = 3 teaspoons grated peel

FRESH GRAPEFRUIT:
- Grapefruit, medium 1 = 10 to 12 sections
- Grapefruit, medium 1 = ⅔ cup juice
- Grapefruit, medium 1 = 3 to 4 tablespoons grated peel

Index

Acorn Squash, Lemon-Glazed, 110–11
Almond(s):
   Dressing and Lemon-Honey Glaze, Roast Turkey with, 74–75
   Salmon Steaks, Mushroom-, Broiled, 54–55
   Seasoned Snack Mix, 224–25
   Shortcake, Tangerine-, 234–35
Antipasto Platter, 29
Appetizers, 15–30
   Antipasto Platter, 29
   Citrus Ice Bowl, 20–21
   Clam(s):
      Dip, Zesty, 24
      Steamed Bucket of, 21
   Dilled Mustard Dip, 28–29
   Eggplant "Caviar," 24–25
   Guacamole, Dilly, 22
   Herbed Cheese with Garlic and Lemon, 17
   Horseradish Dip for Seafood and Vegetables, Creamy, 28
   Hummus Bi Tahina, 25
   Mushroom(s):
      Caps Royale, 106–107
      Easy Marinated, 26
      Marinated, Italiano, 26–27
   Nachos, Lemony Good, 23
   Salmon:
      Dip for Vegetables, 27
      Pâté, 29–30
   Salsa Mexicana, 22–23
   Seafood Cocktail, Western, 27–28
   Seviche Olé, 18
   Shrimp:
      Grapefruit and, with Zippy Cocktail Sauce, 19–20
      Pacifica, 19
   Tuna Cocktail, Slimmers', 23–24
Apple(s):
   Fish rolls, Saucy, 50–51
   Fruit Salad:
      Mariner's, 136
      with Pineapple Dressing, Fresh, 128
   Oatmeal Cookies, Orange and, 218
   Orange Waldorf Salad, 136
   Orange-Yogurt Dip for Fresh Fruit, 207
Apple juice (cider):
   A Gem of a Jelly, 175–76
   Lemon Appleade, 268
   Spiced Punch, Crowd-Pleasing, 280

Index

Apricot(s):
   Orange-Glazed Ham, 95–96
   Sweet and Sour Fish Delight, 44
   Syrup, Grapefruit-, 156–57
Arizona citrus growers, 7
Artichoke hearts for Antipasto Platter, 29
Asparagus, 151
   East-West Sautéed, 101
   Quiche, Springtime, 153–54
   Tuna and, Crêpe Roll-Ups, 57
Avocado:
   and Cashew-Topped Fillets, 49
   Dressing, Lemon-, 143
   Fallbrook's Favorite Salad, 131
   Guacamole, Dilly, 22
   Seafood Cocktail, Western, 27–28
   Triple Decker, Everyone's Favorite, 163
   Tuna-Mac Stuffed, 139

Bacon:
   Cheesy Vegetable Frittata, 152
   Potato Salad, German-Style Hot, 130
   Scallop Sauté with Lemon, 51
   Spinach Salad Flambé, 126–27
Bagels and Orange-Cream Cheese, 166
Banana(s):
   Citrus-Yogurt Sundaes, 205–206
   Flambé, Orange, 203
   Flip, 273
   Fruit Nog, Low Calorie, 272
   Fruit Salad with Pineapple Dressing, Fresh, 128
   and Orange Ice Cream, Fresh, 209
   Orange-Yogurt Dip for Fresh Fruit, 207
   Sim-Yet-Cee (Simple Yet Fancy Ice), 210
   Banana Squash for Winter Squash à l'Orange, 111–12
Basic cartwheel slices, 305
Basil, Tangy Pasta with, and Parmesan, 117
Baskets (garnishes), 290
Bean(s):
   Barbecued Orange Baked, 101
   Three-, Salad, Easy, 135
   see also Garbanzo beans; Green beans; Kidney beans; Lima beans
Beef, 77–85
   Chili, Shirlee K's Grapefruit, 83
   Chuck Roast, Lemon Barbecued, 80
   Flank Steak, Fillmore Marinated, 79
   Meat Loaf:
      "Best Ever," 83–84
      Two-Way Tangerine Meatballs and, 84–85
   Pot Roast, German-Style, 81–82
   Swiss Steak, Orange, 82
   Tangabobs, 80–81
Beets:
   Borscht, Lemon Fresh, 31
   Pickled Eggs and, 155
   Sweet and Sour, 102
Berry(ies):
   Citrus-Yogurt Sundaes, 205–206
   Froth, Grapefruit and, 274
Beverages, 263–83
   Banana Flip, 273
   Coffee:
      Café Brûlot, 281
      Mix, "Made-at-Home" Orange Flavored, 283
   Fruit Nog, Low Calorie, 272

Grapefruit:
  and Berry Froth, 274
  and Orange Cooler, Fresh, 271
Lemon:
  Appleade, 268
  Brandy, 282
  Cran-, Wine Punch, Hot, 277–78
  Hot Buttered Lemonade, 267
  Liqueur, Lively, 282
  Low-Cal Minty Lemonade, 266–67
  and Mint Iced Tea, 269
  Pink Champagne Punch, 278–79
  Real Old-Fashioned Lemonade, 265
  Syrup Base Lemonade, 265–66
  Tangy Orangeade, 267
  Wine, Hot Cran-, 277–78
Minted Citrus Cooler, 270–71
Orange:
  Brandy, 282
  Champagne Punch, Double, 278
  Cooler, Fresh Grapefruit and, 271
  -Cran Nog, Twosome, 272
  "Eggnog" Shake, 274
  Flavored Coffee Mix, "Made-at-Home," 282–83
  Frostee, Strawberry, 273
  Grand Finale, 280
  "Soda," 274–75
  Tangy Orangeade, 267
Punch:
  Citrus Gold Riesling, 277
  Crowd-Pleasing Spiced, 280
  Double Orange Champagne, 278
  Hot Cran-Lemon Wine, 277–78
  Lemon Pink Champagne, 278–79
  Minted Citrus Cooler, 270–71
  Sangría Blanca, 276
  Sangría Burgundy, 276
  Sangría Rosé, 275–76
  Sparkling Fruit, 279
  Ramos Fizz, Old-Fashioned, 275
Tea:
  Hot Russian, 270
  Lemon and Mint Iced, 269
  Spiced Citrus, Iced, 269
Biscuits, Orange Drop, 191
Bite-size pieces, preparing, 305
Blue Cheese Dressing:
  Green and Orange Salad with, 131–32
  Yogurt–, 144
Boats, Lemon (garnishes), 290
Bologna for Submarine Supreme, 163–64
Bow Ties (garnishes), 289
Brandy:
  Café Brûlot, 281
  Fruit-and-, Stuffed Goose with Lemon Sauce Flambé, 72–73
  Orange or Lemon, 282
  Spinach Salad Flambé, 126–27
Bread(s), 181–95
  Corn, Double C Ranch, 183–84
  Crêpes, see Crêpes
  English Muffins, Old-Fashioned, 190–91
  French Toast, Sunrise, 156–57
  Lemon-Granola Quick, 187
  Muffins, see Muffins
  Orange:
    Blender Quick, 186
    Doughnuts and Holes, 192

Bread(s) *(continued)*
  Drop-Biscuits, 191
  –Pumpkin, Fresh, 188–89
  Whole Wheat, and Carrot Loaf, 189
  Pocket, Sesame-Citrus, 194–95
  Popovers, Lemony Good, 183
  Pudding, Hint of Lemon, 200
  Yeast Braid, Luscious Lemony, 193–94
  see also Sandwiches
Breakfast ideas, 147–58
Broccoli:
  Cheesy Vegetable Entrée for Two, 114
  Grapefruit and, Salad, Chilled, 128–29
  Mushroom Caps Royale, 106–107
  Orange-Pasta Salad, Fresh, 125–26
  Orange Vegetable Medley, 114–15
  and Pasta Combo, Fresh, 102–103
  Salmon Supreme, Buffet, 54
Brunch ideas, 147–58
Brussels Sprouts:
  Golden Treasure, 103
  Stir-Fried, and Tangerines, 103–104
Butter:
  Herbed Lemon-, Patties, 118
  Hollandaise Sauce:
    Blender Quick, 57–58
    "Easiest Ever," 119
    Quick Herbed, 45
  Honey Lemon, 184
  Lemonade, Hot Buttered, 267
  Lemon Buttered Cabbage, 104
  Parsley-Dill, 118–19
  Spiced Orange-Pear, 173–74
  Tangy Lemon-Sesame, 119
Butterflies (garnishes), 287–88

Butternut Squash for Winter Squash à l'Orange, 111

Cabbage:
  Borscht, Lemon Fresh, 31
  Coleslaw, Garden Fresh, 137–38
  Lemon Buttered, 104
Caesar Salad, Best-Ever, 129–30
Cake(s), 229–44
  Flowerpot, 239–40
  Fruitcake:
    Grandma's Favorite Molasses, 241–42
    Western Golden, 242–43
  Grapefruit Upside-Down, Spiced, 240–41
  Lemon:
    Karen Ann's, 235–36
    Sweet and Tart, 243–44
  Orange:
    Ambrosia Cake Roll, 233–34
    and Carrot, Fresh, 231–32
    -Cocoa, Fresh, 236–37
    Dark, Loaf, 238
    Molasses Fruitcake, Grandma's Favorite, 241–42
  Tangerine-Almond Shortcake, 234–35
Calamari, Sautéed Lemon, 49–50
California Cioppino, 36
California citrus growers, 6–7
Calorie-Conscious Dressing, 139
Candy, *see* Confections
Carrot(s):
  Borscht, Lemon Fresh, 31
  Cake, Fresh Orange and, 231–32
  California, 105
  Cheesy Vegetable Entrée for Two, 114
  Golden Treasure Brussels Sprouts, 103

Grapefruit-Tarragon Chicken, 65
Loaf, Whole Wheat Orange and, 189
Soup, Orange-, 34
Three "Cs" Rice Bake, 116
Cartwheel Twists, 287
Cashew-Topped Fillets, Avocado and, 49
Cauliflower:
　Orange Vegetable Medley, 114–15
　alla Parmesan, 105
Cereal for Seasoned Snack Mix, 224–25
Champagne punch:
　Double Orange, 278
　Lemon Pink, 278–79
Charlotte Russe:
　Classic Lemon, 259–60
　Tint of Mint Grapefruit, 259
Cheddar cheese:
　Corn Bread, Double C Ranch, 183–84
　Fish Roll-Ups, Company's Coming, 41
　Nachos, Lemony Good, 23
　Salmon Bake for Two, Quick, 56
　Submarine Supreme, 163–64
　Three "Cs" Rice Bake, 116
　Tuna and Asparagus Crêpe Roll-Ups, 57
Cheese:
　Asparagus Quiche, Springtime, 153–54
　Cheesy Vegetable Entrée for Two, 114
　Cheesy Vegetable Frittata, 152
　see also individual types of cheese
Cherry(ies):
　Ambrosia, Grapefruit and, 204–205
　Fruitcake, Western Golden, 242–43

Chicken, 63–70
　Crispy Baked Citrus, 63
　Curried Baked, 68–69
　Far East, Strips and Fruit, 67
　Grapefruit-Tarragon, 65
　Orange Barbecued, 69–70
　Poulet with Orange Sauce, 66
　and Rice, Savory, 68
　Salad:
　　in Grapefruit Shells, Western, 134
　　and Orange Rice, 133
　　Sandwiches, Crunchy, 164
　Slim Jim Baked, Legs, 64–65
　Stock, Old-Fashioned Homemade, 37
　Wonton Soup, 35
　and Zucchini, Lemon, 64
Chick peas, *see* Garbanzo beans
Chiles:
　California Quesadillas, 167
　Crêpes Huevos Rancheros, 149
　Salsa Mexicana, 22–23
Chili, Shirlee K's Grapefruit, 83
Chocolate:
　Dipped Candied Citrus Peel, 227
　Fudge, Fabulous Orange, 225–26
　Glaze, Satin, 237
　and Orange Crêpe Sundaes, 202
Chrysanthemum Flowers, 295
Chrysanthemum Salad Bowls (garnishes), 296
Cinnamon Sugar, 186
Cioppino, California, 36
Citrus growers, 3–4
Citrus Ice Bowl, 20–21
Citrus Ice Ring, 279
Citrus Peel Flowers, 301
Citrus Peel Strips, 292
Citrus Shells, 290
Clam(s):
　California Cioppino, 36–37
　Dip, Zesty, 24
　Steamed Bucket of, 21

Index

Cocktail Sauce, Grapefruit and Shrimp with Zippy, 19–20
Cocoa:
  Cake, Fresh Orange-, 236–37
  Coffee Mix, "Made-at-Home" Orange Flavored, 282–83
Coconut:
  Flan, Orange-, 257–58
  Orange Ambrosia à la Lagomarsino, 204
  Pie Crust, Toasted, 255
Cod:
  Crisp-Coated Fillets with Tarragon Tartar Sauce, 47–48
  Fish Italiano, 42–43
  Fish Rolls, Saucy Apple, 50–51
  Fish Soup, Quick and Easy Lemon, 31–32
  Poached Fish and Wine Sauce, 42
Coffee:
  Café Brûlot, 281
  Mix, "Made-at-Home" Orange Flavored, 283
Coleslaw, Garden Fresh, 137–38
Columbus, Christopher, 5
Confections, 215, 222–27
  Candied Citrus Peel, 227
  Fudge:
    Fabulous Orange, 225–26
    White Citrus, 226
  Lemon Buttered Popcorn, 224
  1000 Palms Stuffed Dates, 225
  Orange Confetti Bars, 222–23
  Orange Popcorn Balls, 223–24
  Seasoned Snack Mix, 224–25
Cookies, 215–22
  Candied Peel Citrus Drops, 217–18

Lemon, Favorite, 221–22
Orange:
  Confetti Bars, 222–23
  Fresh, 219
  Frosted, 220–21
  Oatmeal, Apple and, 218
  Three-Way, 220
Corn:
  Bread, Double C Ranch, 183–84
  on the Cob, Savory, 106
  Relish, Lemon-, 174
  Southwest Stuffed Zucchini or Green Peppers, 112
Cornish Hens, Citrus Baked, 70
Crab for California Cioppino, 36
Cranberry(ies):
  Orange Dressing for Pork, Favorite, 94–95
  -Orange Muffins, 185
Cranberry juice:
  -Lemon Wine Punch, Hot, 277–78
  Twosome Orange-, Nog, 272
Cream cheese:
  Bagels and Orange-, 166
  Clam Dip, Zesty, 24
  Frosting, Zesty Citrus, 244
  Herbed, with Garlic and Lemon, 17
  Mustard Dip, Dilled, 28–29
  Pie, Orange-, 256
  Salmon Pâté, 29–30
  Spread, Fresh Orange, 232
Cream Puffs with A'Peel, 258
Crêpe(s):
  Hint of Lemon, 189–90
  Hint of Orange, 190
  Huevos Rancheros, 149
  Sundaes, Chocolate and Orange, 202
  Tuna and Asparagus, Roll-Ups, 57
Cucumber(s):
  Lemon, 293
  Sauce, Creamy, 58
  Soup, Chilled Lemon, 33–34

Curls (garnishes), 289
Curry(ied):
  Baked Chicken, 68–69
  Sauce, Fish Steaks with Orange-, 48
Custard, Slow Cooking Rice, 201–202

Dates:
  Fruitcake:
    Grandma's Favorite Molasses, 241–42
    Western Golden, 242–43
  1000 Palms Stuffed, 225
Decorated Cartwheel Slices (garnishes), 286–87
Decorated Wedges, 288
Desserts, 197–212
  Ambrosia:
    Four-Star Citrus, 203–204
    Grapefruit and Cherry, 204–205
    Orange, à la Lagomarsino, 204
    Orange-Kiwifruit, 205
  Citrus-Yogurt Sundaes, 205–206
  Custard, Slow Cooking Rice, 201–202
  Dip for Fresh Fruit, Orange Yogurt, 205
  Fruit Pops, "Just for Kids," 211–12
  Grapefruit Snow, 210–11
  Lemon:
    Curd, Classic, 212
    Gelatine, Fresh, 207
    Sauce, Warm, 201
    Soufflé, Hot, 199
    Tofu Delight, 208
  Minty Orange-Grape Combo, 206
  Orange Banana Flambé, 203
  Pears, Spiced Poached, 206–207
  Pudding:
    Hint of Lemon Bread, 200

  Rice, Best-Ever Baked, 199–200
  see also Cake(s); Cookies; Ice cream; Pastries; Pie(s)
Dill(ed):
  Butter, Parsley-, 118–19
  Guacamole, Dilly, 22
  and Lemon Sauce, 151
  Orange Scramble, Dilly, 152
  Potatoes, Scandinavian, 107
Dips:
  Clam, Zesty, 24
  Eggplant "Caviar," 24–25
  Horseradish, for Seafood and Vegetables, Creamy, 28
  Mustard, Dilled, 28–29
  Orange-Yogurt, for Fresh Fruit, 207
  Salmon, for Vegetables, 27
  Salsa Mexicana, 22–23
Double Cartwheel Twists (garnishes), 287–88
Doughnuts and Holes, Orange, 192
Dressing:
  Almond, and Lemon-Honey Glaze, Roast Turkey with, 74–75
  for Pork, Favorite Orange, 94–95
  Salad, see Salad dressing(s)
Duckling with Honey-Orange Sauce, Roast, 71

Egg(s):
  Antipasto Platter, 29
  Cheesy Vegetable Frittata, 152
  Crêpes Huevos Rancheros, 149
  Devilish, 154
  Dilly Orange Scramble, 152–53
  French Toast, Sunrise, 156–57
  Greek Lemon Soup, 33

Eggs *(continued)*
  Hollandaise Sauce:
    Blender Quick, 57–58
    "Easiest Ever," 119
    Quick Herbed, 45
  Lemon Curd, Classic, 212
  Mayonnaise:
    Lemon Fresh, 142
    Lemony Low Sodium, 142–43
  Meringue, *see* Meringue
  Omelette à l'Orange, B.J.'s, 150
  Pickled, and Beets, 155
  Potato Salad, Zesty Molded, 125
  "Puff" Pancake, Orange, 155–56
  Quiche, Springtime Asparagus, 153–54
  Salmon Omelet with Dill and Lemon Sauce, 150–51
  Soufflé, Hot Lemon, 199
Eggplant "Caviar," 24–25
English Muffins:
  Monterey, 166
  Old-Fashioned, 190–91
Equivalent measures, 319

Fans (garnishes), 288
Feta cheese for Lemon Greek Salad, 126
Fettucini Salad, Cindy's Garden, 127
Fish, 39–58
  Avocado and Cashew-Topped Fillets, 49
  California Cioppino, 36–37
  Crisp-Coated Fillets with Tarragon Tartar Sauce, 47–48
  Italiano, 43
  Oven-Fried, with Lemon Ponzu Sauce, 46
  Poached, and Wine Sauce, 42
  Rolls, Saucy Apple, 50–51
  Roll-Ups, Company's Coming, 41
  Soup, Quick and Easy Lemon, 31–32
  Steaks in Foil, Easiest Ever, 47
  Steaks with Orange-Curry Sauce, 48
  Sweet and Sour, Delight, 44
  see also individual types of fish
Flan, Orange-Coconut, 257–58
  see also Pudding
Florida citrus industry, 6, 10
Flounder Fish Roll-Ups, Company's Coming, 41
Flowerpot Cake, 239–40
Flowers (garnishes), 287–88, 295, 297, 298, 301, 302
Fluted Cartwheel Slices, 286
French Dressing, Low Calorie Lemon, 144
French Toast:
  Broiled Orange or Grapefruit Toppers, 157–58
  Sunrise, 156–57
Frosting:
  Lemon, 222
  Lemony, 235–36
  Orange, 221
  Orange Cream Cheese Spread, Fresh, 232
  Whipped Topping, 240–41
  Zesty Citrus, 244
  see also Glaze(d); Icing
Fruit:
  -and-Brandy-Stuffed Goose with Lemon Sauce Flambé, 72–73
  desserts and ice creams, 197–212
  Far East Chicken Strips and, 67
Fruitcake:
  Grandma's Favorite Molasses, 241–42
  Western Golden, 242–43
Nog, Low Calorie, 272

Orange-Yogurt Dip for Fresh, 207
Pops, "Just for Kids," 211–12
Salad:
  Fresh, and Pineapple Dressing, 128
  Mariner's, 136
  see also individual fruits
Fruit Growers Supply Company, 8
Fruit juices:
  "Just for Kids" Fruit Pops, 212
  preparation of citrus, 308
  see also Beverages
Fudge:
  Fabulous Orange, 225–26
  White Citrus, 226

Garbanzo beans:
  Hummus Bi Tahina, 25
  and Macaroni Soup, Hearty, 32
  Three-Bean Salad, Easy, 135
Garnishes, fresh citrus, 285–302
  Baskets, 290–91
  Bow Ties, 289
  Butterflies, 287–88
  Cartwheel Twists, 287
  Chrysanthemum Flowers, 295
  Chrysanthemum Salad Bowls, 296
  Citrus Peel Flowers, 301
  Citrus Peel Strips, 292
  Citrus Roses, 298
  Citrus Shells, 290
  Curls, 289
  Decorated Cartwheel Slices, 286–87
  Decorated Wedges, 288
  Double Cartwheel Twists, 287–88
  Fans or Quarter Cartwheel Slices, 288
  Flowers, 287–88

  Fluted Cartwheel Slices, 286
  Kabobs, 300
  Lemon Boats, 290
  Lemon Cucumbers, 293
  Lemon Rings, 151*n*., 293
  Lemon Twists, 292
  Oblong Slices, 288
  Orange Peel Flowers, 297
  Star Cups, 294–95
  Star Garnishes, 294
  Tangerine Flowers, 302
  Tiki Sails, 299
Gelatine:
  Fresh Lemon, 207
  Grapefruit Snow, 210–11
  Lemon Tofu Delight, 208
Gin, Old-Fashioned Ramos Fizz, 275
Glaze(d):
  Acorn Squash, Lemon-, 110–11
  Chocolate, Satin, 237
  Citrus, 217
  Fresh Peach Pie, 257
  Lemon:
    Fresh, 243
    -Honey, 75
    Tart, 243–44
  Orange, 219, 233–34
    Fresh, 243
    Ham, 95–96
  see also Frosting; Icing
Goose, Fruit-and-Brandy-Stuffed, with Lemon Sauce Flambé, 72–73
Granola, Quick Bread, Lemon-, 187
Grape(s):
  Citrus-Yogurt Sundaes, 205–206
  Fruit Salad:
    Mariner's, 136
    with Pineapple Dressing, Fresh, 128
  Minty Orange-, Combo, 206
Grapefruit:
  -Apricot Syrup, 156–57

Grapefruit *(continued)*
  and Berry Cooler, 274
  Candied Citrus Peel, 226–27
  Charlotte Russe, 259
  and Cherry Ambrosia, 204–205
  Chicken Salad in, Shells, Western, 134
  Chili, Shirlee K's, 83
  Citrus-Yogurt Sundaes, 205–206
  equivalent measures, 319
  Far East Chicken Strips and Fruit, 67
  Four-Star Citrus Ambrosia, 203–204
  garnishes, *see* Garnishes, fresh citrus
  Halves, 308
  history of, 5
  information about, 309–18 *passim*
  -Mint Dressing, 140
  and Orange Cooler, Fresh, 271
  Pie:
    Chiffon, 254–55
    Meringue, 251
  preparation techniques, 303–308
  Salad:
    and Broccoli, Chilled, 128–29
    and Pineapple Mold, Sunny Fresh, 132
    and Spinach, 129
    and Shrimp with Zippy Cocktail Sauce, 19–20
  Snow, 210–11
  -Tarragon Chicken, 65
  Toppers, Broiled, 158
  Upside-Down Cake, Spiced, 240–41
Grape juice for Crowd-Pleasing Spiced Punch, 280
Grated peel, 306
Greek Lemon Soup, 33
Greek Salad, Lemon, 126
Green beans for Easy Three-Bean Salad, 135
Green pepper(s):
  Chicken Strips and Fruit, Far East, 67
  Southwest Stuffed, 112
Guacamole, Dilly, 22

Haddock:
  Avocado and Cashew-Topped Fillets, 49
  Fish Roll-Ups, Company's Coming, 41
  Fish Soup, Quick and Easy Lemon, 31–32
  Poached Fish and Wine Sauce, 42
Halibut:
  Broiled Lemony, with Quick Herbed Hollandaise, 45
  California Cioppino, 36–37
  Crisp-Coated Fillets with Tarragon Tartar Sauce, 47–48
  Fish Steaks in Foil, Easiest Ever, 47
  Fish Steaks with Orange-Curry Sauce, 48
  Oven-Fried Fish with Lemon Ponzu Sauce, 46
  Seafood and Orange Kabobs, 52
  Seviche Olé, 18
  Sweet and Sour Fish Delight, 44
Ham:
  Monterey English Muffins, 166
  Orange-Glazed, 95
  Submarine Special, 163–64
  Triple Decker, Everyone's Favorite, 163
Herbed Cheese with Garlic and Lemon, 17
Herbed Lemon-Butter Patties, 118

Herb Seasoning, High-Flavor
     Low-Sodium, 178
Hollandaise sauce:
  Blender Quick, 57–58
  "Easiest Ever," 119
  Quick Herbed, 45
Honey(ed):
  Dressing, Citrus-, 141
  Fruit Salad Dressing, Rosy's, 143
  Lemon Butter, 184
  Lemon-, Glaze, 75
  Muffins, Orange, 184–85
  -Orange Sauce, Roast Duckling with, 71
Horseradish Dip for Seafood and Vegetables, Creamy, 28
Hubbard squash for Winter Squash à l'Orange, 111–12
Hummus Bi Tahina, 25

Ice Cream, 197
  Chocolate and Orange Crêpe Sundaes, 202
  Lemon, Easy Fresh, 208–209
  Orange:
    Easy, 209
    Fresh, 232
    Fresh Bananas and, 209
    Sim-Yet-Cee (Simple Yet Easy Fancy Ice), 210
  Orange "Eggnog" Shake, 274
  Orange Grand Finale, 280
  Pie, Frozen Lemon, 252–53
  3 Orange "Soda," 274–75
Icing:
  Orange, Fresh, 237
  see also Frosting; Glaze(d)
Information on Western citrus, 309–18

Jam, Easy Fresh Orange, 175
Jelly, a Gem of a, 175–76
Juice, fresh citrus, preparation, 308

Kabobs (garnishes), 300

Kidney beans:
  Chili, Shirlee K's Grapefruit, 83
  and Macaroni Soup, Hearty, 32
  Three-Bean Salad, Easy, 135
Kiwifruit:
  Ambrosia, Orange, 205
  Fallbrook's Favorite Salad, 131

Lamb, 77, 86–88
  Barbecued Butterflied Leg of, 86
  Kabobs, Herbed, 88
  Shanks, Lemony, 87
Lemon(s):
  Acorn Squash, -Glazed, 110–11
  beverages, see Beverages, Lemon
  Borscht, Fresh, 31
  Breads:
    -Granola Quick, 187
    Lemony Good Popovers, 183
    Yeast Braid, Luscious, 193–94
  -Butter:
    Herbed, Patties, 118
    Honey, 184
    Sesame, Tangy, 119
  Buttered Cabbage, 104
  cake, see Cake(s), Lemon
  Calamari, Sautéed, 49–50
  Candied Citrus Peel, 226–27
  Candied Peel Citrus Drops, 217–18
  Charlotte Russe, The Classic, 259–60
  Chicken and Zucchini, 64
  Chuck Roast, Barbecued, 80
  Citrus Ice Bowl, 20–21
  Cookies, Favorite, 221–22
  -Corn Relish, 174
  Crêpes, Hint of, 189–90
  Curd, Classic, 212

Lemon(s) *(continued)*
  Dill and, Sauce, 151
  equivalent measures, 319
  Four-Star Citrus Ambrosia, 203–204
  Frosting, 222, 235–36
  Fudge, White Citrus, 226
  garnishes, *see* Garnishes, fresh citrus
  Gelatine, Fresh, 207
  Glaze:
    Citrus, 217
    Fresh, 243
    Tart, 243–44
  Greek Salad, 126
  Herbed Cheese with Garlic and, 17
  history of, 5
  -Honey Glaze, 75
  Ice Cream, Easy Fresh, 208–209
  information about, 309–18 *passim*
  with lamb, *see* Lamb
  Marmalade, Shimmering, 176
  Mayonnaise:
    Fresh, 142
    Low-Sodium, 142–43
  Muffins, Fresh, Cake, 185–86
  -Mustard Sauce, 55–56
  Nachos, Lemony Good, 23
  Pie Crust, Hint of, 252
  pies, *see* (Pie(s), Lemon
  Ponzu Sauce, 46
  Popcorn, Buttered, 224
  Pork Chops, Barbecued, 92
  Port Jelly, 176
  preparation techniques, 303–308
  Preserves, Tomato and, 173
  Salad Dressing:
    -Avocado, 143
    French, Low Calorie, 144
    -Sesame, 140–41
  Sauce Flambé, 73
  Sauce, Warm, 201
  Scallop Sauté with, 51
  -Seasoned Pepper, 177
  Shrimp Alfresco, 52–53
  Soufflé, Hot, 199
  Soup:
    Cucumber, Chilled, 33–34
    Fish, Quick and Easy, 31–32
    Greek, 33
  Spinach à la, Creamed, 110
  Tartar Sauce, 58
  Tofu Delight, 208
  Veal Piccata, 85
  Vinegar, Herbed, 145
Lemonade, *see* Beverage(s), Lemon
Lima beans, Lemon Buttered, 104
Limes, 314

Macaroni:
  Broccoli and Pasta Combo, Fresh, 102–103
  Fish Soup, Quick and Easy Lemon, 31–32
  Orange-Pasta Salad, Fresh, 125–26
  Soup, Hearty Bean and, 32
  Tuna-, Stuffed Avocado, 139
Margarita Cocktail Pie, 255–56
Marmalade, 171
  Lemon, Shimmering, 176
  see also Preserves
Marshmallows for Fabulous Orange Fudge, 225–26
Mayonnaise:
  Lemon Fresh, 142
  Lemony Low Sodium, 142–43
Meringue, 211
  Five-Egg, 251
  Four-Egg, 253
  Three-Egg, 249
  see also Pie(s)
Minced peel, 307
Mint:
  Citrus Cooler, 270–71

Grapefruit-, Dressing, 140
Iced Tea, Lemon and, 269
Lemonade, Low-Cal, 266–67
Monterey Jack cheese:
   California Quesadillas, 167–68
   Hungryman's Grilled
      Sandwiches, 167
   Monterey English Muffins, 166
   Nachos, Lemony Good, 23
Muenster cheese for
   Hungryman's Grilled
      Sandwiches, 167
Muffins:
   Cranberry-Orange, 185
   Fresh Lemon Cake, 185–86
   Orange-Honey, 184–85
Mushroom(s):
   -Almond Broiled Salmon
      Steaks, 54–55
   Antipasto Platter, 29
   Caps Royale, 106–107
   Marinated:
      Easy, 26
      Italiano, 26–27
   Stir-Fried Zucchini and, 113
Mustard:
   Dip, Dilled, 28–29
   Sauce, Lemon-, 55–56

Nachos, Lemony Good, 23
Nutrients in citrus fruits, 314–18

Oatmeal Cookies, Apple and
   Orange, 218
Oblong Slices, 288
Olives:
   Antipasto Platter, 29
   Lemon Greek Salad, 126
Omelettes, see Egg(s)
Orange(s):
   Ambrosia:
      Four-Star Citrus, 203
      Kiwifruit, 205
      à la Lagomarsino, 204

Baked Beans, Barbecued, 101
Banana Flambé, 203
beverages, see Beverages, Orange
breads, see Bread(s), Orange
cake, see Cake(s), Orange
Candied Citrus Peel, 226–27
-Carrot Soup, 34
Chicken:
   Barbecued, 69–70
   Curried Baked, 68–69
   Poulet with, Sauce, 66
Citrus Ice Bowl, 20–21
Citrus-Yogurt Sundaes, 205–206
Coleslaw, Garden Fresh, 137–38
Confetti Bars, 222–23
cookies, see Cookies, Orange
-Cream Cheese, Bagels and, 166
Cream Cheese Spread, Fresh, 232
Crêpes, Hint of, 190
Crêpe Sundaes, Chocolate
   and, 202
-Curry Sauce, Fish Steaks
   with, 48
Dilly, Scramble, 152–53
Dressing for Pork, Favorite, 94–95
Duckling with Honey-,
   Sauce, Roast, 71
English Muffins, Monterey, 166
equivalent measures, 319
Fallbrook's Favorite Salad, 131
Flan, -Coconut, 257–58
Frosting, 221
Fruit Salad:
   Mariner's, 136
   with Pineapple Dressing,
      Fresh, 128
Fudge:
   Fabulous, 225–26
   White Citrus, 226

Orange(s) *(continued)*
  garnishes, *see* Garnishes, fresh citrus
  Glaze, 219
    Fresh, 243
  Green and, Salad with Blue Cheese Dressing, 131–32
  history of, 4–7
  ice cream, *see* Ice cream, Orange
  Icing, Fresh, 237
  information about, 309–18
  Jam, Easy Fresh, 175
  Minty, -Grape Combo, 206
  Muffins:
    Cranberry-, 185
    -Honey, 184–85
  Neptune Pocket Sandwiches, 165
  Omelette à la, B. J.'s, 150
  Pasta Salad, Fresh, 125–26
  -Pear Butter, Spiced, 173–74
  pies, *see* Pie(s), Orange
  Pigs on a Blanket, 157
  Popcorn Balls, 223–24
  Pork:
    Barbecued, Chops, Tipton, 93
    Barbecued, Ribs, 70
    -Glazed Ham, 95–96
    Golden, Sauce for, 96
    preparation techniques, 303–308
  "Puff" Pancake, 155–56
  Relish, Nutty, 177
  -Rice Pilaf, Pork Chops with, 90
  Rice Salad, Chicken and, 183
  Seafood and, Kabobs, 52
  Shrimp with, Oriental, 53
  Shrimp Pacifica, 19
  Spinach, Oriental, 109
  -Sweet Potato Bake, 108–109
  Swiss Steak, 82
  Toppers, Broiled, 158
  Triple Decker, Everyone's Favorite, 163
  Vegetable Medley, 114–15
  Waldorf Salad, 136
  -Yogurt Dip for Fresh Fruit, 207

Pancake(s):
  Broiled Orange or Grapefruit Toppers, 157–58
  Orange "Puff," 155–56
  Pigs on a Blanket, 157
Parmesan cheese:
  Cauliflower alla, 105
  Pasta with Basil and, Tangy, 117
Parsley-Dill Butter, 118–19
Pasta, 99
  with Basil and Parmesan, Tangy, 117
  Fettucini Salad, Cindy's Garden, 127
  Fresh Broccoli and, Combo, 102–103
  macaroni, *see* Macaroni
  Salad, Fresh Orange, 125
Pastries, 247, 257–60
  Charlotte Russe:
    Classic Lemon, 259–60
    Tint of Mint, 259
  Cream Puffs with A'Peel, 258
  Orange-coconut Flan, 257–58
  see also Pie(s), Crust
Pâté, Salmon, 30
Peach Pie, Glazed Fresh, 257
Pear(s):
  Butter, Spiced Orange-, 173–74
  Spiced Poached, 206–207
Peas, Wild Rice-Filled Tomatoes, 137
Peeling methods, 303–304
Pepper, Lemon-Seasoned, 177
Perch for Fish Rolls, Saucy Apple, 50–51
Pie(s), 247–57
  Crust:
    All-Purpose, 260

Hint of Lemon, 252
Pretzel Crumb, 256
Toasted Coconut, 255
Grapefruit:
  Chiffon, 254–55
  Meringue, 251
Lemon:
  Double Crust, 253–54
  Ice Cream, Frozen, 252–53
  Meringue, Easy, 250
  Meringue, Fresh, 249
Margarita Cocktail, 255–56
Orange:
  -Cream Cheese, 256
  Meringue, 250–51
Peach, Glazed Fresh, 257
Pineapple:
  Chicken Strips and Fruit, Far East, 67
  Dressing, Fresh Fruit Salad with, 128
  Fruitcake, Western Golden, 242–43
  Mold, Sunny Fresh Grapefruit and, 132
Ponce de Leon, Luis, 6
Ponzu Sauce, 116
  Lemon, 46
Popcorn:
  Lemon Buttered, 224
  Orange, Balls, 223
Popovers, Lemony Good, 183
Poppy Seed Dressing, Lemon-, 140–41
Pork, 77, 89–96
  Bacon, see Bacon
  Chops:
    with Citrus Rice, Skillet, 91
    Lemon Barbecued, 92
    with Orange-Rice Pilaf, 90
    Tipton Orange-Barbecued, 93
  Crown Roast of, 93–94
  Dressing for, Favorite Orange, 94–95
  Golden Orange Sauce for, 96

Ham, see Ham
Meat Loaf:
  "Best Ever," 83–84
  Two-Way Tangerine
  Meatballs and, 84–85
Pigs on a Blanket, 157
Ribs:
  Barbecued, Orange, 70
  BR's Good Country-Style, 89
  sausages for Pigs on a Blanket, 157
Potato(es), 99
Salad:
  German-Style Hot, 130
  Zesty Molded, 125
  Scandinavian Dilled, 107
  Skinny-Minny's Baked, Wedges, 108
  Sweet, Bake, Orange-, 108
Poultry, see Chicken; Cornish Hens; Duckling; Goose; Turkey
Preparation techniques, citrus, 303–308
Preserves, 171
  A Gem of a Jelly, 175–76
  Lemon and Tomato, 173
  Spiced Orange-Pear Butter, 173–74
  see also Marmalade
Pudding:
  Bread, Hint of Lemon, 200
  Rice, Best-Ever Baked, 199–200
  see also Flan
Pumpkin Bread, Fresh Orange-, 188–89
Punch, see Beverages, Punch

Quarter Cartwheel Slices, 288

Rabbit au Vin, 96–97
Raisins:
  Fruitcake, Grandma's Favorite Molasses, 241–42

Raisins *(continued)*
  Nutty Orange Relish, 176–77
Red Snapper for Seviche Olé, 18
Relish, 171
  Lemon-Corn, 174
  Nutty Orange, 177
  Sauce, Versatile Vegetable, 120
Rice, 99
  Chicken and, Savory, 68
  Citrus, Skillet Pork Chops with, 91
  Custard, Slow Cooking, 201–202
  "Open Sesame," Pilaf, 116–17
  Pork Chops with Orange-, Pilaf, 90
  Pudding, Best-Ever Baked, 199–200
  Salad, Chicken and Orange, 133
  Salmon Bake for Two, Quick, 56
  Three "Cs", Bake, 116
  Wild, –Filled Tomatoes, 137
Rings, Lemon, 151*n*., 293
Roses, Citrus, 298

Salad(s), 123–39
  Caesar, Best-Ever, 129–30
  Chicken:
    in Grapefruit Shells, Western, 134
    and Orange Rice, 133
    Sandwiches, Crunchy, 164
  Coleslaw, Garden-Fresh, 137–38
  Fallbrook's Favorite, 131
  Fettucini, Cindy's Garden, 127
  Fruit:
    Fresh, with Pineapple Dressing, 128
    Mariner's, 136
    Orange Waldorf, 136
  Grapefruit:
    and Broccoli, Chilled, 128–29
    and Pineapple Mold, Sunny Fresh, 132
    and Spinach, 129
  Greek Lemon, 126
  Green and Orange, with Blue Cheese Dressing, 131–32
  Pasta, Fresh Orange-, 125
  Potato:
    German-Style Hot, 130
    Zesty Molded, 125
  Salmon Mold, Show-Off, 134–35
  Spinach, Flambé, 126–27
  Tangerine Spinach, with Calorie-Conscious Dressing, 138–39
  Three-Bean, Easy, 135
  Tuna-Mac Stuffed Avocado, 139
  Wild Rice-Filled Tomatoes, 137
Salad Dressing(s), 123, 140–45
  Blue Cheese:
    Green and Orange Salad with, 131–32
    Yogurt–, 144
  Calorie Conscious, 139
  Citrus-Honey, 141
  Fresh Orange, 133
  Fruit Salad, Rosy's Honeyed, 143
  Grapefruit-Mint, 140
  Lemon:
    -Avocado, 143
    French, Low Calorie, 144
    -Sesame, 140–41
    -Sesame, Junior-Size, 141
  Pineapple, 128
  see also Dressing
Salami for Submarine Supreme, 163–64
Salmon:
  Bake for Two, Quick, 56

Balls with Lemon-Mustard
    Sauce, 55–56
Buffet, Supreme, 54
Dip for Vegetables, 27
Fish Steaks in Foil, Easiest
    Ever, 47
Fish Steaks with Orange-
    Curry Sauce, 48
Mold, Show-Off, 134–35
Mushroom-Almond Broiled,
    Steaks, 54–55
Omelet with Dill and Lemon
    Sauce, 150–51
Pâté, 30
Salsa Mexicana, 22–23
Sandwiches, 161–68
    Bagels and Orange-Cream
        Cheese, 166
    California Quesadillas, 168
    Chicken Salad, Crunchy,
        164
    Everyone's Favorite Triple
        Decker, 163
    Hungryman's Grilled, 167
    Monterey English Muffins,
        166
    Neptune Pocket, 165
    Submarine Supreme, 163–64
Sangría:
    Blanca, 276
    Burgundy, 276
    Rosé, 275–76
Sauce Italiano, 43
Sausages for Pigs on a
    Blanket, 157
Scallop(s):
    California Cioppino, 36–37
    Sauté with Lemon, 51
    Seafood and Orange Kabobs,
        52
Sea Bass:
    California Cioppino, 36–37
    Seviche Olé, 18
Seafood, 39–58
    California Cioppino, 36–37
    Cocktail, Western, 27–28
    and Orange Kabobs, 52

see also Fish; *individual types of
    seafood*
Sectioning method, 304
Segments, citrus, 305
Sesame seed:
    -Citrus Pocket Bread, 194–95
    Dressing, Lemon-, 140–41
        Junior-Size, 141
    Hummus Bi Tahina, 25
    "Open Sesame" Rice Pilaf,
        116–17
Seviche Olé, 18
Shark:
    Oven-Fried Fish with Lemon
        Ponzu Sauce, 46
    Seafood and Orange Kabobs,
        52
Shrimp:
    Alfresco, 52–53
    California Cioppino, 36–37
    Fettucini Salad, Cindy's
        Garden, 127
    Grapefruit and, with Zippy
        Cocktail Sauce, 19–20
    with Oranges, Oriental, 53
    Pacifica, 19
    Seafood Cocktail, Western,
        27–28
Slivered peel, 307
"Smiles," unpeeled, 306
Sole:
    Crisp-Coated Fillets with
        Tarragon Tartar Sauce,
        47–48
    Fish Italiano, 42–43
    Fish Rolls, Saucy Apple, 50–
        51
    Fish Roll-Ups, Company's
        Coming, 41
    Fish Soup, Quick and Easy
        Lemon, 31
    Poached Fish and Wine
        Sauce, 42
Soufflé:
    Chilled Grapefruit, 255
    Hot Lemon, 199
Soup, 15, 31–37

Soup *(continued)*
  Bean and Macaroni, Hearty, 32
  Borscht, Lemon Fresh, 31
  California Cioppino, 36–37
  Chicken Stock, Old-Fashioned Homemade, 37
  Cucumber, Chilled Lemon, 33–34
  Greek Lemon, 33
  Lemon Fish, Quick and Easy, 31–32
  Orange-Carrot, 34
  Wonton, 35–36
Sour cream, *see* Dips; Salad dressing(s)
Southern California Fruit Exchange, 7, 8
Southern Pacific Railroad, 7–8
Spaghetti:
  Fish Italiano, 42–43
  Salmon Supreme, Buffet, 54
Spinach:
  Creamed, à la Lemon, 110
  Fettucini Salad, Cindy's Garden, 127
  Fish Roll-Ups, 41
  Oriental Orange, 109
  Salad:
    Flambé, 126–27
    Grapefruit and, 129
    Tangerine, with Calorie-Conscious Dressing, 138–39
Squash à l'Orange, Winter, 111
Star Cups, 294–95
Star Garnishes, 294
Steak, *see* Beef
Stock, Old-Fashioned Homemade, 37
Strawberry(ies):
  Citrus-Yogurt Sundaes, 205–206
  Grapefruit and Berry Froth, 274
  Orange Frostee, 273

Sunkist Growers, Inc.:
  heritage of, 7–8
  licensed products of, 12
  processed products of, 11
  today, 8–9
Swiss cheese:
  Southwest Stuffed Zucchini or Green Peppers, 112
  Submarine Supreme, 163–64
Swordfish:
  Fish Steaks in Foil, Easiest Ever, 47
  Oven-Fried Fish with Lemon Ponzu Sauce, 46
  Sweet and Sour Fish Delight, 44
Syrup, Grapefruit-Apricot, 156–57

Tangerine(s):
  -Almond Shortcake, 234–35
  Beef Tangabobs, 80–81
  Citrus Rice, Skillet Pork Chops with, 91
  Four-Star Citrus Ambrosia, 203–204
  garnishes, *see* Garnishes, fresh citrus
  history of, 5
  information about, 309–18 *passim*
  Meatballs and Meat Loaf, Two-Way, 84–85
  preparation techniques, 303–308
  Spinach Salad with Calorie-Conscious Dressing, 138–39
  Stir-Fried Brussels Sprouts and, 103–104
  -Yogurt Dip for Fresh Fruit, 207
Tarragon:
  Chicken, Grapefruit-, 65
  Tartar Sauce, 48
Tartar Sauce:
  Lemon, 58

Tarragon, 48
Tea:
   Citrus Gold Riesling Punch, 277
   Hot Russian, 270
   Lemon and Mint Iced, 269
   Spiced Citrus, Iced, 269–70
Tibbets family, 6–7
Tiki Sails, 299
Tofu Delight, Lemon, 208
Tomato(es):
   Antipasto Platter, 29
   Eggplant "Caviar," 24–25
   Preserves, Lemon and, 173
   Wild-Rice Filled, 137
Tomato sauce:
   Salsa Mexicana, 22–23
   Sauce Italiano, 43
   Tuna Cocktail, Slimmers', 23–24
Tortillas:
   California Quesadillas, 168
   Nachos, Lemony Good, 23
Tuna:
   Antipasto Platter, 29
   and Asparagus Crêpe Roll-Ups, 57
   Cocktail, Slimmers', 23–24
   -Mac Stuffed Avocado, 139
   Mariner's Fruit Salad, 136
   Neptune Pocket Sandwiches, 165
Turkey:
   Barbecued, Drumsticks, 73–74
   Roast, with Almond Dressing and Lemon-Honey Glaze, 74–75
Twists, Lemon, 292

Veal Piccata, 85
Vegetable(s), 99–116
   Entrée for Two, Cheesy, 114
   Frittata, Cheesy, 152
   Medley, Orange, 114–15
   Relish Sauce, Versatile, 120
   Tempura, 115–16
   see also individual vegetables
Vinegar, Lemon Herbed, 145
Vodka for Lively Lemon Liqueur, 282

Waffles:
   Broiled Orange or Grapefruit Toppers, 157–58
   Pigs on a blanket, 157
Waldorf Salad, Orange, 136
Walnuts for Nutty Orange Relish, 176–77
Wedges, unpeeled, 306
Whole Wheat Orange and Carrot Loaf, 189
Wine, *see* Beverages, Punch
Wisniewski, Tony, 3
Wolfskill, William, 6
Wonton Soup, 35–36
Worldwide citrus industry, 9–10

Yam Bake, Orange, 108–109
Yogurt:
   –Blue Cheese Dressing, 144
   Sundaes, Citrus-, 205–206
   see also Dips; Salad dressings(s)

Zucchini:
   Cheesy Vegetable Entrée for Two, 114
   Cheesy Vegetable Frittata, 152
   Chicken and, Lemon, 64
   Southwest Stuffed, 112
   Stir-Fried, and Mushrooms, 113